Archibald Henry Sayce

An Assyrian grammar for comparative purposes

Archibald Henry Sayce

An Assyrian grammar for comparative purposes

ISBN/EAN: 9783742841797

Manufactured in Europe, USA, Canada, Australia, Japa

Cover: Foto ©Andreas Hilbeck / pixelio.de

Manufactured and distributed by brebook publishing software (www.brebook.com)

Archibald Henry Sayce

An Assyrian grammar for comparative purposes

AN

ASSYRIAN GRAMMAR,

FOR COMPARATIVE PURPOSES.

BY

A. H. SAYCE, M.A.,

FELLOW AND TUTOR OF QUEEN'S COLLEGE, OXFORD;
MEMBER OF THE GERMAN ORIENTAL SOCIETY,
AND OF THE SOCIETY OF BIBLICAL ARCHÆOLOGY.

LONDON:
TRÜBNER & CO., 8 AND 60, PATERNOSTER ROW.
1872.
[*All Rights reserved.*]

PRINTED BY
STEPHEN AUSTIN AND SONS, HERTFORD.

PREFACE.

The distinction between the material and formal parts of a language is nowhere better illustrated than in the case of one which is being gradually recovered from its native records. A dictionary, in the true sense of the word, is impossible: we can have only a vocabulary which is being continually enlarged and corrected. But although the power of speech in producing new words is unlimited, the number of forms under which these words find expression is practically closely defined. A comparatively small number of written works will afford sufficient material for the outlines of a grammar: more extensive means of comparison serve merely for correction and greater detail. Until, however, we know all the actual forms possessed by a language at the various periods of its literary career, we cannot be said to have more than a general acquaintance even with its formative part; we can deal only with its coarser features, and these would be probably much modified by a more intimate knowledge of the niceties and finer texture of the grammar. And while this is of the highest importance for an accurate interpretation of the language itself, it is of still higher importance for the purposes of comparative philology.

Assyrian, it is now recognized, is of the greatest value for Semitic philology. And the time has come when it is possible to give a grammar of the language which may bear some comparison with those of Hebrew or Ethiopic. Of course our acquaintance with the new study is constantly growing; but it is growing rather upon the side of the lexicon than of the grammar. In spite of the prejudice which naturally existed in the minds of Semitic scholars against an upstart science which threatened to dwarf the old objects of study, and the results of which were at once startling and revolutionary, while the decipherers were not always distinguished by scholarship or caution, the method of interpretation has at last won its way to general acknowledgment, so that even Ewald and Renan venture to use the statements of professed Assyriologues. Indeed, rational scepticism is no longer possible for any one who will take the trouble seriously to investigate the subject. The history of the decipherment need not be told over again. No scholar now questions the decipherment of the Persian inscriptions; and when this had once been accomplished, the translation of the Assyrian transcripts with their numerous proper names, and with the aid of the immense stores of comparison which the discoveries at Nineveh and elsewhere afforded, could only be a matter of time. The language disclosed was found to be Semitic in grammar and vocabulary, and the sporadic phenomena which at first offended Semitic scholars have turned out either to be errors on the part of the decipherers, or to admit of sufficient explanation. The contents of the inscriptions, again, have thoroughly verified the method of interpretation. Not only are they consistent, but the names and facts are such as are required by historical criticism. The greatest stumbling-block in the way of the sceptics has proved to be one of the most striking verifications of the method. It was urged that the existence of polyphones—that is, characters with more than one value—was sufficient to condemn the whole theory. Polyphones, however, actually exist in Japanese for the same reason that they existed in Assyrian;[1] and we find that the Assyrians, in their use of polyphones, observed certain general laws, so that the transliteration of a word (unless it be a native proper name) is very rarely doubtful. Still these polyphones were felt by the Assyrians themselves to be the weak point in their system of writing, and Assur-bani-pal accordingly caused syllabaries to be drawn up in which the several

[1] See Léon de Rosny, "Archives Paléographiques," 2me Livraison, pp. 90–100. This is referred to by Mahaffy, "Prolegomena to Ancient History," p. 207, whose Fourth Essay on the History of Cuneiform Decipherment is very good, and suited to the popular understanding. The want of acquaintance with Assyrian on the part of the author, however, has led to a few mistakes, most of which I have pointed out in the *Academy*, December 15th, 1871, p. 564.

signs have their different phonetic values attached. Now the various powers which the decipherers assigned to the same character are found assigned to it in the native syllabaries. Thus the character which by itself denotes a lion is variously used as *ur, liq, tas*; and a syllabary gives us the same sign explained *u-ri, li+iq,* and *ta-as*. The syllabaries also explain the origin of these polyphones. The cuneiform characters were primarily hieroglyphics (like the Chinese), and were invented by a Turanian population of Babylonia. These in their several dialects[1] assigned various names to the object denoted by the same hieroglyphic, and when the latter came to be used as a phonetic character, the various names became so many phonetic sounds. Every character, however, continued to be employed as an ideograph as well as phonetically; consequently when the Semitic Assyrians adopted the written system of their Turanian predecessors, they translated the Accadian word into their own language, and in some cases employed this (stripped of its grammatical inflexion) as a new phonetic value.

The tablets also give other evidence in favour of our system of interpretation. Some of them contain lists of Assyrian synonymes, and each synonyme is often a well-known Semitic word. Thus *bi-is-ru* (בשר) is equated with *se-ru* (שאר), and *al-pu* (אלף) with *su-u-ru* (שור).

[1] Berosus ap. Syncelli Chron. p. 28:—ἐν δὲ τῇ Βαβυλῶνι πολύ πλῆθος ἀνθρώπων γενέσθαι ἀλλοεθνῶν κατοικησάντων τὴν Χαλδαίαν.

A last and conclusive corroboration of the method is afforded by bilingual inscriptions in Phœnician and Assyrian, on private contract-tablets and duck-weights. The *maneh* of the Phœnician is *ma-na* in Assyrian; the proper names in the two legends agree, as well as the chief facts of a "sale," and of the chattels sold, which are stated in both.[1]

The following pages will show to how great an extent I am indebted to Dr. Oppert's Grammar (second edition). He possesses the great merit of having first made Assyrian available to other Semitic students by formulating the general grammatical principles of the language. And this merit will outweigh all the disadvantages of arbitrary conclusions upon insufficient evidence, which have resulted not only in minor errors, but in three radical misconceptions—of an emphatic state, of the want of a Perfect (or Permansive) and

---

[1] Thus *tadāni Arb'-il-khiret*, "the giving up of A." appears in the Phœnician legend as דנת ארבלחר; *pan Mannuci-Arb'-il*, "in the presence of M.," as למנגארבל. Harkavy (*Révue Israélite*, 1870, p. 20) says:— "A présent, grâce au zèle indefatigable et à la persévérance du petit corps d'assyriologues, cette défiance et cette réserve diminuent et disparaissent peu à peu. Le vote solennel de l'Académie des inscriptions et belles-lettres, qui a décerné à notre célèbre correligionnaire M. Oppert le prix de la plus grande découverte dans le domaine de la philologie,— l'explication des légendes bilingues, araméennes et assyriennes, au Musée britannique, par Sir H. Rawlinson,—la trouvaille, a l'isthme de Suez, d'une inscription quadrilingue, malheureusement endommagée, se sont succédé coup sur coup, et ont contribué à attirer aux études cunéiformes la confiance de tous, sauf naturellement de ceux qui ferment les yeux à la lumière."

Passives, and in a confusion between the Present Kal and the Pael—which make his book a dangerous one for beginners. I have entered into the arena of controversy wherever I have thought it needful; but this, I hope, does not prevent me from bearing testimony to Dr. Oppert's scholarship, research, and acuteness. His grammar lacks completeness, it is true, as well as accuracy; but this is due to the progressive nature of Assyriology; and the same plea is needed for my own pages. The most defective portion of his work is the chapter on syntax, and this might have been remedied.

To Dr. Hincks my obligations are even greater. It will be seen that in most of the points of dispute between him and Dr. Oppert, independent investigation has made me follow the Irish scholar. The student of Assyrian may well deplore his loss.

I have also made considerable use of Mr. Norris's "Assyrian Dictionary" (the third volume of which is about to appear),[1] and of Mr. G. Smith's "Annals of Assur-bani-pal." Such books are greatly wanted to lighten the labour and facilitate the research of other students. I can only regret that Mr. Norris has not yet got beyond his second volume, and that Mr. Smith's promised "Annals of Sennacherib and Essarhaddon," upon the same plan as his former work, are still un-

---

[1] The volume has been published since the above was written. It brings the list of nouns as far as the end of N. The next volume will begin the verbs.

published. It is with the same regret that I am obliged to finish my labours without having had the advantage of consulting the two Papers by Dr. Schrader upon the Assyrian language, which are expected by readers of the "Zeitschrift der Deutschen Morgenländischen Gesellschaft."

Before concluding, I would express my thanks to Mr. G. Smith, for his courtesy and kindness in enabling me to consult the original texts.

The cuneiform has been throughout transliterated into Roman characters, partly because the original type would be at once expensive and cumbrous, and partly to facilitate the comparative studies of Semitic scholars who are disinclined to commit to memory the complicated Assyrian syllabary. I have avoided confusing my text with references, so far as was possible; and have only broken the rule in points where dispute might arise.

A. H. SAYCE.

QUEEN'S COLLEGE, OXFORD,
May 11*th*, 1872.

ABBREVIATIONS USED.

W. A. I. = Cuneiform Inscriptions of Western Asia, Vols. I., II., III. (the fourth volume containing translations of Accadian hymns, is expected to be published before the end of the year).

S. H. A. = Smith's History of Assur-bani-pal, 1871.

[In the transcription of Æthiopic words, *shewa* is denoted by *ĕ* and *y*.]

CONTENTS.

	PAGE
PREFACE	v
CONTENTS	xiii

INTRODUCTION.

The habitat and character of the Assyrian language	1
Comparison of it with Hebrew, Arabic, Æthiopic, and Aramaic	1–3
Peculiarities of the Assyrian: the dialectic differences between Assyrian and Babylonian	3
How far Assyrian varied at different epochs, and in the mouths of the common people	4
Notes to the above, filling up the details	5–15
Traces of degeneracy in the language	15
Use of the masculine for the feminine not a mark of antiquity	16

LITERATURE OF THE ASSYRIAN LANGUAGE.

The grammatical tablets of Assur-bani-pal	17
List of modern publications	18

PHONOLOGY.

Origin of the Assyrian syllabary	23
Transcription of the alphabet	25
Phonetic changes and affinities of the several letters	26–35
Use of the diphthongs	35
The Assyrian alphabet compared with the Hebrew and Arabic	36
The accent in Assyrian	36

THE PRONOUNS.

The Separative Personal Pronouns; their use and affinities	37
Note on their origin	40
The Demonstrative Pronouns (*suatu, sasu, aga, ammu, annu, ullu*)	41
The Relative Pronoun and its affinities	45
The Interrogative and the Indefinite Pronouns	46
The Reflexive Pronoun	47

THE VERB.

Character of the Assyrian verb	48
The Six Principal and Five Secondary Conjugations	49
Other rarer Conjugations (see Appendix, p. 185)	49
The Passives	52
Quadriliterals	51
The Five Tenses; Permansive, Aorist, Perfect, Present, and Future	52
The Aorist divided into the Apocopated, the Telic (ending in *u*), the Conditional (with *a* the Augment of Motion), and the Paragogic (with the mimmation); also the termination of the Aorist in -*i*	54
The Four Moods: Precative, Subjunctive, Imperative, and Infinitive	56
The Participle	59
The Persons (Singular, Plural, and Dual)	59
Origin of the Person-endings	61
Proof of the existence of a Permansive Tense against Dr. Oppert	61
Proof of a Present Tense in Assyrian	68
Traces of *Waw Consecutivum*	69
Contracted Forms	69
The Strong Verb in Kal	71
In Iphteal (and Iphtaneal)	74
In Niphal	77
In Ittaphal	78
In Pael	78
In Iphtaal (and Iphtanaal)	79
In Shaphel	80
In Istaphal	81
In Aphel and Itaphal	82
In Shaphael	82
In Istaphael	83
The Passives	83

THE DEFECTIVE VERB.

 Verbs פ״י 84
 Verbs פ״א, פ״ה, פ״י, פ״ו (with Istataphal) 85
 Concave verbs (with Niphalel, Palel, Papel, and Palpel) . . 91
 Verbs ל״א, ל״ה, ל״ו, ל״י, ל״ע (with Niphael) 94
 Verbs containing ע 95
 Verbs doubly defective. 96
 Quadriliterals. 97
 The Pronominal Suffixes of the Verb 98

THE NOUNS.

 Two genders: want of an Article: the Singular, Plural, and
  Dual. 101
 The Three Case-terminations -u, -i, -a 102
 The Mimmation. 102
 Dr. Oppert's ascription of an Emphatic State to the Assyrian
  controverted 102
 Derivation of Nouns: Primitive Nouns 104
 The verbal nouns with three radicals 105
 Nouns from defective verbs 107
 Nouns formed by the Prefix *m*- 108
 By the affix -*ânu* (-*inu*) 109
 By *t* affixed (to build abstracts) 109
 By *t* prefixed 110
 By a prefixed vowel. 110
 Gentile nouns. 111
 Quadriliterals and Pluriliterals. 111
 Letter-changes in Primitive Roots 112
 Turanian origin of biliteral roots 113
 Number and Gender 114
 Origin of the terminations of the feminine, the plural, and the
  dual 121
 The Cases. 123
 The Construct State 125
 The Pronominal Suffixes of the Noun. 127

	PAGE
THE NUMERALS	130
Origin of the Semitic Numerals	133
The Ordinals	138
Fractions, etc.	139
Weights and Measures	140
THE PREPOSITIONS, SIMPLE AND COMPOUNDED	141
THE INTERJECTIONS	143
THE ADVERBS	143
THE CONJUNCTIONS	145
THE SYNTAX.	
Of the Noun	146
Of the Numerals	150
Of the Pronouns	155
Of the Verbs	157
Of the Particles	161
PROSODY.	
Order of the sentence	172
Assyrian poetry	172
Analytical specimens of translation	173
CORRECTIONS AND ADDITIONS	179
NOTE ON THE GRAMMATICAL VIEWS OF DR. HINCKS	188

N.B.—*The reader is requested to refer to the additional notes in the Appendix.*

AN ASSYRIAN GRAMMAR.

INTRODUCTORY.

The Assyrian language was spoken in the countries watered by the Tigris and Euphrates. It was bounded on the north by the Aryan populations of Armenia and Media, and on the east by the Turanian dialects of Elam. With the exception of one or two doubtful words preserved in classical writers, such as πανδοῦρα (Pollux, iv. 60), *Armalchar* (Plin. H. vi. 30), all that remains of it is to be found in the cuneiform inscriptions. These, though fragmentary, are copious, and are met with in Assyria (1), in Babylonia, and in Persia. The Semitic character of the language is unmistakable (2); indeed, the fulness, antiquity, and syllabic character of its vocabulary and grammar would claim for it the same position among the Semitic tongues that is held by Sanskrit in the Aryan family of speech (3). It has borrowed its syllabary from the primitive Turanian inhabitants of Chaldæa; and this, though not without grave inconveniences, has yet had the fortunate result of preserving the vocalic pronunciation of the Assyrians. Every character is syllabic, as in Æthiopic.

The Semitic dialects to which the Assyrian shows most affinity are the Hebrew and Phœnician. It agrees with these in its preservation of the sibilants (4), which are not changed as in

Aramaic, in its fuller expression of the vowels (5), in its want of an Emphatic State, in its construct plural, in the forms of the personal pronouns, in the possession of a Niphal, and in the general character of its vocabulary (6). Next to Hebrew, it has most affinities with Arabic. Like the latter, it retains the primitive case-endings of the nouns, though these in the later inscriptions have begun to lose their strict value (7), and agrees with it in the variously modified forms of the imperfect (8), in the use of the participle (9), in the conjugations (10), in the possession of a dual by the verb, in the *mimmation* which replaces (as in Himyaritic) the Arabic *nunnation*, in the simplicity of the vocalic system, and in the formation of the precative (11). It does not possess, however, any broken plurals (12). Its points of resemblance to the Æthiopic are not so great as might have been expected from the similar position of the two languages—outposts, as it were, of the Semitic family, in constant contact with non-Semitic populations, whom they had dispossessed of their former country, and using a syllabic mode of writing which ran from left to right. Like the Æthiopic, the Assyrian has split up its imperfect into two tenses (13), has chosen the guttural form of the first personal pronoun in the Permansive tense (14), has no article, has borrowed many foreign roots (15), and has adopted several peculiar prepositions (16).

Of all the branches of the Semitic family, the Aramaic is furthest removed from the Assyrian. In the one the vowel-system is very meagre, in the other it is correspondingly simple and full (17). They stand in much the same relation to one another that the Sanskrit does to the Latin. The only points of likeness are the existence of a shaphel and an aphel (18), the use of *ana* with the accusative as לְ in Aramaic (compare 2 Chron. xvii. 5; Ezr. viii. 16), and the formation of the precative. Peculiar to the Assyrian is the change of a sibilant into a liquid before a dental (19), as well as the form of the third personal pronoun,—which is, however, met with in South Arabic (20); the extended use of the secondary conjugations with an inserted dental (21), the division of the imperfect into an aorist, present, and future (22), and the adverbial ending (23).

The Assyrians seem to have dispossessed the Turanian population of their cities and country in the sixteenth century B.C. (24), and the oldest inscriptions which we have written in the language are two or three centuries later. The original home of the Semitic people was apparently Arabia (25), whence the northern branch moved into Palestine, and then into Mesopotamia and Assyria. About B.C. 1270 (26), under the name of כשדים (= Assyrian *casidi*, "conquerors") (27), the Assyrian Semites took possession of Babylonia, subduing the Sumiri (? שנער) or Cassi (Cush), and the Accadi or "highlanders," the inventors of the cuneiform system of writing, who claimed kindred with the Turanian Elamites. A peaceful Semitic population had already been settled in Chaldæa for some centuries, in subordination to the dominant Turanian race. One of the first Babylonian Semitic inscriptions of which we know belongs to Khammurabi (? Semiramis) (28), and records the construction of the Nahr-Malka, the great canal of Babylon, whose two towers were called after the names of the king's father and mother. The Assyrian and Babylonian dialects differed in several respects. Thus the Assyrian *p* becomes *b* in the Southern dialect (*e.g.*

Sardanapalus and Merodach-Baladan, *u-se-pi-sa* Assyrian, and *u-se-bi-s* Babylonian, *episu* Assyrian, and *ebisu* Babylonian); ס becomes *sh* (compare בלשאצר and סרגן, like the sharper pronunciation of the northern Ephraimites, Judg. xii. 6); *k* is changed into *c* and *g* (as in *katu* "hand" Assyrian, *gatu* Babylonian, *sanaku* "chain" Assyrian, *sanagam* Babylonian); ע sometimes replaces א (׳), e.g. *ri-e-su* for *ri-'i-su* "head," *er-si-tiv* for *ir-tsi-tiv* "earth," which is also an instance of the interchange of צ and ט; *i* represents the third person singular and plural aorist Kal of verbs פ׳י in Babylonian, while in Assyrian the first and third persons are identical (beginning with *e*); *lu* is used before substantives as in vulgar Assyrian; and generally the Babylonian presents us with a much greater fulness of vowel-sounds, and has a preference for tne mimmation.

The Assyrian itself varies slightly in the oldest and the latest inscriptions (29). Thus *Nabiuv* became *Nabuv*, and Assur-bani-pal's inscriptions present us with such grammatical irregularities as *sal-la-ṭi* ("spoil") for *sal-la-at*, and *ic-su-du* for the dual *ic-su-da*. The doubling of letters is frequently omitted (30). Masculine verbs are even found with feminine nouns, e.g. *Istaru yu-sap-ri* "Istar disclosed." The language also in the mouths of the common people was to some extent corrupted, and these corruptions may occasionally be detected in private tablets, and even in the royal inscriptions. Dr. Oppert instances *kham-sa* by the side of *khan-sa* "five"; and we may add *e-rab-bi* for *i-rab-bi* or *i-rab-bi-u*, *ippalacoita* for *ippaloita*, *i-ta-tsu* for *it-ti-si*, *sa* used without any antecedent, as in *ina sa Gar-ga-mis* for *ina mana sa*, "according to the standard of Carchemish," *umma*, "thus" "that," inserted as in Greek before quotations, and on Michaux's stone and elsewhere *irin*, "he gave," for *idin* (*iddin*). In Assur-banipal's inscriptions *umma* is generally preceded by *ciham*. The contract tablets also offer us examples of the change of *u* to *i*, as *iddini* for *iddinu* (31). In the Persian period the Assyrian experienced considerable changes. New words were introduced, such as *birid* "among," *uku* ("people," Accadian originally), *hagá*, *hagáta*, *haganet* "this," "these" (which, prefixed to the personal pronouns, and the demonstrative, passes into an article—compare too *aganet mati* "these lands"); *ul* is used with nouns and pronouns instead of *la*; and an Aryan order of words even is followed, as in *Kam-bu-zi-ya mi-tu-tu ra-man-ni-su mi-i-ti*, "Cambyses by the death of himself dead." The same cause seems to have produced such ungrammatical sentences as *istin in itehme madu'utu*, or even *istin itehme madútu* and *madutu in itahime* (!), "one among many lawgivers" (32).

1. *Assur* was originally the name of the primitive capital of the country, now called Kileh-Shergat. It was of Turanian origin, and the name is explained in the bilingual tablets as compounded of *a* (= *mie*, מים) and *usor* (= *siddu*, שׂדה). Two or three brick-legends belonging to its early Turanian princes, called *patsi'is*, are in our possession. They are placed in the nineteenth century B.C., by a chronological reference in the inscription of Tiglath-Pileser I.

2. Had scholars not been prejudiced, this might have been concluded from the few Assyrian words preserved in the Bible or classical writers, viz., *Rab-shakeh*, *Rab-saris*, רחבות עיר, *Belus*, *Zab* (=λύκος), *Zabate* ("caprea"), and Pliny's *Narrage* or (*N*)*ar-malcha* (="flumen regium") mentioned above. And see Ia. xxxiii. 19.

3. The Assyrian would take this rank as furnishing us with some of the earliest examples of Semitic literature. The simplicity of its vowel-system evidences its antiquity, as well as its so-called case-terminations, which are identical with those of the aorist. The Semitic languages have marked their decay by modifications of the three primitive vowels, which alone

appear in Assyrian and classical Arabic. The large number of conjugations preserved in Assyrian, as well as the form of the third personal pronoun and the first person singular of the Permansive, are archaic. So also is the mimmation and the use of shaphel. Lastly, the vocabulary is extremely large, and it is unfortunate that we have to explain Assyrian from Hebrew and not Hebrew from Assyrian. Obscure points in Hebrew lexicography have already been cleared up (*e.g.* עָשָׂה יִשְׁתֵּי has been explained by Dr. Oppert as Assyrian *istin*, "one," masculine). Even in the Persian period we get *u-ta-h-me* or *i-te-h-e-me*, "lawgiver," from שׂים, formed by the prefix *u* or *i*, traces of which are to be found in such Hebrew proper names as יִצְחָק, יַעֲקֹב, or the Arabic يربوع.

4. The following table will show this clearly:—

ASSYRIAN.	HEBREW.	ARABIC.	ARAMAIC.	ÆTHIOPIC.
שׁ	שׁ	ش, س, ث	ת, שׁ, ס	s, š
ס	ס	س, ش	ס	s, š
צ	צ	ص, ض, ظ	ע, ט, צ	ṣ
ז	ז	ز, ذ	ד, ז	z

Thus Assyrian *šal-ši*=שָׁלֹשׁ, Arabic ثلث, Aramaic תלת, Æthiopic *šalastu*; Assyrian *irtsituv*=אֶרֶץ, Aramaic אַרְעָא; Assyrian *tsalulu*=צלל, Arabic ظلل, Aramaic טלל, Æthiopic *tsalala*; Assyrian *zicaru*=זכר, Arabic ذكر, Aramaic דכר, Æthiopic *zacara*.

The Assyrian *š*, however, frequently replaces *s* both in Hebrew and in Assyrian itself, especially where Hebrew has שׂ; e.g. *šiba'* and *siba'*, "seven," *šarru*=שַׂר, *iš'amu*=שׁהם.

5. E.g. *Catim*=קָבַל, Aramaic *k'bal*.

6. Thus we have *nadinu* (נתן) instead of Aramaic *y'hab*, *ôdu* (בוא) instead of *'atah*, *radu* (ירד) for *n'khat*, etc. So כון, as in Hebrew, = "to establish:" it has not passed, as in Arabic, Æthiopic, and Phœnician, into the general idea of "existence." The inserted ר is absent, as in Hebrew; e.g. *cussu*=כִּסֵּא, in Phœnician כרס׳, Aramaic *corsai*, Syriac *curs'ya*, Arabic *curs'ya*.

Assyrian differs from Hebrew chiefly in its rare use of the perfect and *waw conversivum*, its want of an article (except perhaps in the Achæmenian period), its plural, its extended use of the secondary conjugations, its substitution of *pael* for *piel*, and its want of the inseparable prepositions, and (except in the later inscriptions) of the accusative prefix. The feminine always ends in *t* (like classical Arabic, Æthiopic, and Phœnician) both in noun and verb. With Hebrew must be classed Phœnician and Moabite (as found in the inscriptions of Mesha). Phœnician agrees with Assyrian in the scanty use of an article and of *waw conversivum*, in the use of the participle for tenses, in the substitution of the relative ש for אשר (as in the northern dialect of Judges and Canticles), and in the older form of the feminine suffix ת for ה. In most cases, however, where Phœnician and Hebrew differ, Assyrian agrees with the latter; e.g., *raglu* "foot," not פעם, *dhabu* "good," not נעם, *sani* "years," not שנות, *nadinu*, not יתן. In many instances the Assyrian employs words common in Phœnician, but poetical in Hebrew, e.g., *pilu* = פעל (Hebrew usually עשה), *alpu* = אלף (Hebrew usually שור), *arkhu* = ירח (Hebrew usually חדש).

It often happens that the Assyrian agrees only with the poetical (archaic) words and forms of the Hebrew, e.g., חזה (Assyrian *khazu*), the plural in ן, the sparing use of the article and the accusative prefix את, and the lengthened form of the pronoun-suffixes ימו, etc., which preserve the final -*u* of the Assyrian (*sunu*).

7. The syllabaries carefully give the typical form in *u* or *um*, but we find in the inscriptions numberless instances of a wrong use, more especially of the oblique cases. Thus, Assur-bani-pal has *pu-lukh-tu* for *pu-lukh-ti*, *di-e-ni* for *di-e-nu*, *libba* for *libbu*; while in Babylonian inscriptions we even meet with such instances as *ana da-ai-nuv tsi-i-ri*, "to the supreme judge," for *ana da-ai-na tsi-i-ra*; and the astrological tablets have *khibi essu*, "recent lacuna."

8. These also are liable to be interchanged in the later inscriptions: e.g. in Assur-bani-pal we have indifferently *as-lu-lu* and *as-lu-la*, "I carried away;" *is-ta-nap-pa-ra* and *is-ta-nap-pa-ru*, "I wished to be sent forth;" though perhaps *a* stands here for *u-a* (*wa*), as in *aslula*, "They carried away."

9. More properly, verbal adjectives, as in Arabic, one denoting the agent (e.g., *mâlicu*, "ruling;" *asibut*, "habitantes;" *dûcu*, "slaying;" *limattu*, for *limantu*, "she who injures;" *limuttu*, for *limuntu*, "she who is injured;" *dîcu*, "slain"). The participles of the conjugations (Kal excepted) are formed by the prefix *mu*.

10. The Assyrian possessed a passive for every conjugation (except Kal, which used Niphal instead), formed as in Arabic; e.g., in the Pael, *sar-ra-ap*, "to burn," *sur-ru-up*, "to be burnt."

Every conjugation, again, had a secondary one (intensive), formed by the insertion of *t*, as in the Arabic eighth conjugation. So also the nasal Assyrian conjugation (e.g. *istanappar*) may be compared with the Arabic fourteenth and fifteenth. In Moabite we find an *ifta'ala* (for Niphal) הִלְתָּחֵם, infinitive בְּהִלְתָּחֲמֹה, imperfect אֶלְתָּחֵם), imperative הִלְתָּחֵם.

11. The precative formed by the prefix *l* is compared by Dr. Oppert with the Arabic precative prefix لِ, the ל of the Talmud, and with the Aramaic forms לֶהֱוֵא, לֶהֱוֵין. But it is better to regard these last as equivalent to the usual preformative of the imperfect ', with the intensive particle *lu* prefixed. This has been united with the verb, causing the elision of the person-determinative, and in Syriac has been corrupted into *n*.

12. Broken plurals are a later formation in the Semitic languages, and were originally merely singular nouns of multitude. In Himyaritic the Arabic plural *actab* occurs by the side of the ordinary plural (e.g., *sheb*, "tribe," plural *ashób*). Broken plurals, common in Æthiopic, have become the rule in Arabic. As in Hebrew and Aramaic, there are no certain traces of them in Assyrian. Dr. Hincks believed he had detected two or three: *balu*, plural of *ablu*, "son" (but this word means "power"), *rid*, plural of *ardu*, "servant" (but *rid* is singular referring to Assur-izir-pal, explained as equivalent to *mil-cu* (מֶלֶךְ) and *admu* (אָדָם) ii., 30.3; like *li-du* by the side of *a-lit-tuv*, ii. 36.2.), *ri-i-mu*, plural of *ar-mi*, "bull" (but this explanation of *ar-mi* is doubtful), and *ni-si* from *anis* (but the latter word is not found). Assyrian differs from the Arabic chiefly in its consonantal system (besides agreeing with Hebrew in the sibilants, it does not possess the modern Arabic modifications (ض, ث, خ); in its want of an article (אלקוש is *alu Kus* or *Kis*, "the town of Kis" in Babylonia); in its want of auxiliary tenses; and in its vocabulary (e.g., *mā* in Arabic, as in Syriac, is negative, in Assyrian only interrogative).

13. This will be proved further on. The Assyrian present *igabbir* or *igabir* answers exactly to what Ludolf calls the present in Æthiopic *yĕgabĕr*, and the aorist *igbur* (or *igbar*) to his subjunctive *yĕgbar*.

14. Assyrian *gabracu* or *gabrae* stands side by side with the Æthiopic *gabarcu*. So in Mahri (*zegidek*, "I strike") and Amharic (*zegadhu*). In the second person, however, the Assyrian has the *t* of the other dialects (*gabirta*, *gabirti*), herein departing from the Æthiopic and Mahri, as well as the Samaritan. The ך seems more original than ת when we compare the substantive suffixes throughout the Semitic dialects, and the absolute form of the first personal pronoun (Assyrian *anacu*, where *ana* is explained by the root הנא). For the change of ת and ך, conf. שָׂדֶה and

אֱכָל. It appears to belong to the oldest period of the languages. The inhabitants of Raïma near Zebîd still say *kunk* for *kunt*.[1] Assyrian agrees also with Æthiopic and Himyaritic in one of the forms for the plural—*ánu* (*án*); as well as in forming many adverbs by means of the accusative affix *s* (as also Arabic), e.g., *bazza*, "as rubbish," *be-'e-la*, "much." So, too, we find such forms as *manzazu*, "fixed," like Æthiopic *maf'rey*, "fruitful," where Arabic has *u*, and Hebrew and Aramaic *shewa*. Himyaritic, again, possesses the mimmation, as in the genitive *Marthadim*; and Amharic and Hararic have a nunnated accusative, *ĕn*, *ĭn*. The Æthiopic *shĕnālem* is an old mimmated accusative.

15. Few, if any, are derived from an Aryan source. This is the more strange, as Aryan nations (Medes, Armenians, Tibareni, Comagenians) surrounded them on the north, the people of Van even adopting their mode of writing. Perhaps *urdhu*, given in a tablet as a synonyme of *tilla*, "high," is the Zend *eredhwa*, etc., but I have never met with the word in inscriptions. *Alicani*-wood, again, one of the trees introduced into Assyria by Tiglath-Pileser I., is possibly אֶלְגַּנִּים, Sanskrit *Valgu* (*ka*), "sandal." On the other hand, a large number of Accadian vocables were borrowed by the Assyrians, after being Semitized. Thus *muq* becomes *muk-ku*, *gal* or *gula gal-lu*, *naga nangu'u*. Though words of more than one syllable have been thus taken, the roots are more commonly monosyllabic; and the proximity of the remote ancestors of the Semitic family to the Turanians of Chaldæa seems to make it probable that a considerable proportion of the monosyllabic radicals common to the Semitic tongues were originally foreign. A curious example of this may be found in *khirat*, *khirtu*, "woman," a Semitic feminine formation from the Accadian *kharra*, "man" (? חִי, Syriac *khîra*). Some roots, lost in the other dialects, are found in Æthiopic and Assyrian alone: e.g. *basu*, "to exist," has been well compared by Dr. Oppert with Æthiopic *bisi*, "man." There are no traces of Egyptian influence unless it be *pirkhu* given as a synonyme of "king," on a tablet (II. 30., 3). More probably, however, this merely means "a young man" (מְדוּ). *Ammat* (אַמָּה), "cubits," is Semitic. *Mana* is of Accadian origin, as is shown by the famous law-tablet.

16. *Ana*, *ina*, *assu*, are not less Semitic than *diba* and *ribba*. The other Assyrian prepositions are common to the surrounding dialects. *Ana* and *ina* are merely accusative cases used adverbially: *ana* I would derive from אֵת, أَنِي, "to be suitable," and *assu* from the common root *assu*,

---

[1] V. Maltzan (Zeitschrift d. D. M. G. 1871, p. 197).

אשש, "establish." The inseparable prepositions of Hebrew and Arabic are merely contracted forms of roots which bore much the same meaning, ב of בית, ל of לוה (just as we have מ for מן and כ for כה). In Assyrian also *cima* is contracted into *ci* (e.g., *ci pi*, "according to the tongue"), and *limetu* (לוה) is also found as *li* (ל). So, too, before a consonant we sometimes have *an* for *ana*, and *it* for *itti*. Another point of resemblance between Assyrian and Æthiopic is the violent change of sounds usual in both. Thus in Assyrian a sibilant before a dental regularly changes into *l*. So again Æthiopic, Himyaritic, and Mahri, like Assyrian, have no article. *Sunu*, "illi," may be compared with Himyaritic and Arabic *humu*, Æthiopic *wetomu*, *m* becoming *n*, as in the plural of nouns. *Su, sa, si*, must be ranged with the Mahri *sé*, "she," with plural *sén*, and Himyaritic *s*.

17. As already remarked, the consonantal character of Assyrian agrees with Hebrew, not with Aramaic; compare תרין and *sand*. Mendaite, perhaps, most exhibits the degenerating tendency of Aramaic. In this dialect the three quiescent letters are vowels; and the gutturals are all pronounced as א, as is sometimes the case in Galilee, in the Talmud, in Nabathean, and on the Jewish bowls found at Babylon by Layard. These, it is important to notice, present a complete contrast to the Assyrian, which goes so far as to permit the doubling of ה as well as of ר. Assyrian ה, however, was frequently dropped in writing, and the language resolves the final ה into *u*, as Aramaic does into א. The guttural sound of ע, again, was not known, it being always a vowel (thus, עזה is written *Khazitu*). *Imiru*, however, is not חמר, but Phœnician אמר ("lamb"). The numerous contractions and agglutinations of Mendaite are altogether alien to Assyrian. Assyrian, so far as I know, has but one example of the substitution of *n* for the reduplication of a letter, usual in Aramaic and Mendaite. This is the word *pulunge*, "regions," once used by Sargon; which is, moreover, an Aramaic use of the usual *palgu*, "a canal" (but found also in Phœnician).

This unlikeness of Assyrian to the peculiarities of Aramaic marks it off from the dialects of Yemen (which have an emphatic termination *o*, the Aramaic postfixed vowel, and such words as *bar*, "son"), or the Siniatic inscriptions (which have *bar* and *di* for the relative pronoun).

The vocabulary, again, is strikingly non-Aramaic (note 6). Thus we find לקח instead of קבל, and מלך rather than שלט, *ab-lu* (יבל) and *binu* instead of בר. So *admu*, "man," is found only in Hebrew, Phœnician, and Himyaritic.

Other points of contrast between Assyrian and Aramaic will be the want of the emphatic termination (the postfixed article), the formation of the passive by vowel-mutation, the want of compound tenses (in which Arabic agrees with Aramaic), the use of *isu* (יֵשׁ) instead of אוֹת, and the rarity of substantives expressing abstract ideas by the help of final terminations.

18. Traces of *shaphel* are to be found in Hebrew (e.g., שַׁלְהָבֶת). But the conjugation is presupposed by Arabic *istactala* and Æthiopic *êstagabbara*. *Istaphel* is possessed by the Mahri. *Aphel* from *shaphel* (*hiphil*), Arabic and Æthiopic *aetala*, is found in Assyrian only in verbs י"ע.

Other points of resemblance will be the want of the article, the usual loss of emphatic א in the *status constructus* like the loss of the case-endings in Assyrian, and the circumscription of the genitive by the relative pronoun (as in Æthiopic *za*), which is, however, *sa* (not Aramaic דִי or Himyaritic ד). So, in both languages, the superlative is formed by the insertion of the relative between the positive and the genitive plural.

Before the decipherment of the cuneiform inscriptions, philology had shown that the so-called Chaldee was really the language of Northern Syria, and did not encroach upon Palestine and Chaldæa until after the overthrow of the Babylonian empire. Isaiah xxxvi. 11 merely shows, what we know to be the case from private contract tablets extending from the reign of Tiglath-Pileser II. to that of Sennacherib, that after the fall of Tyre Aramaic, together with its alphabet, had become the language of commerce and diplomacy (like French in modern Europe). It was not yet understood by the lower orders, but was regarded as the language of politics. Ezra iv. 7 bears out this fact: with the Persian supremacy, the native dialects of east and west began to pass away before the influence of the Aramaic. Daniel ii. 4 only exhibits the unhistorical character and late date of the book, which cannot be brought into harmony with the inscriptions. Laban (Genesis xxxi. 47) was a Syrian of Mesopotamia (xxviii. 5). *Sahadutha*,[1] neither in form nor root, is found in Assyrian. *Igaru* (יְגַר), however, is common, answering to the Accadian *isi* or *is*.

19. This is the regular change (e.g., *mikhil-tu* for *mikhits-tu*, *iltanappar* for *istanappar*; *ulziz* for *ussiz*), but it is often disregarded, especially in the later inscriptions. The comparison of Χαλδαῖοι with כשדים has been brought forward as an instance of this phonetic change; but though a sibilant becomes a labial, the converse never takes place; and the *Caldai* are first met with in inscriptions of the eighth century, as a small Elamite tribe on the lower Euphrates. They gradually advanced north-

---

[1] With the suffixed article of the Aramaic emphatic state, the Assyrian would be *Sahaduthi*. Contrast רב־שׂקה = *Rab(u)-sakku*.

ward; and under Merodach-Baladan, son of Yagina, got possession of Babylon. The sibilant must have been changed into *r* before it could have become *l*.

20. This alone would claim for Assyrian a standard place among the Semitic tongues, as retaining archaic forms. The ה of the other dialects has long ago been shown to have been originally שׁ, just as Hiphil presupposes Shaphel. It is curious that in the sub-Semitic dialects the third personal pronoun has a sibilant. Thus Harar *zo* or *so*, "he," *sinyo*, "they;" Barber (suffixed) *es*, *as* (singular), and *sen* or *asen* (plural masculine), *sent*, *asent* (plural feminine). Haussa *shi*, "he," *su*, "they," *sa*, "him." Mahri again gives us *sé*, "illa," *sén*, " illæ," and the suffixes -*es*, -*senn*.

21. The dental was originally inserted at the beginning, as in Assyrian verbs י״ע (e.g. *it-bu-ni*, "they went,") or פ״ע (*it-ebus*, "he made"). In the eighth and tenth conjugations of the Arabic the dental has been inserted into the form. So too in the Æthiopic *estagabòara*, Mahri *shakhber* (for *stakhber*), and Aramaic *eshtaphal*. Compare also Hebrew forms like הִסְתַּבֵּל.

The uniformity of the Assyrian in using this conjugation with *t* by the side of every other conjugation, seems rather to be the result of a secondary striving after uniformity than the relic of original usage, when it is considered that the dental primitively stood before the root and had a reflexive meaning.

22. I cannot help believing that this was influenced by the neighbourhood of their Turanian neighbours. The Accadian had an aorist and a present, and with the machinery already possessed by the Assyrian verb, it was not difficult to set apart one form for the aorist signification, and another for the present. The same phenomenon re-appears in Æthiopic, which was similarly situated in close neighbourhood to a non-Semitic population. A grammatical form was not borrowed by the Assyrian (comparative philology would protest against such an assumption); but the existing forms were specialized to suit the requirements of a bilingual people. The elaboration of a future was easy: it is merely the older and fuller form of the present, just as future time is an extension of present time by dwelling longer upon it. The fuller form of the aorist had a tendency to express a similarly extended action: it is used rather where the Aryan languages would employ a perfect or a pluperfect, just as, conversely, in Arabic and Hebrew, the apocopated form denotes energetic, immediate action. The Assyrian inscriptions, however, will not allow us to draw the same distinction of meaning between the shorter and longer forms of the past tense that must be drawn between the shorter and longer forms of the present.

The difference was only felt in an indistinct way; the language never definitely and consciously expressed it.

23. The adverbial ending in -*is* has been admirably explained by Dr. Oppert as a contraction of the third personal suffix-pronoun attached to the oblique case of the noun. Thus *sallatis*, "as a spoil," will be for *sallati-su*. The pronoun is often found in a contracted form; e.g. *yussi-limus*, "he conferred on him," *balus*, "his power."

24. The names of the chief cities of Assyria are Accadian, and are generally written ideographically with the Accadian *si* ("land") affixed. Shalmaneser seems to mention Bilu-snmili-capi as the founder of the Semitic monarchy. Sennacherib brought back from Babylon (in B.C. 700) a seal which belonged to a former Assyrian king, Sallimmanu-ussuru (whose name and legend are Semitic), 600 years previously. Before that event alliances had been made with (non-Semitic) kings of Babylonia by Assyrian kings who bear Semitic names (Assur-yupallat, Buzur-Assur).[1] The two *patesis* of Assur, however, who founded the great temple there, and who are stated by Tiglath-Pileser I. (1120) to have built the temple 701 years before his time, have Turanian names and inscriptions. The first known inscription of the Semitic Assyrians is the seal above referred to; Shalmaneser's predecessors are only known through a tablet which gives a synchronous history of Assyria and Chaldæa.

25. The Semitic traditions all point to Arabia as the original home of the race. It is the only part of the world which has remained exclusively Semite. The racial characteristics—intensity of faith, ferocity, exclusiveness, imagination—can best be explained by a desert origin. Palestine would seem to have been originally occupied by non-Semitic tribes, the Zamzummim, etc., the giants of old days. The Phœnicians were said to have come from the Persian Gulf (Strab. i. 2, 35, xvi. 3, 4; 4, 27; Justin, xviii. 3, 2; Plin. N. H. iv. 36; Hdt. i. 1, vii. 89; Schol. to Hom. Od. iv. 84). The myth of Kepheus and the Æthiopians at Joppa might point in the same direction. Egypt would seem to have been colonized by a ruling Semitic caste at an early period; in this way we can best explain the Semitic colouring of the grammar, and the strange mixture of an elevated Semitic religion with Nigritian beast-worship; and the Semites could only have crossed from Arabia. Apparently, also, Palestine was not Semi-

[1] In this way, perhaps, we may account for Accadian kings with Semitic names and inscriptions (Naram-Sin, the destroyer of Carrak, for instance) in the sixteenth century B.C. In the case of Naram-Sin, however, it must be borne in mind that there seems to have been another contemporary monarch in Babylonia, Rim-Sin (unless the two names are identical).

tized in the fourth millennium B.C. No affinity can be shown to exist between the Semitic and Aryan families of the speech. They are radically different in genius and in grammar. One is based upon monosyllabic roots: the other presupposes triliterals. All attempts to compare single roots in the two families are unscientific; we have no Grimm's law, neither do we know the original meaning and form in many cases: and coincidences often happen in the most diverse languages (e.g. Mandschu *sengui* and Latin *sanguis*). Words like נף compared with κέπας are borrowed; and onomatopœia has played a great part in the origin of all languages, producing similar sounds for the same idea.

26. This date comes from Berosus: here begins his Assyrian (Semitic) dynasty, headed by Semiramis, for 526 years (cf. Hdt. i. 95). The date is confirmed by the scanty hints of the inscriptions: all the older Chaldæan kings have Turanian names and legends; Semitic begins with Merodach-iddin-akhi, the contemporary of Tiglath-Pileser I. (B.C. 1110). The mutilated records of the cylinder of Nabonidus point in the same direction.

27. *Casadu* is a common Assyrian word ("to possess"); *casidu* will be the nomen agentis. If "Ur of the Casdim" is to be identified with the Chaldæan Huru,[1] it will be the Semitic name attached to the old Accadian "moon-city" (however pronounced). The Semites changed the names of the Babylonian cities in many cases: thus *Ca-dimirra*, "the gate of God," became *Bab-ilu*. Chesed was brother of Huz and Buz and uncle of Aram (Gen. xxii. 21), and Arphaxad was son of Shem.

28. This Khammurabi was the leader of a dynasty which was not Accadian, but Elamite, though speaking a language allied to Accadian. It would seem to be the *Arabian* dynasty of Berosus. Probably 'Αρδβιοι is a corruption of the final part of Khammurahi (? or for 'Αυρδβιοι). The Nahr-Malk was ascribed to Semiramis. S'ammnramat was the name of an Assyrian queen, whose name, I think, was confounded by Greek writers with Khammurabi.

29. The plural of *yumu*, "day," is made feminine (W.A.I. iii. 44), *yumāti* instead of *yumi*, and the curious phrase *ana yumati*, "for ever," used. So, again, we must notice the use of *im* (אם, e.g. *im matima*, "if any one"). Assur-hani-pal's inscriptions give us the first examples of

---

[1] *Huru* or *'uru* simply meant "the city," and I have found the name used for the whole of Babylonia. '*Uru*, I believe, was borrowed by the nomad Semites under the form of עיר. Cities were a product of Accadian civilization; and the Assyrians retained in their usual term for "a city" *alu* (=אהל) a remembrance of their original tent-life.

־תֶא with the accusative pronouns; e.g., *attu-a* and *attu-cunu* (S. H. A., 190, 23). We also get *anacu* used with a preposition (*assu*) in *assu anacu*, "of myself" (S. H. A., 190, 24). Assur-bani-pal, again (S.H.A. 187 *k*), has the strange form *ikhallici* for *ikhallic* after *pani*, where the final vowel seems to have a conditional force. So the astrological tablets have *ikhkhar, ikhkhiram*, with initial *m* suppressed from *makharu*.

30. Not only is this common in the verbs (which always admitted the omission more or less), but we even find *yu-tag-gil-a-ni* for *yu-tag-gil-an-ni*, "he confided to me;" as well as the converse (e.g. *i-sac-can-nu* for *isaccanu*, "they place").

31. So, again, *ma-na-e*, as plural of *mana*, and *ta-a-din* (or *ta-din*) for *taddin*. Similarly we find the ungrammatical form *abbattiv-va* (S.H.A. 189, 13), instead of *abattiv*.

32. Besides the use of a quasi-article, תֵא with the accusative became common, especially in the case of the first personal pronoun, e.g., *at-tu-a*, "me" (אֵתִי). The change of ו into י, which is already effected in Hebrew (except in a few archaisms like וְלִד, Gen. xiv.), has also begun in Achæmenian Assyrian (e.g. *itahma* by the side of *utahma*).

In spite of its preservation of many archaic forms, Assyrian has entered upon a stage of corruption and degeneracy. The attempt at system displayed in its secondary conjugations is perhaps an instance. The dual has for the most part perished; it is only found in a few nouns (as in Hebrew) which express duality; and it is rarely met with in the verb.[1] The apocopated aorist has become the most usual form. Niphal has acquired a passive signification. The cases of the noun which are accurately distinguished in the earliest inscriptions tend to be more and more improperly used until in the Persian period even *-u* has ceased to be the mark of the nominative.[2] The same

[1] So it has disappeared from the verb in modern Arabic, and was wanting in Æthiopic.
[2] Traces of the case-terminations are to be found in Hebrew (ו Genesis i. 24, Numbers xxiv. 3, 15, Psalms cxiv. 8; י in construct, e.g. Genesis xlix. 11, Isaiah i. 21; ה local). So, too, in proper names, *Methu-selah, Methu-sha-el* (where the Assyrian sign of the genitive appears), *Penu-el, Khammuel* (1 Chronicles iv. 26), etc. In the Sinaitic inscriptions the

has been the fate of Arabic; in most dialects of modern Arabic they have even disappeared altogether. The Assyrian third plural of the verb-tenses has lost its final terminations *na* and *su*, which Hebrew has in some rare cases retained: probably this was in great measure caused by the addition of *ni*, the characteristic of the subjunctive. Both *su* and *na* have been weakened to *ni* in the perfect and future. The plural of nouns has degenerated into *an*, and even *i* or *e* for masculine, and *at* or *et* for feminine. Hence, in many instances, the plural and the second case of the singular have exactly the same form. Verbs י"ע undergo contraction, as in the allied dialects (though the nomen agentis takes the same form as in Arabic and Aramaic, e.g. *da-i-is* or *da-is*, "trampling on," instead of קָם or קוֹם). Verbs ע"ע are regular, except that a preceding *u* assimilates *e*.

Dr. Hincks believed that in an early stage the Assyrian made no distinction between the genders of the personal pronouns. A bilingual tablet of Accadian laws reads *atta* for *atti*, and *su* for *sa*, besides *isir* for *tasir* and *igtabi* for *tagtabi*;

nominative in proper names and titles only ends in *u*, and the genitive takes *i* if the nomen regens and the nomen rectum are connected so as to form a compound. *Gashmu* in Nehemiah (vi. 6), elsewhere *Geshem* (ii. 19), is another instance. In the old Egyptian monuments names of places in Palestine, which end in a consonant in the Old Testament, have *u* final; thus נגבו = *Negeb*, בעלו = *Baal*. So in Phœnician *Hasdrubal*, etc., while Samaritan shows -*u* and -*i* in certain words before suffixes (especially כ); similarly Aramaic. The Abd-Zohar coins (Levy, Z. D. M. G. xv.) have י (e.g. in מזרי) before יו, and the proper names, as in the inscriptions of Palmyra, the Hauran, and the Nabathean kings, terminate in ו. In Æthiopic the sign of the accusative *a* has been preserved (also the termination of the *status constructus*). According to Palgrave, the three terminations are still to be heard in central Arabia; further south and east *a* stands for *i*, and nearer the coast all three have entirely disappeared. Nöldeke disputes, to a certain extent, the existence of the case-endings in Hebrew, and affirms that they are peculiar to Arabic. Assyrian, however, opposes this conclusion.

and he compared the (supposed) archaic use of הוּא and נַעַר as of common gender in the Pentateuch. But the tablet states that it was written in the reign of Assur-bani-pal, and it is a mere assumption that it is a transcript of an older translation. We do not find any disregard of gender in the inscriptions of Tiglath-Pileser I. Moreover, it is very possible that the translator was an Accadian, and but imperfectly acquainted with Assyrian. This is rendered almost certain by the ungrammatical use of the verbs, which follow the genderless Turanian idiom. The same looseness of grammar characterizes a letter to Assur-bani-pal from the Elamite king Umman-aldaśi (S. H. A., p. 252); and in one place we even have *su* for the feminine (*mahaśśu* for *mahad-sa*, S. H. A., 291, *m*).

The introduction of *attu* to form the accusative shows that already in the time of Assur-bani-pal the case-endings had begun to lose their meaning, and we are not surprised, therefore, to find the different terminations confounded one with the other.

LITERATURE OF THE ASSYRIAN LANGUAGE.

The first conscious attempts at the formation of a grammar —older probably than the earliest of the Hindu grammarians —seem to have been made by the Semitic Assyrians. It was found necessary to explain the Accadian language, the original possessor of the cuneiform system of writing, in which were contained, stored up in the libraries of Hurn and Senkereh, which Sargina had founded in the sixteenth century B.C., all the treasures of borrowed Assyrian science and religion. By the command, therefore, of Essar-haddon and

Assur-bani-pal, syllabaries, grammars, dictionaries, and translations were drawn up. The last king states that Nebo and Tasmitu had inspired him to attempt the re-editing of the "royal tablets," which no previous king had attempted, and at the same time to explain and chronicle all the difficulties, "as many as existed," "for the inspection of his people." This implies that there was a considerable amount of culture in the country at the time. The nouns are always given in the nominative, generally with the mimmation added, which was therefore considered the typical form of the word. The third persons singular and plural of the aorist and present are the only parts of the verb which we find; it would seem that they took the place of the nominative of the nouns; from them the other persons could at once be derived. The most important fact which we have to notice is the full recognition of triliteralism. No radix consists of less than three letters, and the rule is accurately observed in the defective verbs: thus we have *da-'a-cu* (דוך), *ba-'a-bu* (בב), *si-'i-mu*, *pu-'u-ru*, *ma-lu-'u* (מלא), *ka-bu-'u* (קבה) Just as Sanskrit grammar begins with the recognition of monosyllabic roots, Semitic grammar begins with the recognition of a triliteral basis. Assyrian passed away before the encroaching influence of Aramæan, but as late as the reign of Antiochus we have the cuneiform characters (and apparently the language also) still used. Since the decipherment of the inscriptions the following works upon the subject have appeared:—

E. Botta, "Mémoire sur l'écriture cunéiforme Assyrienne" (in Journ. Asiat.), 1847. De Saulcy, "Recherches sur l'écriture cunéiforme Assyrienne," Paris, 1848. E. Botta and E. Flandin, "Monument de Ninive," 5 vols., Paris, 1849–50.

(The inscriptions in vols. iii. and iv. contain Sargon's annals from Khorsabad.) Sir H. Rawlinson, "Commentary on the Cun. Inscr. of Babylon and Assyria," London, 1850. E. Hincks, in Transact. of R. Irish Soc., 1850 (the names of Sennacherib and Nebuchadnezzar identified). Dr. G. F. Grotefend, in the Götting. Gelehrt. Anzeigen, 1850, No. 13 (on the age of the Black Obelisk). E. Hincks, Journ. of R. Asiat. Soc., xiv., 1851, pt. 1. H. Ewald, in Götting. Gel. Anz., 1851, No. 60. A. H. Layard, "Inscriptions in the Cuneiform Character from Assyr. Monum." (Brit. Mus.), 1851 (untrustworthy copies; contains the inscr. of the Black Obelisk). Grotefend, "Bemerkungen zur Inschrift eines Thongefässes mit Niniv. Keilschrift," Göttingen, 1850-51 (Grotefend had already published a memoir on this inscription in 1848, and had attempted the Assyrian inscriptions in a paper, "Zur Erläuter. d. Babylon. Keilschr.," 1840); "Die Tributverzeichniss d. Obelisken aus Nimrud nebst Vorbemerkungen über d. verschied. Ursprung u. Charakter d. persischen u. Assyr. Keilschr.," Göttingen, 1852; "Erläuter. d. Keilinschr. Babylon. Backsteine," Hanover, 1852. Dr. E. Hincks, "On the Language and Mode of Writing of the Ancient Assyrians," read before the Brit. Asso., 1850. In Transact. of Royal Irish Soc., xxii., 1852, xxiv., 1854 (the numerals made out, and the Babylonian characters deciphered). J. Bonomi, "Nineveh and its Palaces," London, 1852. Grotefend, "Erläuter. der Babyl. Keilinschr. aus Behistun," Göttingen, 1853. Rawlinson, "Memoir on the Babylonian and Assyrian Inscriptions," 1854. De Saulcy, in Journal Asiatique ("Traduction de l'Inscription Assyr. de Behistoun"), 1854-55. C. C. Bunsen, "Outlines of a Philosophy of Universal History," vol. i.,

London, 1854. Grotefend, "Erläuter. zweier Ausschr. Nebukadnezar's in babyl. Keilschr.," Göttingen, 1854. Hincks, "On Assyrian Verbs," in Journ. of Sacred Literature, 1855–56 (extremely valuable, the foundation of an Assyrian grammar). J. Brandis, "Ueber d. histor. Gewinn aus d. Entziffer. der Assyr. Inschriften," Berlin, 1856 (he had already published, in 1853, "Rerum Assyriarum tempora emendata," Bonn). Fox Talbot, "On Assyrian Inscriptions," in Journ. of Sacred Lit., 1856. M. von Niebuhr, "Geschichte Assur's u. Babel's seit Phul," Berlin, 1857. Rawlinson, Fox Talbot, Hincks, and Oppert, "Inscr. of Tiglath-Pileser I. transl.," 1857. J. Oppert, in Journ. Asiat., v., tom. 9, 10, 1857–8. J. Ménant, "Inscriptions Assyriennes des briques de Babylone (Essai de lecture et d'interprétation)," Paris, 1859; "Notice sur les Inscriptions en caractères cun. de la collection epigraphique de M. Lothoi de Laval," Paris, 1859. Hincks, "Babylon and its Priestkings," in Journ. of Sacred Lit., 1859. Fox Talbot, "Annals of Essar-Haddon," in same, 1859. Oppert, "Eléments de la Grammaire Assyr.," Paris, 1860 (first attempt to form a full grammar; very useful to the student). Ménant, "Recueil des Alphabets pour servir à la lecture et l'interprétation des écritures cun.," Paris, 1860. Hincks, "Arioch and Belshazzar," in Journ. of Sac. Lit., 1861. Rawlinson and Norris, "The Cun. Inscr. of Western Asia," vols. i., ii., iii., London, 1861, 66, 70 (lithographed for the Brit. Mus.). Ménant, "Les Noms propres Ass.," Paris, 1861; "Principes élémentaires de la lecture des Textes Ass.," Paris, 1861; "Sur les Inscr. Assyr. du Brit. Mus.," 1862–3. G. Rawlinson, "Herodotus," vol. i., London, 1858 (contains valuable essays by his brother)

"The Five Great Monarchies of the Ancient Eastern World," vol. i., London, 1862. Hincks, "The Polyphony of the Assyrio-Babylonian Cun. Writing" (reprinted from the Atlantis), 1863 (valuable). Oppert, "Expédition scientifique en Mésopotamie," vols. i., ii., 1863. Ménant, "Inscr. Assyr. de Hammourabi," Caen, 1863. Oppert and Ménant, "Les Fastes de Sargon" (trad.), Paris, 1863 (important to the historian; a commentary and vocabulary are added); "Grande Inscription de Khorsabad, publ. et comment.," two vols., Paris, 1865. Ménant, "Eléments d'Epigraphie Assyr.," second edit., Caen, 1864 (first edit. 1860). J. Olshausen, "Prüfung des Charakters d. in d. Assyr. Keilinschriften enthaltenen semit. Sprache," in the Abhdl. d. Kön. Akad. d. Wiss. zu Berlin, 1864 (valuable attempt at a comparison of Assyrian with the cognate languages; Oppert's grammar criticized). Rawlinson, in the Journ. R.A.S. 1864 (on the bilingual, Ass. and Phœnician inscriptions). Ménant, "Inscr. des revers des plaques du Palais de Khorsabad trad.," Paris, 1865. Hincks, "On the Assyrio-Babylonian Measures of Time," 1865; "Specimen Chapters of an Assyr. Grammar," in Journ. R. A. S., 1866 (the most important contribution to Assyrian Grammar yet made). E. Norris, "Specimen of an Assyrian Dictionary," J.R.A.S., 1866. Fox Talbot, "Assyrian Vocabulary," in J.R.A.S., 1867-9 (full of unscientific comparisons). Ménant, "Exposé des éléments de la grammaire Assyrienne," Paris, 1868 (Oppert's first edition enlarged; inaccurate and incomplete). Oppert, "Grammaire Assyrienne," second edit., Paris, 1868 (very good and useful, but disfigured by the theory of a stat. emphat. and an incomplete theory of the verb). Norris, "Assyrian Dict.," vols. i., ii.,

1868, 70 (useful, but premature; has not as yet advanced further than *l* in the nouns). D. Haigh, G. Smith, Oppert, and Lenormant, in the Zeitschrift für Aegyptische Sprache, 1868-70 (mostly on Assyrian history; the question of the canon reviewed by Lepsius in the Abhdl. d. Berl. Akad., 1870). Lenormant, in the Rev. Archéologique, 1869. G. Smith, in the North British Review, 1869-70 (especially an important paper on "Assyrian and Bab. Libraries"). E. Schrader, in the Zeitschr. d. D. Morgenl. Gesellsch., xxiii., 1869 (proof of the decipherment and its results); also pp. 82-5 in his edition of De Wette's "Lehrbuch," Berlin, 1869. Ménant, "Le Syllabaire Assyrienne" (useful, but too long and incomplete). A. Sayce, in the Journal of Philology, 1870 (attempt to form an Accadian grammar). Renan, in Mémoires de la Société de Linguistique de Paris, 1869, "Sur les formes du verbe Sémit." (Assyrian grammar compared with those of the cognate languages). M. A. Harkavy, Revue Israélite, 1870, Nos. 2, 6, 8, 10, 12, and 14. G. Smith, "History of Assur-bani-pal," 1871 (cuneiform texts, translated); "Phonetic Values of the Cuneiform Characters," and "Chronology of the reign of Sennacherib," 1871. Lenormant, "Lettres Assyriologiques" (on Media and Armenia), 1871. Criticism of the interpretations (more or less favourable). Ewald, in the Götting. Gel. Anz., 1857, 58, 59, 60, 68. Renan, in Journ. des Savants, 1859. F. Hitzig, "Sprache u. Sprachen Assyriens," (attempt to compare Assyrian with Sanskrit by rejecting polyphons!) Leipzig, 1871. Ch. Schöbel, "Examen critique du déchiffrement des inscr. cun. Assyr.," Paris, 1861. Assyrian used for comparative purposes in Rödiger's Gesenius' Heb. Gram., 20th edit., 1869. Ewald,

"Abhandlung über d. geschichtliche folge d. Semitischen Sprachen," Gött., 1871 (Assyrian is placed in the same (second) stage of development of Semitic speech as Æthiopic). We may be allowed to refer to the dreams of Dorow ("Die Assyr. Keilschrift erläut. durch 2 Jaspis-Cylinder aus Nineveh u. Bab.," Wiesb., 1820), W. Drummond (Classical Journ., 1812), C. Forster ("One Primæval Language," 1856), and Comte de Gobineau ("Traité des Écritures cun." two vols., Paris, 1864; "Lect. des textes cun.," Paris, 1859).

PHONOLOGY.

The syllabary, as we have seen, was of non-Semitic origin, and primitively hieroglyphic. Its inventors spoke a variety of Turanian idioms, and inhabited the lowlands of Chaldæa. Every character was an ideograph, denoting some object or notion, sometimes more than one, as in Egyptian and Chinese. Different sounds, consequently, were attached to the same character, either because the object or idea admitted of different names, or because the various tribes of Chaldæa did not always agree in their vocabulary. When these characters came to be used phonetically, polyphony was the necessary result. The Assyrians adopted the system of writing, along with the science and mythology, of their predecessors. When space was an object, the characters were used ideographically, and this was generally pointed out by the addition of the (Semitic) grammatical termination. Thus ideographs came to take the place of the Hebrew *literæ dilatabiles*. Ordinarily, however, the words were spelled out phonetically: in this case, the sounds attached to the characters by the Accadians, which had ceased to have any meaning for people who spoke another language, were employed as phonetic values. As these sounds (words once, but now replaced by Semitic roots if the characters were used ideographically) were manifold, almost every character had at least more than one power attached to it. This would seem to introduce an element of confusion into the orthography; but such is not the case. The different powers were used in accordance with rule—the Assyrian writing was to be read, not puzzled out—and it is but seldom that the transliteration is doubtful. Homophones are rare. Owing to the hieroglyphic origin of the writing, the number of characters is very large, almost every possible combination of two or three letters (one being a vowel) being found.[1] Many are of rare occurrence, some are only to be met with in the syllabaries. Were these perfect, this part of the subject would be complete. A syllabary, generally, sets the character to be explained in the second of three parallel columns; the first column representing the Accadian word (a mere phonetic sound in Assyrian), and the third the Assyrian root, which translated the Accadian of the first column and was the pronunciation when the character was employed as an ideograph. Thus we have a character, whose usual value is *is*, explained *i-si* in the first column, *sa-du-'u* ("mountain") in the third: then in the next line the same character with *ta-khar* in the first column, *ip-ru* ("dust") in the third. Again, a character, whose ordinary power is *mi*, is given thrice following as *mi-e* in the first column, successively translated *ku-lu* ("assembly"), *ka-'a-lu* ("assemble") and *tam-tsu* ("weight") in the third;

---

[1] Mr. G. Smith gives 389 in his "Syllabary," about 200 being compounds, but he has not given all the characters that are found.

then the same sign with *i-si-ip* in the first column and *ra-am-cu* ("herd") in the third. It will be seen that when a closed syllable of two consonants is not used, two characters which respectively end and begin with the same vowel take its place, the two vowels coalescing in a long syllable. For the syllabary the reader is referred to Ménant's "Grammaire Assyrienne," pp. 11—36, or his "Syllabaire Assyrienne,"[1] or to Norris's "Assyrian Dictionary," vol. i. (beginning), with supplement in vol. ii.

My transcription of the Hebrew alphabet is as follows:—
א = 'a, ב = b, ג = g, ד = d, ה = h, ו = 'u, ז = z, ח = kh, ט = dh, י = i, כ = c, ל = l, מ = m, נ = n, ס = s, ע = ̒, פ = p, צ = ts, ק = k, ר = r, שׁ = s, ת = t.

The Assyrian syllabary made no difference between *b* and *p* final; similarly between *f, c* and *k* final, or *z, s* and *ts* final, or *t, d* and *dh* final. Unless, therefore, the syllable is doubled, and the initial letter of the next character determines the value of the last preceding, we have to be guided by comparison alone in fixing upon the root. Between initial *p* and *b*, again, when followed by *u*, and between initial *s* and *ts*

---

[1] This will contain all that is needed by the student of Assyrian grammar. At the same time the syllabary is very incomplete (*e.g.* the character under *lak* has further values of *gal* and *issep*, that under *du* of *gub, sū, rā*, and *dun*, that under *kap*, which does not require a query, is the Assyrian *sumilu*, "left"), and a considerable number of rarer characters are not given at all. *Rām* is Assyrian ("high"), not Accadian, which is *aca*. The character marked 15 in p. 34 of the Grammaire was phonetically *gā*, No. 16 is *ur* Accadian, not connected with Semitic אוֹר; 14 was *ucu* (*sivan*); 13 was *uru*; 12 was (Accadian) *urud*, Assyrian *eru* ("metal"), and so on. The characters in p. 86 are similarly deficient. The first meant "south"; 8 is "a goat" (Assyrian *caranu*); 9 meant "limb" or "body" (Assyrian *si-'i-ru*); 10 was in Accadian *cit*, just as 2 was *ugudili*.

Since the above was written, Mr. G. Smith has published his "Syllabary," which leaves but little to be desired in this part of the subject.

when followed by *a*, as well as between initial *dh* when followed by *a* or *i*, there was the same confusion. The Assyrians did not improve upon the syllabary which they borrowed, and which in some respects was not well adapted to express a Semitic speech.

א is expressed by the same letter, whether it denotes a syllable or merely a long vowel (1). Thus *ta-'a-ru* (תאר, "to return, become") and *khar-sa-a-nu*, *kharsānu*, "forests," have both the same character. The same holds good of *i* and *u*. *A*, as the weaker letter, is lost after or before *u*, e.g. *usalic* for *a-usalic*, *u'ulla* for *u-alla*. It is very commonly weakened to *i*, as in the cognate dialects. In this case the Babylonian dialect generally had *e* in place of the guttural; e.g. *rēsu*, "head," Assyrian *risu* (like *recutu* for רחק). *A* with *h* following coalesces into a long syllable, as *dlu* = אהל or *nāru* by the side of *nahru*. In correct orthography *h* is written when a syllable is denoted; thus we have indiscriminately *na-h-ru* and *na-'a-ru*, "a river." *H* is sometimes used to represent the diphthong *ai*: thus "house" is either *bi-ya-he*, *ba-h-tu*, *bi-'i-tu*, or more commonly even *bi-tu*.[1] *H* also stands for ע, e.g. *ri-h-u-tu* and *ri-e-u-tu*, "rule" (from רעה), *rah(i)mu* and *remu*, *bu-h-i*, "seeking" (from בעה). It sometimes expresses the breathing before verbs which have a vowel as first radical, e.g. *ah-a-bid*, "I perish," *u-h-a-bid*, from אבד, *u-sa-h-lid*, *ah-al-du* from אלד (2).

---

[1] This is an instance of the tendency of the Assyrians to corrupt their language by breaking down the syllables. In this respect they are the Latins of ancient Semitism. Another instance of this tendency is shown in the fact that ע is always a vowel simply. The confusion of syllables is carried so far that we get ה dropped altogether; e.g. for *u-tu-h-ut* (הואת), the later inscriptions give us *utut*.

ו as a consonant is not distinguished from *m*. This is a fault of the original system of writing, but it has had great influence upon the Assyrian. In this way the mimmation has hardened into a long vowel (*tum, tuv, tū*). The conjunction after a verb which ends in a vowel is represented by a character which usually stands for *ma*, but here is *va*. Hence, after the mimmation, it is impossible to say whether *ma* or *va* is to be read; probably the former (see below). "The suppression of *m* or *v*," Dr. Oppert says, "is more frequent than in the other Semitic languages." Conversely, we find *acmu*, "I burned" (כמה), Hebrew כוה, *amaru*, "seeing," Hebrew אור (but also *urru*), etc. So in Æthiopic *m* and *v* interchange, e.g. *masaca* and *vasaka* (3).

As a vowel, *u* is expressed by three different characters, properly *hu, u,* and *va*, though this distinction is not always observed. The cuneiform could not express either *yu* or *uy;* consequently these sounds had to be expressed by *u*. Hence the first and third persons of pael, iphtaal, etc., are *written* in precisely the same way, though pronounced *u-* and *yu-*. So, again, we have *abu'a, katu'a* for *abu-ya, katu-ya*. This want of inventiveness and adaptation on the part of the Assyrians argues against the Semitic origin of the Aramaic alphabet. *U* hardened easily into *va*, as in all Semitic tongues: thus, *yunakkaru-va*, "he shall destroy, and"; *kharri va bamāti*, "the valleys and heights"; *iššukh-va*, "it was removed and." In both the latter instances we should usually have had *u*, since, as in Hebrew, the conjunction inclines to a vowel-sound before a labial. This *va* sometimes becomes simple *a*, the *u* being lost altogether, as in *sukalula* for *sukalul-va*, or *dhābu* for *dhăvăbu*. *U* passes readily into the weaker *i*, e.g. *sunu* by the side of *sina*, *uraps-inni* for *urapsu-inni* (comp. *optumus*, *optimus*).

B before *v* is generally assimilated, e.g. *eruv-vá*, "he descended and," for *erub-vá*. Conversely, *vá* becomes *ma* after a preceding mimmation, as *abnum-má*, "I built and," where the second *m* merely expresses the length of the preceding syllable, which has been lengthened by the enclitic, and the loss of *w* (or *v*).

Z as in Hebrew never changes to a dental. *Z* in Babylonian may take the place of *ts*, as in *erzitiv* for *irtsitiv*. In Babylonian, also, we find *Bar-zi-pa* taking the place of the Assyrian *Bar-śi-ip*, or *Bar-śa-ip* (where we have again to notice the confusion between *ai* and *ī*). Rarely *s* and *ts*, when followed by *i*, are confused; e.g. we find both *takhāzi* and *takhātsi*, "battle," (מָחִיץ) and *arzip* by the side of *artsip*, "I built," (רָצַף). Compare זָעַק and צָעַק, זִין, and צִיץ, etc., in Hebrew. The Assyrian tendency to soften the pronunciation is exemplified in their use of ט (though their preference for צ in many cases, and their preservation of the sibilants show that this tendency had not gone far). Once we find the extraordinary assimilation of *śkh* into *zz*, and *śś* in *śazzaru*, "small," for *śaśkharu*, and *śiśśeru* for *śiśkhiru*.

Kh like *r* can be invariably doubled, as in Arabic (like מָרָה Prov. xiv. 10; שָׁרֵךְ Ezek. xvi. 4). It is occasionally used to express the guttural sound of the Hebrew ע, as in *Khazitu*=עַזָּה *Gáza*. Conversely, we have חִדֶּקֶל for *Idiklat*. This, however, was Accadian, not Assyrian; and the Assyrian *imiru* is not חֲמוֹר, but Phœnician and Aramaic אֲמָר. The Assyrian tendency towards a soft pronunciation showed itself in sometimes omitting the medial or final ה of a root, its place being supplied by the simple aspirate: e.g. פָּתַח is always *pitu'u*, and *katu*, "hand," is perhaps from לָקַח, the Assyrian form of which is *ilkū*, "he took." *Rukutu*, again, "distant," is the Assyrian form of רָחַק. In Babylonian it is *ri-e-ku-tu* or *ri-e-ou-tu*, where ע replaces ח. So also *apte'e* instead of the ordinary *apti* from פָּתַח.

Dh is found for *t* after a guttural: e.g. *akdhirib*, "I approached," the iphteal of קָרַב. So *d* replaces *t* after *m* or *n*; e.g. *imdanakharu*.

I is regularly found in the place of the Hebrew א, whenever this last varies with י, either in Hebrew itself or in the cognate dialects: e.g. *ris* = רֹאשׁ (רִישָׁן), Targ. (רִים), *sibu* = ذيب ذَاب. In Assyrian itself, *a*, first weakened to *i*, was absorbed by an *i*: e.g. *yutir*, "he restored," from *ta'aru* (for *yuta'ir*), *bitu* for *bi-ya-tu* or *ba-hi-tu* (בַּיִת), etc. So in the third person *ispur*, *ispuru* for *yaspur*, *yaspuru*. Hebrew, Aramaic, Æthiopic, and Himyaritic, show a similar weakening. *I* interchanges also with *e*: e.g. *ci-i-nu* (Assyrian), and *ci-e-nu* (Babylonian), *tsa-'i-ri*, *tsa-yā-ri*, and *tsa-e-ri*, and the oblique cases and plurals of masculine nouns.

I, like *u* and *a*, is never doubled.

C rarely takes the place of ג and (more frequently) ק in the cognate dialects: e.g. *kakkaru* = כִּכָּר (comp. עָכַר), *cirbu* = קָרַב, *ca'ari*, *carie* = קִיר, קָרָה, *cutsbam*, "beautifully" = קָצַב.

C and *ts* are frequently combined in roots, where Hebrew, etc., prefer the softer consonants: thus *actsur* (from *catsiru*) = גָּזַר, *cutsalu* = גּוֹזָל, *cinitsu* = גָּנַן.

In Assyrian itself an interchange of *c* with *k* and *g* sometimes occurs; e.g. *cabru* and *gubru*; *kinnātu* ("female slave") is on Michaux's stone *cinātu*. The latter was apparently the vulgar pronunciation common in Babylonian. In fact, in the Babylonian, *g* commonly takes the place of *k*, e.g. *gatu* for *katu*, *sangute* for *sankute*, "chains." This pronunciation began to prevail in Assyria in the later days of the empire. Dr. Oppert remarks that *c* seems to have had a softened sound, which assimilated it to the Hebrew ג; thus *Tukulti* = תגלת, *S'arru-cinu* = סרגון, *Sacanu* = סגן. *Tiglath*, however, answers to the Assyrian *tiglat* or *tigulti*; *Sargon* is not the Assyrian *S'arru-cinu*, but the Accadian original *S'argina;* and *Sacanu*, by which, I suppose, either *Sacnu* or *Saccanacu* is meant, was non-Semitic. On the other hand, *c* and ג answer to one another in *Nebuchadnezzar*, *Calah*, and *Accad*.

L is the pronunciation generally, though by no means necessarily, assumed by a sibilant before a dental: e.g. *khamistu* and *khamiltu* ("five"), *istu* and *ultu* ("from") *asdhur* and *aldhur* ("I wrote"), *astacan* and *altanan* ("I fought"), *lubustu* and *lubultu* ("clothing"), *mikhistu* and *mikhiltu* ("strong"). *L*, however, never becomes a sibilant. This change of consonant, peculiar to Assyrian, must have been effected through *r* into which the sibilant first passed. Compare the mutations of final *s* in Sanskrit. Before a second hard sibilant, *s* may also become *l*; as in *ulsis* for *ussis*. In common pronunciation *l* seems to have been somewhat *mouillé;* thus verbs ending in *l* generally have *a* attached even in cases which would hardly permit the conditional suffix, e.g. *aslula;* while on the other hand the case-terminations are sometimes improperly dropped before a following *l*, as in *ana gurunit la agrun*, "to a heap I heaped."

M usually, but not always, becomes *n* before a sibilant, a dental, or a guttural: thus we have *dhen-su* from טעם, *khansa* and *khamsa* ("five"), *khandhu* (חמם), *tsindu* and *tsimdu* ("a yoked-chariot"), *muntakhitsu* for *mumtakhitsu* ("fighting"), *dumku* and *dunku* ("lucky"). In this way is explained the change of the plural-ending into *n*, like the change of mimmation into nunnation. So in Æthiopic, *m* before dentals and labials passes into *n*. A double *b* or *p* may be replaced by *mb*, *mp* (e.g. *inambu* for *inabbu*), and a double dental by *nd*, *nt*, (e.g. *inandin* for *inaddin*) just as in Æthiopic. *M* first changed to *n* can be assimilated to a following consonant, as in *ikhkhar* from *makhiru*, *takhatsi* (for *takhkhatsi*) from מחץ.

N, as in Hebrew, is assimilated generally to the following radical. This is the rule with verbs פ'נ, though we meet with *inandin* for *inaddin* ("it is given"). Contrary, however, to Hebrew, *n* is assimilated (regularly) before *t* and *s*; e.g. *limuttu* for *limuntu* ("injured"), *libittu* for *libintu* ("brick-work"), *maddattu* or *madattu* ("tribute") for *mandantu* (*mandattu* is found); *cissu* ("much," "collected") from כנס (Targum. כנש). So in Hebrew אמת for אמנת, אף for אנף.

S rarely represents a Hebrew שׁ as in *khursanis* from חרש, *ti'amu* = שהם, *siba*, "seven" (W.A.I. ii., 19, 66). Where the Hebrew has ס and שׂ, Assyrian also has *s* and *s;* e.g. *sarru* and *saru* ("king"), *cabis* and *cabisu*, "trampling." *S* seems to have been preferred by the Assyrians, *s* by the Babylonians (see *suprá*). Just as the example of סרגן = *Sarru-cinu* shows that the Assyrian pronunciation of *s* was hard, so the fact that *t-s* is frequently expressed by *s* points to a similarly hard pronunciation of the latter. Thus *sarrut-su* ("his kingdom") is also spelt *sarruśu, kat-su* ("his land") becomes *kaśśu* for *ka-śu*. The difference between *ś* and *ts* in Assyrian was probably that between *t-s* and *t-z*. Hence a final dental followed by the sibilant of the third personal pronoun is very commonly represented by *ś*; e.g. *dannuśu* for *dannut-su, illaśu* for *illad-su*. Conversely, *s* followed by the dental of the secondary conjugation is often written *ś* (like *st* pronounced *sh* in the tenth conjugation of the Mahri), as *aśacan* for *astacan, aśicin* for *asticin, aśarap* for *astarap*. Probably, however, the sibilant in vulgar pronunciation changed the place of the dental, just as, conversely, in Hebrew the dental of Hithpael followed the sibilant. In the inscription of Khammurabi *s* takes the place of *ś* in *tsirrasina* = *tsirraśina* (*tsirrat-sina*). This hard pronunciation of *ś* would once have been universal among the Semites, as is implied by the Greek pronunciation of *samech* (ξ). The interchange of *ś* and *s* in Assyrian (mostly in the later inscriptions) would show that a softened pronunciation was becoming usual. Similarly in Babylonian we find *usalbis-śu*, "I covered it" (for *su*).

E is always a vowel. Occasionally, however, it answers to a Hebrew ה; e.g. *ecilu* ("place") = Aramaic חקל, or *rēcutu* in Babylonian = רחק. There must, therefore, have been a time when the guttural pronunciation of ע was known to the Assyrians. *E* sometimes replaces א (as in *erinu* = ארן); conversely we have *ra-'a-du* ("thunder") = רעד, *aggullu* ("wheel") = עגל. Hebrew ע is also sometimes represented by *u* or *i*, e.g. *uzalu* ("gazelle") = غزال, *Istar* = עשתר. Its pronunciation differed but slightly from that of *i*, as is shown by the interchange of the two vowels (see *suprà*), and the fact that many characters have indifferently *e* and *i* as their vowel-sound. At the same time the presence of radical *e* was always observed; verbs with *e* radical are full. *E* with *u* fell away; thus from עלה we have *ul-la-'a* in Assyrian, and *u-'ul-la-'a* in Babylonian. Babylonian sounded it more clearly than Assyrian (so *ci-e-nu* for *ci-i-nu*). So from עפש, Assyrian has *epsit*, Babylonian *e-ib-sit*. On the other hand, generally in Babylonian and Achæmenian *e* was assimilated to *i*, while in Assyrian the converse took place; thus Assyrian *ebusu* = Babylonian *ibusu*. In both the weaker sound *a* was lost before *e*; e.g. *ebus*, "I made" (for *a-ebus*); but *a* following assimilated even a radical *e*; e.g. *isma'a* for *isme'a* from שמע. Occasionally *e* is interchanged with *a* in roots, owing to the guttural aspirate common to both, like נעל and גאל, אנם and ענם in Hebrew. Thus *agu'u*, "crown," is given also as *e-gu'u* in a syllabary, from the Accadian *ega* (compare ענה), and *eliah* and *aliah* are used indifferently; so *ersituv* for *irtsituv* in Babylonian, which often replaces by *e* an Assyrian *i*, where this has been weakened from an original '*a*. In the Babylonian *recutu* (Assyrian *rukutu*) *u* has been lost before *e*, which here replaces *kh*.

P prevails in Assyrian where *b* appears in Babylonian, and (often) in the cognate dialects (e.g. Assyrian *epis*=Babylonian *ebis*, *pursu*=برغوث). Conversely we have *bislu*=פסל. The two sounds interchange in Assyrian itself; thus we find *iskhupar*, "he overthrew," *sikhubartu*, "overthrow," *paldhuti*, "surviving," *baladhu*, "house" (פלם). In one instance *u* seems to replace פ; *etstsuru*, "a bird,"=Arabic عصفور, Hebrew צפור.

R, though, like *l*, sometimes used to form quadriliteral roots (e.g. *parsidu, palcitu, iskhupar*), is much more scantily employed than in the cognate dialects. Thus we have *cuśśu'u*, not כרשה, *annabu* ("hare"), not ארנב.

S was never aspirated, as in ancient Hebrew and Phœnician *Samsu*=שמש. Dr. Oppert gives a long list of words where Hebrew has שׂ and שׁ, but Assyrian simply *s* in both cases: *sumilu*=שׂמאל, *siptu*=שׂפת, *sarru*=שׂר, *pasku*=פשׂק, *dussûtu*=דשׁן, *distu*=דשׁא. Already in the seventh century B.C. the Hebrew pronunciation seems to have inclined towards an aspirated *s*; this would explain the transcription of Sargon, etc., by ס. In Assyrian itself we have a word like *bis-śu, bis-śate*, and in Assur-bani-pal's inscriptions *taśbusu* is a variant of *taśbuśu*. In Arabic (and Æthiopic for the most part) *s* (*ś*)=Northsemitic *sh*, and *sh*=Northsemitic *s* (*ś*). Before a dental, *ts* might become *s*, as in *marustu* (and *marultu*) for *marutstu*. So *bislu*=Hebrew פסל, *isid*=יסד.

T servile, in the secondary conjugations, is assimilated to a preceding צ, ז, ד, and ט (e.g. *itstabat* becomes *itstsabat*, "he takes," *iztacir* becomes *izzacir*, *astacan* becomes *aśacan*. After a guttural, *t* servile may change to *d* or *dh*, e.g. *igdamir* for *igtamir*, *ikdhirib* for *iktarib*, *ikdhabi* for *iktabi*. We find even *amdhakhits* for *amtakhits* ("I fought"), according to Dr. Oppert through the influence of the following צ, though after *m* or *n t* more usually becomes *d*. *Bd* in Assyrian, again, was regularly changed into *pt*; e.g. *captu*, "heavy" (כבד), *aptati*, "ruins" (אבד). There is one instance of *d* in Assyrian and Babylonian replacing a ת of the other dialects: נתן is always *nadin*. *T* replaces *dh* in Babylonian in *tub*=*dhub* (so in Æthiopic *cadana*=כתן, כתם, *damana*=

טָמֵן, *dabyr* = טוּר). The syllabary had no special character for *dha*. In *iotil*, *t* replaces Hebrew ט, as in Æthiopic.

The Assyrian avoided the use of diphthongs: *au* is very rare; perhaps the foreign name *Khauran* is the only certain example of it. *Ai* and *ya* are much more common. The Gentile termination is *ai*, e.g. *Madai*, "the Medes." *Ai* has a tendency to become *ya* or *yā*;[1] thus *ayāsi* (אַיִשׁ) is more usually *yāsi*; *aibut*, "enemies," also appears as *yābut*; *yanu* or *yānu* = אַיִן. More frequently *ay* or *ya* passed either into *ah* (*bāhtu* = *biyatu*) or *i;* while in proper names an initial Hebrew י was always *ya* (e.g. *Yahua, Yahukhazi*), in roots it was more generally *i* (e.g. *imnu* = יָמִן, *irad* = יָרַד, *isibu* = יָשַׁב, *isara* = יָשָׁר). Even when answering to אַ, *ai* became *i;* e.g. *inu* = אַיִן. To prevent a compound vowel, *hemza* was largely employed, as in *abu'a* for *abu-ya*, "my father." As in modern Arabic, *hemza* tended more and more to be lost: in the Babylonian period it is very generally replaced by a long vowel: so even *utut* for *utuhut*.

1. As in all ancient Semitic alphabets, '*a* was a consonant, a soft breathing, namely, followed by the vowel *a*. This will explain how it is that *ai* is represented by '*a*+'*a*. The second breathing here passed into *y*, so that we have '*aya*; and hence *ai*.

2. ‏H‎ is another instance of the ambiguity arising from the employment of a foreign alphabet. It stood for *h*, *ah*, and *hi*. More usually the value is *ah*.

3. In the Babylonian inscriptions the *m* final very often appears as a separate character, implying that the mimmation was more strongly pronounced in Babylonia than in Assyria. The interchange of מ and ב in the cognate languages argues the weaker and later pronunciation of ב as *v*. Assyrian does not exhibit any interchange of *b* and *m*. *B* reduplicated, however, may be changed into *mb*, e.g. *innambu*, "he is proclaimed," for *innabbu*, just as we find *ambuba* for אַבּוּב, Ἰερομβάαλ for יְרֻבַּעַל, σαμβύκη

[1] This is properly אַי; e.g. *yarru* = יָאר.

for סַבְכָא; and conversely סִימְפֹנְיָה from συμφωνία. The change is an Aramaising one, and therefore exceptional in Assyrian: more frequently in (mercantile) contract tablets of late date.

There is no trace of aspiration in Assyrian in the letters *b, g, d, c, p, t*. In Hebrew also the *dagesh lene* would be of late introduction, caused by Aramaic influence, as the alphabet, like the cuneiform syllabary, uses but one character for both sounds. So, too, in Arabic and Æthiopic. Equally unknown to Assyrian are the sounds elaborated by Arabic ظ, ض, غ, خ, ث, (ش), and ذ; or (as in modern Aramaic) the *f* of Arabic and Æthiopic. The soft pronunciation of *gimel*, again, is not found.

The accent, as in Arabic, is thrown back as much as possible. Without doubt, this was also the usage of ancient Hebrew (as is shown by the segholates) before the necessities of a rhythmic intonation of the Old Testament changed the accent. The accent is upon the antepenult, unless the penult has a long vowel or is a closed syllable. The accent is often indicated by the incorrect insertion of a long vowel or a double letter. Besides accent, Assyrian observed the laws of quantity. A long vowel was according to rule expressed, though in many cases omitted (as in the case of the double letters). In the *nomina verbi* a short vowel in the second syllable was generally dropped before the case-endings. The accent and the quantity seem to have coincided, as in Arabic, whenever a word possessed a long syllable not further back than the antepenult or not in the last syllable. There was a tendency to shorten vowels and words in the later period; thus the Babylonian inscriptions give us *labri*, for which the Assyrian is always *labiru* ("old"). When a word consisted of three short syllables, the second vowel was generally dropped, making the first a closed syllable long by position; thus *málicú* becomes *malcu*. The enclitic threw back the accent upon the preceding syllable, even though this had a long syllable before it; e.g. *illicúniv-va* (for *illicúni-va*), *ikhdu'uninni* (for *ikhdhúni-ni*).

The doubling of a consonant was frequently disregarded even in *pael*[1]—sometimes it was replaced by a long vowel, more often by the accent merely, as in *lí-mu* for *lim-mu* in contract tablets.

THE PRONOUNS.

The personal pronouns in the Semitic languages, as in the Aryan, are formative elements of the verb, and therefore must be considered first.

SINGULAR.

I, me = *anacu*; *yāti, yati, yātima*.
Thou, thee (masculine) = *atta*; (feminine) *atti*; *cāta* (*cāti*).
He, him (masculine) = *su'u, su*; (feminine) *si'i, si*.

PLURAL.

We, us = [*anakhni*].
You (masculine) = *attunu*; (feminine) [*attina*].
They, them (masculine) = *sunu, sun, sunutu*; (feminine) *sina, sin, sinatu*.

Attina has not been found, but analogy would lead us to this form. *Anakhnu* or *anakhni*, Dr. Oppert's conjecture, is probably right. The word is met with only in a mutilated part of the Behistun inscription (l. 3), where Sir H. Rawlinson's cast reads doubtfully *a-ga-ni*. As the suffix of the noun is *-ni*, the form *anakhni* is to be preferred, *u* being weakened to *i* through a false analogy of the plural termination.

[1] So in Hebrew, Æthiopic, etc.

Anacu is Hebrew אָנֹכִי, Phœnician אנך, for which in the other dialects we have only *ana*, *ani*, or *ono*. Traces are found in the Æthiopic tense-ending *-cu*, Mahri *-k* (Arabic and Hebrew *tu* and *ti*). The plural in all the dialects is manifestly formed from it, *c* becoming *kh*. In Coptic (and Old Egyptian) *anok* (and *nuk*)="I," *anen*="we"; so in Berber *nekki*="I," *nekni*="we." The relation of these sub-Semitic dialects to the Semitic family is very questionable. Vulgar Assyrian used *anacu*, in the place of the suffix pronoun, after a preposition, e.g. *assu anacu*, "as regards myself" (S.H.A. 190).

The Arabic and Æthiopic *ana*, Hebrew *ani*, point to another form of the pronoun in *ya*. This has lost the final vowel in Hebrew and the initial vowel in the other two languages. It is the form that appears as the suffixed pronoun in Assyrian *ya*, later *i* and *a*, in Hebrew, Arabic, and Aramaic *i*, in Æthiopic *ya*. The Assyrian alone uses this without the verbal root *an* preceding, substituting for the latter the abstract termination *tu*, *ti*, as in *sunuti* by the side of *sunu*, or *ristu*, "chief," from *ris*, "head" (compare Æthiopic *we'tu*, "he," and *ye'ti*, "she"). *Yâti* is often shortened to *yati*, just as in Arabic *'ana* is used by the poets as a word of two short syllables. *Yatima*, "me here" (e.g. *cima yâtima*, "like me here"), has the demonstrative *ma* added (as in *suma*), for which see below. *Yâti* is for the most part used only at the beginning of a sentence, but we find also *ikbi yati*, "he told me." I have not found it, except in Babylonian inscriptions, and those of the later Assyrian empire (after Sennacherib). *Yâti* is not to be confounded with *yâsi* or *aisi*, "myself." This is *yasu* (אִישׁ), "man," (used for "self," compare 1 Kings xx. 20, etc.), with the pronoun-suffix of the first person added (*yās-i*). *Yā'a* (S.H.A., 37, 9) is irregularly lengthened from *yā*, like *ma'a* for *ma*. The survival of the old word for the first personal pronoun in Assyrian is parallel to the existence of א as third personal pronoun in the Phœnician—a form pre-supposed by the third person of the verb.

In the second person, again, Assyrian agrees with Hebrew in assimilating the nasal to the dental, while the other dialects have *anta* and *ant*. The Coptic *ntok* and Berber prefixed pronoun *swent* have been compared. The interchange of guttural and dental already noticed appears in the Æthiopic tense-ending *ca*, *ci* (Mahri -*k*, -*sh*). Hebrew has in most instances shortened the feminine to *att'*, just as Aramaic has contracted the masculine. In the plural, *antumu* has become in Assyrian *attunu*, like Aramaic *antún* and the feminine plural in all the dialects. Assyrian and Æthiopic alone preserve the case-ending of the masculine, though it is found also in Arabic poetry. Like *sunuti* and *yāti*, *attunu* is used in vulgar Assyrian as an accusative after the verb in place of the suffixed pronoun (e.g. *altapra attunu*, "I sent to you," where the preposition is ungrammatically omitted). *Cāta* (in the accusative) is employed for the sake of emphasis after a preceding verbal-suffix *ca*, which is changed into a separate pronoun by the abstract termination *tu*, *ta* (e.g. S.H.A., 180, *usamkhar-ca cāta*, "I cause thee, even thee, to be present," as tributary).

The verbal root with which the pronouns of the first and second persons are compounded is regarded by Dr. Hincks as אִין, "adesse," whence the preposition *ana*. I should prefer

אָנָה. Dillmann regards it as the pronominal element *n* or *na*, "there," whence נָא, הִנֵּה, etc., with *a* prefixed. The demonstrative *annu* is referable to the same source. The third personal pronoun is peculiar, but apparently exhibits a more primitive form than is the case in the cognate dialects. See page 12.

'*U* in *su'u*, and '*i* in *si'i*, answer to Arabic *wa* and *ya* in *huwa* and *hiya* (1). They are more often found in their contracted forms (as in Hebrew and Aramaic). The full form of the plural was *sunuti* (*sunutu*), frequently shortened to *sunut*,[1] and still more frequently to *sunu*. This, again, especially before consonants, might be still further shortened to *sun*, just as we find in the singular *s* for *su*, e.g. *usadlimu-s*, "they conferred on him." It is in these pronouns, the words most in use, that we find the first tendency to drop the case-endings: besides the third personal pronoun, in the first person of the permansive tense we have *pitlukhac* ("I worship") for *pitlukhacu* (2).

1. *I* is a weaker vowel than *a* or *u*, and therefore more fitted to express the feminine. So in the Aryan languages we have *ayam*, "this," masculine, *iyam* feminine.[2]

2. To compare these pronouns *acu*, *ta*, and *su'u* with the Aryan personal pronouns is unscientific. We have no standard of comparison: it is impossible to say in what form an Aryan guttural or dental would appear in

---

[1] *Sunuti*, *sunut*, are specially separate forms; *sunu* generally, and *sun* always, being used as suffix-pronouns. The second case-ending -*i*, the weakened -*a*, is used rather than -*a* because the ideas of motion towards a place and rest are not so prominently brought forward as in the case of the ordinary substantive. *Susutav*, however, is sometimes found, and even *sunutu*.

[2] So in Mantschu *ama* = "father," *eme* = "mother," *chacha* = "old man," *cheche* = "old woman"; in Carib *baba* = "father," *bibi* = "mother." Compare the list of pronominal words in Tylor, "Primitive Culture," vol. i., p. 199.

Semitic. Moreover, the original Aryan first personal pronoun was *me*; the nominative was of later formation. *Ac* and *ta* are primitive sounds, and we do not know what form they originally had. Phonetic decay would tell primarily upon the pronouns, and *su'u* has preserved its dissyllabic origin owing to its want of a supporting prefix. At an early stage in the language the guttural and dental seem to have been interchangeable: just as in the verbs the first person appears in Hebrew and Arabic as *ti* or *tu*, so in Æthiopic (and Mehri) the second person is *ca, ci, cymmu, cyn, (cem, cann)*. And the guttural is always found in the suffixed pronouns. (Comp. שתה and שקה.) The evidence of the sub-Semitic languages may also perhaps be adduced. Coptic gives both dental and guttural combined for the second person *ntek*, and in Berber we have *kecchi* (masculine), *kemmi* (feminine), and in the plural *kunwi* (masculine), *kunwith* (feminine). This may lead us back to a stage of language when, as in Japanese and other Allophylic tongues, there were no words set apart specially for the different pronouns, but some root of general meaning ("servant," "one," etc.) was employed sometimes for one person, sometimes for another, according to the context. Comparison would lead us to infer that the original root used for the first two persons was *'eteq, 'eceq*, or *'ecet* (the initial being retained in *acu*), and this reminds us of אחד, "one."[1] For the change of ד and ח compare אנכי and אנחנו. For *su'u* we may have שוה, "like," "companion," which in Assyrian takes exactly the same form as the pronoun *su'u*.

The suffixed pronouns will be treated of under the verbs and the substantives (see below).

The Demonstrative Pronouns.—The Assyrian was rich in these. The usual demonstratives "this," "that," were declined as follows:—

SINGULAR.

Masculine { *su'atu.* / *su'ati.* / *su'ata.* }   Feminine { *sa'atu, siatu.* / *sa'ati.* / *sa'ata.* }

PLURAL.

Masculine { *su'atunu, su'atun.* / *su'atu'ni.* / *su'atuna.* }   Feminine { *sa'atinu, sa'atin.* / *sa'atini.* / *sa'atina.* }

---

[1] Two objections must be set against the assumption of this root: אחד seems to be of Turanian origin (see below), and *d* is not *t*. Perhaps the original root may better be sought in Arabic *'acea*, "amavit," or Æthiopic *acata*, "to honour," "thank."

Another form of the pronoun, which seems to be employed indifferently with it, is *sasu* :—

SINGULAR.
Masculine—*sāsu (sa'asu)*.   Feminine—*sa'asi, sa'asa*.

PLURAL.
Masculine—*sāsunu, sāsun*.   Feminine—*sa'asina, sa'asin*.

Both forms immediately follow their substantive. *Sâsu* may be used alone in place of the separate personal pronouns. *Su'atu* is merely a secondary form of the third personal pronoun, in which the radical *a* (as in הוא) is preserved by the termination *t-u*. The feminine is formed similarly from *sâ*, the form taken by the third pronoun when suffixed. *A* has been weakened to *i* in *si'i* on account of the following *i*: in *sa'atu*, however, it is preserved by *ā* following, though we also find *siatu*. *Sasu* is a compound of the relative and the third personal pronoun; so that *bitu-sasu* would be literally " house which (is) it," *i.e.* " that house."

In the Achæmenian period we find a new demonstrative in common use, *'agā* or *'agah* :—

SINGULAR.
Common gender—*agā, agah*.   Feminine—*agata, agāta*.

PLURAL.
Common gender—*agā*.

This is compounded with the demonstrative *annu* and the personal pronouns so as to strengthen the determinative idea; thus :—

SINGULAR.   PLURAL.
Nominative—*agannu*.   Masculine—*agannutu*.
Accusative—*aganna*.   Feminine—*agannitu, aganēt*.
aga-su'u, " he namely," *aga-sunu*, " they namely."

The word is often employed like a mere article, as ה(ל) in

Hebrew, ذٰلِك in Arabic: thus while it usually follows its noun, we meet with *agannituv mati*, "these countries," and both *aganet mati* and *mati aganet*. So, too, *aga-su'u* by the side of *su'u aga*, which also occurs at the beginning of a sentence. The origin of the word is obscure: it can hardly be the Accadian demonstrative *gan*. In Himyaritic *agi* has been doubtfully read as the relative pronoun. According to Dillmann *ca* is the Semitic demonstrative root for indicating the further object, as in ذٰلِك (?), דְּךְ, Æthiopic *sycu* ("that"). As the word, however, does not make its appearance until the Achæmenian period, perhaps it is best to regard it as of foreign origin.[1]

In classical Assyrian three demonstratives are used to express determinative distance, *ammu* or *ma* ("hic"), *annu* ("iste"), *ullu* ("ille").

	SINGULAR.		PLURAL.
Masculine	{ [*ammu*]. [*ammi*]. [*amma*], or *ma*, *mā*. }	Masculine	{ [*ammutu*], *mā*. [*ammuti*]. [*ammuta*]. }
Feminine	{ [*ammātu*]. *ammāte*. }	Feminine—	[*ammate*].

Ma, the shortened form of *amma*, is appended as an enclitic to nouns and pronouns: e.g. *sar Assur-ma*, "king of this same Assyria" (*i.e.* "also"), *racibu-sin dicu-ma*, "their charioteers were killed here," *yatima*, "I here" ("for myself"), *ina asariduti-ya-ma*, "in this my pre-eminence," *ultu usmani annite-ma*, "from that camp here," *ina lime anni-ma*, "in the eponym of this person here" (*i.e.* "myself"). *Annima* is frequently contracted into *anma*, and once we have

[1] Prof. Schrader regards it as an Aramaism, referring it to דֵּךְ, דָּךְ.

annimma. Su-ma, "that," is also used absolutely for "him." We even find *ina sanati-ma siati,* "in this very year." The explanation of this word is due to Mr. Norris. *Ma* is irregularly lengthened to *mā* or *ma'a,* and is then often used as a conjunctive particle (like *sa*) with the meaning "since," "that being so." We have one instance of *mā* employed absolutely with a plural verb (S.H.A. 156, 50), *mā sa icbudu,* "one of them who laboured." *Suma* in its demonstrative sense follows the noun (like הוא) and is interchanged with *su,* as in *ina yumi suva* or *su,* "on that day." We may compare the Phœnician third person singular pronoun suffix ־ם, as also the Hebrew ־מו.

	SINGULAR.		PLURAL.
Masculine	*annu.* *anni, anni'i.* *anna, anna'a.*	Masculine	*annutu.* *annuti.* [*annuta*].
Feminine	*annātu* *annāte.*	Feminine—*annetu, annitu.* Common gender—*anne.*	

Another form of this pronoun, more nearly representing the Hebrew הנה, הן, is *'a'anati* (S.H.A. 103), and *'a'anni* (W.A.I. II. 60, 11).

From *annu* we get the prepositions *anna, inna* (to be distinguished from *'ana, 'ina*); like *ulli* ("among") from *ullu.*

	SINGULAR.		PLURAL.
Masculine	*ullu.* *ulli, ullā.* *ulla.*	Masculine	*ullutu, ullūtu, ulluai* (Achæmenian). *ulluti.* *ulluta.*
	Feminine *ullātu.*	Feminine [*ulletu*].	

Ullu is also used absolutely in the common phrase *ullu ullu,* "from that (old) time." In an Achæmenian inscription *ullu* is joined with *ma, ullumma,* "that thing." *Ulluai* is a product of the Persian period, and Xerxes even gives us the monstrous compound *akhulluai ullî*, "those shores," for *akhi ullutu*.

Ullu is Hebrew *ēl*, *ēlleh*, Aramaic *illēyn*, *illeyq*, Arabic *al*, *ilâ*, *ulai*, *ûlai*, Æthiopic *yllâ*, *yllû*, *yllântu*, *yllontu*: *annu* connects itself with the Æthiopic *yntyq* and *ynta*; and *ammu* is one of the archaic forms preserved in Assyrian which make this language so valuable to the philologist. Traces of it are found in אִם (Assyrian *im*), Arabic *in*, Æthiopic *ema*: *annu* pre-supposes *ammu*, just as the plural affix has changed from *amu* into *anu*, or Arabic *am* into *in*.

The Relative Pronoun.—This is *sa*, identical with the Phœnician שׁ and northern and later Hebrew שׁ (in Canticles, Judges, and Ecclesiastes), which appears again in Rabbinic שׁ. Here, again, Assyrian and Hebrew agree. In the other dialects we have a different root employed: Æthiopic *sa*, Aramaic *di*, Syriac *d'*, Himyaritic *d*, Sinaitic *dî* (Hebrew זוּ, זֶה), Arabic *allazi* (הַלָּזֶה) and *sû*. *Sa* is often used pleonastically to introduce a sentence (like *que* in French patois), "as regards which." The genitive, when the relation is not expressed by the construct state, is formed by the relative pronoun (e.g. *sarru sa Assur*), as in Æthiopic, Himyaritic, Sinaitic, Aramaic, etc. We have traces of this in Hebrew, e.g. *Methu-sa-el*. The Phœnician uses שׁ in this sense exactly as in Assyrian (e.g. הבנם שׁאבנם, "the builders of stone"). We find also *sa ana* used rarely to express the genitive, like אֲשֶׁר לְ and Rabbinic שֶׁל (compare Canticles i. 6, iii. 7). In relative sentences *sa* may be omitted, as in Hebrew and Arabic. "That which is not," is *sa-lâ*. *Sa* must not be connected with אֲשֶׁר (? = אֲתַר, asaru, like so, "place," "which," in Chinese), while the Phœnician אִשׁ (ys) is probably אִישׁ. Sa was originally the demonstrative, and stood by the side of su, sa, si. Himyaritic and Æthiopic show traces of a pronoun s. Like אֲשֶׁר, sa is indeclinable. In vulgar Assyrian it was often used without an antecedent (e.g. ina sa Gargamis, "after (the maneh) of Carchemish").

The Interrogative Pronoun.—This is *mannu, mânu*, or *man*, "who?" contracted by the vulgar pronunciation into *má*. *Ma* appears in the adverb *matima*, "at any time" (Hebrew מָתַי, "when"), where the demonstrative *ma* is attached to the interrogative with *ti* affixed. In the later inscriptions *matima* is used as an interrogative, e.g. *sa matima*, "of what place." *Mê* or *mi*, weakened (because either a neuter or an enclitic) from *má*, is found attached to *mannu*, which is thus reduplicated; e.g. *mannu-mê attâ akhû*, "who (art) thou brother?" *Mânu* is Æthiopic *manu, mi, ment;* Arabic *man, mâ;* Aramaic *man, mâ;* Hebrew *mi, mah*. *Mi* was also used by the Assyrians, as is proved by the indefinite *mimma* and the existence of *mê*. The interrogative enters into the composition of

The Indefinite Pronouns. — These are *mamman, mamma, manumma*, or *manamma* in Assyrian, *manama* in Babylonian, *manma* in Achæmenian, "aliquis." In *manama* or *manamma* and *manumma* (where the double letter merely expresses the accent), the interrogative precedes the demonstrative;[1] in *mamman* (where the accent again occasions the double letter) the converse is the case. Dr. Oppert compares ὅστις. Just as in Arabic, etc., the interrogative becomes conjunctive: thus at Behistun we have *manu atta sarru*, "whatever king you

[1] So in *sanumma* and *sanamma*, "another," from *sanu*, "second," and *ma*.

may be" (so in בְּמוֹ בְּמָה, Aramaic *c'mah*, Arabic *cam, camâ*, Assyrian *cima*). "Whatsoever" was *mimma*, from the neuter *mi*. Followed by *lâ* before the verb, *manama* = " nobody ": in the Achæmenian period the negative might be dropped, *manma* having acquired a negative sense like *personne*, etc., in French; e.g. *manma isallimma*, "no one accomplishes." Just as *manu* has become מָה in Hebrew, so in Assyrian we find *mamma* (for *manama, manma*) like *mê* used as an enclitic: *lû aba lû khallû manma*, "whether an officer or any common man whatever."

Another indefinite pronoun is the indeclinable *mala, mal*, "as many as," whose meaning was first pointed out by Dr. Hincks. *Mala* would be compounded of the conjunctive *manu, ma*, and the demonstrative *la*, which we have repeated in Æthiopic *lala*, "he himself," and which may possibly be related to *ullu*, אלה, Æthiopic *al;* just as the two negatives אַל and לֹא, Assyrian *ul*, and *lâ* or *la* stand over against one another.

"Some"—"others," is expressed by *anute—anute* and *akhadat—akhadat* or *akhadi—akhadi*. As an adjective "other" is *akharitu*. *Sanumma* is "another." We also find *estin ana estin*, "one to another."

The Reflexive Pronoun.—This is *ramanu, ramani, ramana, raman*, so excellently explained by Dr. Oppert. He first pointed out its true meaning and derivation. The first syllable is long, for *rahmanu*, from *rahamu*, the Assyrian form of רחם which we get in *rihma*, "mercy," and *ra'im misari*, "lover of justice" (whence אברהם according to Harkavy, Rev. Israél., March, 1870). *Ramanu*, therefore, is primarily "bowels," then "self," עצם. It is combined with the personal pronoun suffixes, so that we have *ramaniya*, "myself," *ramani*$^{oi}_{ca}$ "thyself," *ramani*$^{si}_{su}$ "himself," "herself," [*ramanini*, "ourselves,"] [*ramani*$^{cin}_{cun}$ "yourselves,"] *ramani*$^{sin}_{sun}$ "themselves." The second syllable was accented:[1] hence the nasal is often doubled (*ramannuca*). Sometimes, however, the accent was kept on the (long) first syllable; this necessitated the excision of the second (*ramnisu*). Another word for expressing the same idea is *gadu*, "an individual" ("a piece cut off"), which is sometimes combined with *sâsu* (as *sâsu gadu*). *Sâsu* may also be used alone in the same sense; and *anni-ma* or *anma* is common for "myself" (like ὅδε in Greek). So "myself" is also expressed by *yâs-i* or *ais-i* (see *suprâ*).

Su or *sunu* placed before the noun gives it emphasis, e.g. *su Elamu*, "the Elamite himself."

THE VERB.

The Assyrian verbs are for the most part triliteral. There are very few quadriliterals. This assimilates Assyrian rather to Hebrew, than to Arabic and Æthiopic. Verbal roots will be discussed further on.

The verbs are either complete or defective. The latter will be arranged as in the Hebrew grammar: verbs פ״נ; verbs פ״א, פ״ו (פ״ה) פ״י; verbs ע״ו, ע״י; verbs (ל״ה ל״ה),

---

[1] This is occasioned by the shortness of the last syllable, which obliges the accent to be on the preceding syllable. Properly the vowel of the servile abstract termination in *s* was short (ă) (lengthened in Æthiopic, Hebrew, [and Arabic], though words like Æthiopic *yrgynā*, "age," bear witness to an originally short vowel), thus distinguishing it from the long vowel of the plural termination in *ânu*.

לא; and verbs doubly defective. Verbs ע'ע are not irregular in Assyrian. Instead of verbs ו'ע, י'ע, the language preferred verbs ע'ע, which therefore exist in an unusual number. Verbs א'ע or ע'ה are regular. Verbs ע'ל are conjugated in great measure like verbs ל'ה. Indeed ע radical in any place produces certain peculiarities. Verbs containing ה, however, do not deviate from the ordinary type.

There are six conjugations in ordinary use, each admitting a secondary conjugation. Others are occasionally met with, anomalously, as in Hebrew.

The secondary conjugations are formed by the insertion of *t* (sometimes changed to *dh* or *d*, p. 29) between the first and second radicals. In concave verbs the dental precedes the first radical. The six principal conjugations with their secondary forms are as follows:—

(1.) Kal, as *catim*; aorist *ictum*.
(1a.) Iphteal, as *pitlukh*; aorist *ikdhabi'*.
(2.) Niphal, as *nanzuz*; aorist *issacin*.
(2a.) Ittaphal, as aorist *ittalki'*, *ittapalcit*.
(3.) Pael, as *hallac*, aorist *yunaecir*.
(3a.) Iphtaal, as aorist *yuptadhdhir*.
(4.) Shaphel, as aorist *yusalbis*.
(4a.) Istaphal, as aorist *yultisib* (for *yustisib*).
(5.) Aphel (found only in concave verbs), as aorist *yudhip*.
(5a). Itaphal (found only in concave verbs), as *yutacim*.
(6.) Shaphael (found mostly in verbs ל'ה), as *yusnammir*, *yusrabbi'*.

Traces of other conjugations are also found. The most common of these are an *iphtaneal* (1*b*), an *iphtanael* (3*b*), an *ittanaphal* (2*b*), and an *istanaphal* (4*b*); e.g. *istanahâlu* ("they asked one another") *ictanarrab* ("he approaches

4

near"), *ikhtanabbata* ("he wasted much"), *istanapper* ("he sends forth often"), *istandakhu, ittanallaca* ("he goes repeatedly"). These forms with the inserted nasal may be compared with the fourteenth and fifteenth Arabic conjugations.[1] It is possible that this strengthened form of the secondary conjugations in Assyrian was influenced by the Accadian causative, which inserted *tan* between the pronoun and the verbal root. It retains the original meaning of reciprocity more persistently than the form with a simple dental. Another conjugation rarely found is an *istataphal;* e.g. *yustetesser* or *yustelesir* from שׂטר, *yuctatatsir,* "he marshalled" (*Iphtatael*). A *Pilel* and a *Palel,* also, like Arabic conjugations ix. and xi., are occasionally met with (mostly in concave verbs), as *acsuttu* ("I acquired," for *acsûddu*), *isaccannu* ("they place"), *ipparsiddu,* "they fled"; *yutarru* ("they bring"), compared with *yutaru* Pael present, and *yutirru* ("he returned") compared with Pael aorist; *irtenin,* "he made"; *iddanan,* "he gives." Examples of a *Poel* and *Hithpoel,* Arabic conjugations iii. and vi., are *ilubusu,* "he had put on";[2] *etupusa,* "I made." A Tiphel with passive signification seems to occur in the permansive *tebusu,* "he has been made" (W.A.S. 17, 1, 1). Compare the participle *etpisu,* "constituted." *Illilliq,* "he went," is an instance of a form with the second radical doubled.

Concave verbs have a peculiar conjugation, in which the aorist and present agree with the Pael of regular verbs; the permansive, however, takes the form *niba* ("told"), *dicu*

---

[1] So in Æthiopic a short tonic vowel may strengthen itself by an inserted nasal, e.g. *zyntu* for *zytu.*

[2] This cannot be passive of Pael, as the meaning is against it, and we ought to have *yulubbisu.*

("smitten"), *nikha* ("rested"), with a passive or neuter meaning. So in Arabic we have *kíla*, perfect passive i. of *kulu:* hence we may conclude that the Assyrian *niba* stands for *nivuba* (like *limunu*, see below).

As in Arabic, every conjugation, except Niphal and Ittaphal, possesses a passive formed by means of the obscure vowel *u*. Kal also has no passive, Niphal being used for it.[1] As the signification of Niphal was originally reflexive, not passive, Kal in Assyrian nevertheless wanting a passive, it would seem that the passive was a late addition to the Semitic verb. This is confirmed by its being found only in Arabic and Assyrian. The passives of the other conjugations of the Assyrian verb are as follows:

(3.) Pael makes *nussuku* ("they climbed up"), *surrup* ("he is burned"), *gubbu* ("he is proclaimed"). The Aorist *yunummir*, "it is seen."

(4.) Shaphel makes *sukuru* ("they were made to be called"), *suluku* ("they were made to go"). When the permansive had a vowel attached, the vowel of the second syllable could be irregularly changed to *a*. Thus we find *subaruru* ("he drives away"), and *sukalula* by the side of *sukulula* ("he caused to reach"). The aorist would be *yususlim* ("he caused to be finished"), as we find *yusuti*.

(5.) Aphel seems to make *yudhbu* ("they were made good"). This is rather the aorist than the permansive, which ought to be *udhubu*.

(4a.) Istaphal makes *sutesuru* ("they were kept right"), *sutabulu* from בל.

I have found no examples of a passive in the remaining conjugations.

In (1a) Iphteal, however, we have *latbusa* ("they were covered"), with which we may compare the form of the *nomen mutati* of Kal, as in *darummu* ("a habitation").

[1] In *sipru suatu ippusu*, "this message has been accomplished," *ippusu* is not passive, but a late irregular form (as in Babylonian) of *ebusu* (Kal), "one has accomplished."

Special details will be found under the head of each conjugation.

Quadriliterals are rare in Assyrian. Unlike the Arabic, they have the same conjugations as triliteral verbs, with the exception of a Pael, viz. (1) Kal, or Palel, e.g. Aorist *iskhupar* ("he overwhelmed"), present *ipalcit* ("he comes over"); (1*a*.) Iphtalel, e.g. *yuptalcit*; (2) Saphalel, e.g. *yuspalcit*; (2*a*.) Istaphalel, e.g. *yustapalcit*; (3) Niphalel, e.g. *ippalcit*, present *ippalcat*; (3*a*) Ittaphalel, e.g. *ittapalcit*, present *ittapalcat*; (4) Iphalalla or Niphalella, e.g. *ipparsiddu* ("they fled"), and *iparsiddu*. These four voices are strikingly analogous to the four Arabic conjugations, *saphalel* taking the place of *taphalala* and *niphalel* of *iphanlala*. An instance of the tertiary conjugation (*t-n*) in a quadriliteral is *ittanaprassidu*, "he has fled to" (*ittanaphalel*). Quadriliterals are mostly found in the Niphalel, and generally the Niphal of triliterals is to be compared with them. With Ittaphalel the Hebrew Nitpael is to be compared, so common in the Rabbinic literature. I have found no instance of the Permansive tense.

The Assyrian verb is rich in tenses. It possesses a Permansive, or Perfect as it is generally called in Semitic grammars, of comparatively rare occurrence in the historic inscriptions, but sufficiently common in the tablets; besides four more other tenses. These have been formed out of the Imperfect or Future of ordinary Semitic grammars. This tense was first divided into two forms, the longer expressing present time, and the shorter having an aoristic sense. Exactly the same phenomenon appears in Æthiopic, and would seem in both languages to have been due to non-Semitic influence.

At all events, Accadian possessed an aorist and a present. The two tenses thus gained by the Assyrians were still further modified by attaching a different shade of meaning to the form which ended with the original short vowel and to the apocopated form. Thus, *isallim* is a present, *isallimu* has a future signification. In the case of the aorist this difference of meaning was not so uniformly observed. Generally *isdhuru* has a perfect or pluperfect signification, while *isdhur* is aorist; sometimes, however, the longer form cannot be distinguished in sense from the aorist. We thus have the following tenses:—(1) Permansive, e.g. *sacin* ("he places"); (2) Aorist, *iscun* ("he made"); (3) Perfect or Pluperfect, *iscunu* ("he has had made"); (4) Present, *isaccin* ("he makes"); (5) Future, *isaccinu* "he will make"). The Kal present is only distinguished from the Pael aorist by the person-prefix which is amalgamated with *u* in the Pael; thus, *isaccin* is Kal present, *yusaccin* is Pael aorist. As in Pael, the double letter of the Kal present is frequently dropped; a fault common to all Semitic writing.[1]

In the remaining conjugations Niphal, Pael, and Shaphel, the Present is distinguished from the Aorist by containing *a* instead of *i* in the last syllable: thus, *issacan, isacin; yusaccan, yusaccin; yuca'an, yucin* (כין); *yusascan, yusascin*.[2] The name Permansive is due to Dr. Hincks, who thus marks it off from what he calls the Mutative tenses.

---

[1] Very rarely, and only in ungrammatical inscriptions, such as the Law-tablet, the present takes the form *iraggum*, through the influence of an unfrequent form of the Pael aorist.

[2] *I* is a weakened *a*, and consequently *a* more fitly marks a continuing period of time upon which the mind dwells.

Besides the termination in *u*, the Assyrian aorist resembles the Arabic in possessing two other forms at least. Adopting the Arabic division, we have:

(1.) The Apocopated Aorist, expressing urgency and command, and therefore usually employed in the inscriptions.

(2.) The Telic Aorist, terminating in *u*, denoting the continuance of past time.

(3.) The Aorist of Motion, or Conditional Aorist, terminating in *a*.

(4.) The Paragogic Aorist, expressing energy, terminating in *m* or *mma*.

Besides these, I have detected traces of a termination in *i* —e.g. *yubahi*, "it had sought," *amdakhitsi* as a variant of *amdakhits* ("I fought"), *wracsi* ("I reached"), *usarrikhi* ("I consecrated") in Babylonian. The same termination is pre-supposed by *imma*, which is found (though rarely) by the side of *umma* and *amma*. This termination would seem properly to have been used when the idea expressed in the sentence was subordinate to what went before.

These flexions are identical with those of the noun.[1]

The Apocopated Aorist, from its aptitude to denote vigour, like the Jussive in Arabic and Hebrew, has become the common form in Assyrian, as in Phœnician, Hebrew, Aramaic, and Æthiopic. Not but that all the forms given above, with the exception of that in -*i* (which has been altogether lost in Arabic), are frequently found.

The principal form in -*u*, answering to the nominative of the noun, so conspicuous in Arabic, has acquired in Assyrian

---

[1] As in the noun, *i* is weakened from both *a* and *u*, which would, therefore, be the primary terminations.

for the most part a telic sense, *i.e.* it generally denotes a perfect or pluperfect action. In those persons which end in a vowel, the original termination in *n*, otherwise lost in Assyrian, is preserved, the vowel being attached. This is in a few rare cases *û*, though *i* generally takes its place, *a* not being met with. The prevalence of *i* is to be explained partly by the fact that the additional vowel is mostly found in relative and subordinate sentences, partly by the influence of *ni*, the conditional enclitic. The final syllable of the person-ending was long; hence we often find *yusaldidu'uni* written for *yusaldidûni*. When followed by the enclitic conjunction, the accent was thrown upon the final *i*, which, accordingly, generally has the consonant after it doubled: thus, *ikhdhûniv-va* for *ikhdhûni-va*.

The aorist of motion answers to the accusative of nouns, and hence signifies motion towards a place. Both have in Assyrian the vowel *a*, which corresponds to the termination of the Hebrew Cohortative in the verb and the local case in the noun, long recognized as a relic of the old Semitic accusative.

The long הָ֑ originates in the primitive mimmation (*amma, am*, Arabic, *anna, an*), just as in Arabic *yactulánna* or *yactulán* becomes *yactulá* in pause. Assyrian, when it drops the mimmation, preserves the original short quantity of the vowel. While in Assyrian the aorist in -*a* very frequently signifies motion (e.g. *aslula*, "I carried off"), in many instances it denotes a purely quiescent state (e.g. *ebusa*, "he made"); but in this case it either stands in a conditional sentence or has its object following it, so that the action of the verb is moved forward to the noun. I have not found it used as a cohortative, a sense which arises from the idea of motion in urging oneself or another forward to do a thing, and implies a continuance of the action desired by putting it into effect. When it stands in a relative sentence it exactly corresponds to the Arabic subjunctive, a use of the form originating in the conception of limitation implied in the termination (as in the accusative of the noun)—the action having proceeded to a certain point and no further,—from which also arises the idea of motion. The accusative is the object to which the mind travels. Hence it is expressed by the broad vowel *a*.[1]

The Paragogic or Energic aorist is merely that in which the attached vowels retain the primitive mimmation, once possessed by all noun-cases, and which has become a nunnation in Arabic. The final *ma* is generally the enclitic conjunction ו, in which *v* has been changed into *m* on account of the preceding *m* (see p. 28).[2] Thus we have *abnuv* or *abnum* ("I built"), *iddinûnum* ("they have given"), *isrucunimma* ("they have presented and"), *usetsamma* ("I brought forth and"), *uselamma* ("I brought up and").

The Moods, excluding the Indicative, are four in number: (1) Precative, (2) Subjunctive, (3) Imperative, and (4) Infinitive, though the latter would better be described as a verbal noun.

(1) The Precative is formed from the aorist, as in Arabic

---

[1] We have to distinguish the enclitic *a* for *va*, "and," from this tense-ending. Final *u* coalesces with the *a*; thus *aslulā* for *aslulu-a* (*aslulwa*) "they carried off." The augment of motion is found also with the Present (especially when used cohortatively), as well as with the Imperative and Precative (see below). So, too, the mimmation.

[2] In classical Assyrian this final *ma* is always the enclitic conjunction.

and Aramæan, by means of the prefix *li* or *lu*. So, too, Æthiopic often prefixes *lâ* to the shorter form of the Imperfect in the same sense. In Assyrian, when the first letter of the verb is a vowel, *lu* is used; *a, u,* or *yu* are absorbed by the *u* of the prefix which is lengthened: if, however, the first letter be *i, lu-i* is contracted into *lî*, which becomes *lê* before *e*. This *lu* must be distinguished from the particle *lû*, denoting past time (like *kad* in Arabic, or *sma* in Sanskṛit), which never amalgamates with the verb. Dr. Oppert points out its connexion with the ל of the Talmud and the Aramaic (as in the forms in Daniel לֶהֱוֵא and לְהֵן).[1] The Precative is confined to the first and third persons, the Imperative being used for the second; but it is chiefly found in the third. Examples are *lubludh* (joined with *anacu*), *lucsud* ("may I obtain"), *lusba-'a* (with the augment of motion added) and *lusbim* ("may I be satisfied with"), *lurabbis* ("may he enlarge"), *lutir* ("may he restore"), *lirur* ("may he curse"), *libi'elu* ("may they rule over"), *liscunu*, ("may they place"). Irregularly it was even used in later times with the second person: thus Nebuchadnezzar has *lutippis* ("mayest thou make"). The same form is used for the masculine and feminine of the third person. The subjunctive enclitic *-ni* may be attached to the Precative; e.g. *lissû-ni*, "may they carry away" (in a quotation).

(2) The Subjunctive is hardly to be called a distinct mood. It is formed by the subjunctive enclitic *ni* added either to the Perfect or to the Permansive, e.g. *utsbacuni*. In some cases the enclitic cannot be distinguished in form from the fuller plural

---

[1] This ל, however, may represent the ן of the Aramaic third person of the verb.

termination of the aorist: generally, however, an accusative pronoun is inserted between the verb and the enclitic, e.g. *abilu-sina-ni* ("I have possessed them"), *ikabu-su-ni* ("he calls it"). The enclitic is used after the relative or such particles as *ci*. A common idiom is to use this enclitic without *ci*, followed by *va* ("and") and an aorist (not unlike the use of *waw consecutivum*); e.g. *ilsbatŭniv-va emuru*, "when they had taken, they saw" (where the first *v* does not represent the mimmation, but points out that *i* has the accent thrown back by *va*). *Ni* must be compared with the Æthiopic enclitic *nă* added to *'sca*, "until," shortened probably from *nē*, which is attached to the accusative of motion. Both probably go back to *nā* (as in *nāhu, nawā*), Arabic *anna*, Hebrew נא. Compare Assyrian *eninna*, "again" (?).

(3) The Imperative is confined to the second person, the second person singular feminine ending in -*i*, the second person plural masculine in -*ū* long, feminine -*ā*. The subjunctive augment of motion is sometimes attached to the second person singular masculine, e.g. *sullimă* (pael), "complete." It would be more true to say that the final *a* was the primitive form which was afterwards contracted, the object-vowel (*ă*) being used rather than the subject-vowel (*ŭ*), as in Arabic, because the action passed on from the speaker to the object. The length of the final vowels in the plural is sometimes denoted by otiose characters, as in Arabic: thus, *salkhu'u-su* for *salkhū-su*, "do ye extend it." In Shaphel, the imperative is always formed as if from Aphel: e.g. *suscin* for *sususcin*, as in Hebrew *hactēl* for *hehactēl*.

The Energic Augment may be used (especially in Baby-

Ionian), with both the imperative and the precative, e.g. *surihimam*, "cause to be exalted;" *lusbim*, "may he be sated with," besides *lusbiam*, which combines (like *surihimam*) the Conditional and Energic Augments.

(4) The Infinitive is a verbal substantive, and as such may take the feminine termination. It would be better called, as in Arabic, a *nomen verbi;* and as such will be considered further on.

The participle prefixes *mu* in all conjugations except Kal, and the Pael of concave verbs, as in the other Semitic tongues. This *mu* is the pronoun *ma, mi, manu*, etc., as Ewald has pointed out. Assyrian here agrees with Arabic, as well as really with Hebrew and Aramaic, in which *shewa* is equivalent to the short *u* of the other more conservative languages: Æthiopic alone has retained the original *a*.

THE PERSONS.

As in the other Semitic languages, a distinction is made in the attachment of the person-suffixes in the Permansive and the Aorist. The Permansive is conjugated as follows:—

	SINGULAR.		DUAL.		PLURAL.
1 m. and f.	tsabtacu, tsabtaca,			1 m. and f.	[tsabitni]
	tsabtaq	3 f.	tsabtâ	2 m.	[tsabittunu]
2 m.	[tsabtita]	3 m.	[tsabtâ]	2 f.	[tsabittina]
2 f.	[tsabtiti]			3 m.	tsabtu
3 m.	tsabit			3 f.	tsabtâ
3 f.	tsabtat				

I have taken the greater part of the above from Dr. Hincks. The form of the second singular is restored from the forms of the pronoun in Assyrian, *atta* and *atti*.

The Aorist is conjugated thus:—

	SINGULAR.		DUAL.		PLURAL.
1 m. and f.	asdhur	2 m. and f.	[tasdhurā]	1 m. and f.	nisdhur
2 m.	tasdhur	3 m.	isdhurā	2 m.	tasdhuru
2 f.	tasdhuri	3 f.	isdhurā	2 f.	tasdhura
3 m.	isdhur			3 m.	isdhuru
3 f.	tasdhur			3 f.	isdhurā

The Present will be:—

SINGULAR.

1 m. and f.	asaccin, asaccan, asacin
2 m.	tasaccin, tasaccan
2 f.	tasaccini, tasaccani, tasacni
3 m.	isaccin, isaccan, isacin
3 f.	tasaccin, tasaccan, tasacin

DUAL.

| 2 m. and f. | [tasaccinā, tasacnū] |
| 3 m. and f. | isaccinā, isacnū |

PLURAL.

1 m. and f.	nisaccin, etc.	3 m.	isaccinu, isacnu
2 m.	tasaccinu	3 f.	isaccinā, isacnā
2 f.	tasaccina, tasacna		

In the Perfect and Future we have to add *u* to such persons as terminate in a consonant, and *ni* or *nu* to those that terminate in a vowel.

The dual is very rare: as in modern Arabic, it has almost disappeared from the verb. We find, however, *basa'ā uznā-su*, "his ears always exist," *icsudā katā-su*, "his hands possessed" (with a variant *icsudu*).

The first person of the Permansive is identical in form with the Æthiopic, and refers us to the original form of the first personal pronoun. As in the case of the affixed pronoun *su*, the final *u* may be dropped: this seems almost always to happen in the Babylonian and Achæmenian inscriptions. The form in *a* corresponds with the aorist subjunctive, being used in relative sentences, e.g. *sa anacu tsibāca*, "what I wish."

In the third plural (and dual) the short i has been dropped, as will be seen is often the case.

In the Aorist, *u* following or preceding causes the distinctive *a* to disappear: the first person singular of the Pael is *usaddhir*.

The person-endings in the Permansive are attached to the root as in the Aryan languages; *tsabacu* exactly corresponds to *ad-mi*. In order to distinguish the two tenses, as the Semites did not possess the Aryan machinery of augments, the pronouns were divided in the aorist, the characteristic letter being prefixed, and the rest of the word affixed. *At* (in *atta* and *attin*) was shortened into *t*, -*i* and -*in* being affixed. The *a* of the first person is either the last relic of the ancient guttural *ao* (? from *ácát*) or the pronoun which appears in *yati*. The third person in the aorist seems to have employed a different pronoun from that in common use among the Semitic nations. In the Permansive it is merely the abstract participle, with the feminine termination attached to the feminine (*a* in the plural standing for *an*(*u*); see below). In the Aorist the pronoun seems to be that preserved in the Æthiopic *wĕtu*, *yĕti*, which cannot be derived from *huwa*, *hiya*, by dropping the first syllable, as this is the all-important one, and the Semitic languages in abbreviations dropped the final, never the initial, syllable.

In the preceding it will be seen that I have followed the views of Dr. Hincks in the main, rather than those of Dr. Oppert. The researches of the latter into the Assyrian verb have been vitiated by a refusal to perceive minor differences, and by a pre-conceived theory deduced from the *general* usage of the historical inscriptions. Dr. Oppert, in the second edition of his Grammar, still denies the existence of a Permansive, a Present (which he confuses with Pael), and of a Future or Perfect (which he considers to be interchanged indiscriminately with the shorter forms); while he ignores several facts of importance, such as the existence of a dual, the use of the aorist subjunctive, and the passives. As he has brought forward arguments against the existence of a Permansive tense in Assyrian (now admitted by Mr. Norris and Mr. G. Smith), it will be necessary to show that such really does exist in the inscriptions.

Dr. Oppert seems to admit that *cullu*, "they are holding," and *nasu'u*, "they are carrying," in the Achæmenian inscriptions—to which he might have added *bitlukhu*, "he has been worshipping," *saldhac*, "I am ruling," *tsibāca* and *tsummukhu*—are true perfects; but he objects that the texts in which they are formed belong to a corrupt period of the Assyrian language, and that the forms, therefore, are to be classed with other (Aramaising) peculiarities of the Persian period. The cases, however, are not quite parallel. One, the Permansive, is part of the original stock of the Semitic family of speech; the others are words which could easily have been borrowed from neighbours. How could a people which did not possess the Semitic Perfect ever feel the want of such a tense? Even Semitic scholars find it hard to grasp its fundamental idea. Moreover, forms identical with those just cited, and necessarily construed as finite verbs, are to be found in the older texts. Against the sentence quoted by Dr. Hincks, *epir sepi-sunu . . . pān samie rapsuti catim*, "the dust of their feet . . . the face of the whole heaven is concealing," Dr. Oppert urges that the sentence is not completed here, *illamu-a* being added. But *illamu* is a preposition, "before"; and the case governed by *catim* is *pan*. So that Dr. Hincks's argument still holds good; were *catim* a participle (in that case, by the way, it ought to be *catimu*), it "would stand before what it governs, and would require a verb to complete the sentence." But another instance may be brought forward in which the permansive is absolutely the last word in the sentence. This is *balti ussu pulukhti melamme sarruti itati-su sakhrā-va*, "the strong power of reverence, the fear of royalty, surround its walls; and." This sentence is complete in itself, and, according to Dr. Oppert, the verb ought to be in the aorist. Another instance quoted by Dr. Hincks from Sennacherib is *tebuni gibsu(t)-sun urukh Aocadi itsbatuni-va ana Babila tebuni*, "their forces took the road to Accad and came on to Babylon;" the verb is בוא. Dr. Oppert tries to invalidate this by saying that *te* is a mistake of the engraver for *it*. But the time has not yet come for us to amend our texts: until we know a good deal more of Assyrian than what can be gathered from the uniform phraseology of royal historical inscriptions, we must be content to take what lies before us, and to believe that the Assyrian scribes knew a good deal more about their language than we do.

Moreover, to close all doubt upon the matter, the same word is found in another passage—*sa pan matti mitkharis ana epis tukmati tebūni*, "who to the countries in person to make opposition came on," and Assur-bani-pal's texts have *tebacu*, "I am coming" (S.H.F., 124). The same remarks apply to Dr. Oppert's statement that *tsabtu* (which can only be a verb) is a mistake for *itstsabtu*, "which is often found in the same phrase." But we can match the permansive *tsabtu* with numberless instances. Thus we have *sa ina lanni-sunu ina carbi-su camu'u*, "(the youths) who in their dwellings within it were associated"; *arakh il libni nabu'u sum-su*, "the month of the god of bricks they call its name" (Sivan); *sa ilu ana sarrutiv eri curu sicir-sun*, "whose fame the god hath called to the sovereignty of the city"; *sa la citnusu ana niri*, "who were not submissive to my yoke"; *tsir sukti Nipur .... subat-sun sitcunat-va*, "upon the covers of Nipur .... their abode was situated, and;" *cima selut .... ana same zikipta sacnu*, "like rocks ... to the sky pointed they stood"; *cirkhu-su cima uba'an sade sacin*, "its head like the top of a mountain was standing"; *cima zikip samdhu*, "like a stake they pierced"; *cima zikip ... nādi*, "they a stake ... they were situated"; *tsalui ... sakis nansuzu*, "images ... on high were fixed"; *racibu-sin dicu*, "their charioteers were slain"; *sa cima khirate tsabruni*, "which like women (men) collect"; *nummuru bukhar-sun*, "their excellency was seen"; *sa latbusa*, "which were covered"; *mala basu'u*, "as many as exist"; *sa nubalu-su ... subaruru*, "who drives away his enemies"; *sa ... sursudu*, "which was erected"; "*sa sutabulu cirib-sa*, "which had been carried within it"; *sa ... sukuru*, "which were appointed by proclamation"; *sa ... suluca-va ... nisi ... la ida'a*, "which were made to go and ... men ... did not know of"; *tulu-sa ul ipsi sabat-sa tsukhkhurat*, "its mound was not, its site was small"; *eli sade-sunu martsuti daglu*, "to their rugged mountains they trusted"; *Tarkū ... inacidu-va attu-ni asaba-ni minu*, "Tirhakah will be unfortunate and (men) measure out our habitation to us." In most of these cases the permansive is joined with an aorist and follows its case, so that it can no more be a participle (as Dr. Oppert would have us believe) than any perfect in the Bible. Besides, were the permansives above-given participles, we should require *tsalui nanzuzi* instead of *nanzuzu*, or *sa la citnusi* instead of *citnusu*. *Trukkhurat* and *suluca*, again, would have the prefix *mu*. But, says Dr. Oppert, "the other Permansive forms of Hincks are either participles like *musarbu* or infinitives *sitkunat*, *suhhurat*, etc." Dr. Hincks however, in the first place, never called *musarbu* a Permansive; and, in the second place, the examples given above are sufficient to show that the words instanced are not infinitives. This will be made still plainer by the following sentence from Sennacherib's cylinder: *rucubi adi kurrai-sina sa ina kitrub takhazi danni racibu-sin dicu-ma va sina mussura-va ramanu-ssun ittanallaca*, "the chariots with their horses whose charioteers in the meeting of mighty battle were killed there; then they (feminine) were abandoned and the men themselves went away." Here *mussura* and *ittanallaca* are on exactly the same footing; if one is an infinitive, the other must be so likewise. So, again, in a relative sentence like *abnu . . . sa . . . nussuku*, "the stone . . . which . . . climbed up," an infinitive is out of the question; and the same will apply to the phrases quoted above. The astronomical reports prove the same thing: in which the only verbs that occur are, according to this strange theory of Dr. Oppert, in the infinitive mood! Thus we have *yumu VI. arakhi Nisanni yumu va musi sitkulu*, "the sixth day of Nisan, day and night are balancing one another."

The last argument of Dr. Oppert is directed against the

first person singular of the Permansive! and this is a form which it is difficult to explain away. Accordingly, he asserts that *sarracu*, "I am king"; *sicaracu*, "I am a male," etc., are substantives, with *cu* for *anacu* affixed (!), while *utsbacu(ni)*, *saldhaq*, and *tsibaca* are to be read *yutsbacuni*, *saldha epus*, and *tsiba ieris*. Now the first explanation either means that *sarracu*, etc., are first persons of a Permansive tense, or else introduces an altogether non-Semitic grammatical form. In the latter case we must prefer an explanation which accords with Semitic grammar to one which contravenes its principles. A permansive first person of the form *sarracu* is in accordance with the rules of Semitic grammar; a substantive with a Separate Pronoun-affix cannot be paralleled among the cognate languages. Moreover, the bilingual tablets translate Accadian *verbs*, not substantives, by this form; e.g. *mun-lu* is rendered *tsabtacu*, "I am taking," *mu-s-tugdu* by *khatacu*, "I am honouring." If, however, Dr. Oppert does not wish to introduce a non-Semitic conception, then he is merely using an inaccurate expression to denote the Permansive. No one will deny that in the Æthiopic *gabarcu* the pronoun-affix appears: but equally no one will deny that *gabarcu* is the first singular of the Preterite. The Assyrian, like all other Semitic tongues, employs a different pronoun-affix for substantives, and attaches to the compound an altogether different sense from that which *tsabtacu* bears. If Assyrian be Semitic, it must be interpreted in accordance with the genius of Semitic speech. *Tsabtacu* could by no possibility be a substantive. That would require *tsabituya* or *tsabtuya*, and would have to be translated "my capturer." Next as regards the explanation of the three last words instanced by Dr. Oppert. Two obvious rules for every decipherer are—(1) not to assume ideographs in the text unnecessarily, and (2) to explain in the same way similar forms with similar significations. This will dispose of the monstrosities *saldha epus* (for *saldhaq*, "I am ruling," Persian *patiyakhshiya*) and *tsiba ieris* for *tsiba'aca*, together with many like words, e.g. *pitlukhaq*, "I am worshipping"; *bitugaq*, "I am working at"; *cainaq*, "I am stedfast"; *badhlaq*, "I am failing"; for which I suppose Dr. Oppert would adopt the same desperate explanation. Dr. Oppert seems to imagine that these first person Permansive forms are exceptional. Even in the historical inscriptions, however, this is not the case; and certain tablets, such as those containing prayers, regularly present them; e.g. *puputa rabacu asala dabsacu*, "crops I increase, corn I mature" (where neither form nor syntax allow *rabacu* to be called a substantive); *cinacu ci makhalti*, "I am strong as a fortress"; *tsammiracu ci atani*, "I rejoice like a wild ass (?)"; *sarraku*, "I am king," where the change of guttural implies that the form had become so well established as to obliterate the recollection of its origin. The examples just given are found side by side with *ridā isu*, "I have a servant," and *anacu napāsa*, *anacu nutsbasa*. However possible it may be to imagine a substantive in such intransitive verbs as *sarracu*, *sicaracu*, this is altogether out of the question with *rabacu* and *dabsacu*. These two words alone would be sufficient to establish a Permansive tense in Assyrian. As for *utsbacuni* ("I am stopping," with the subjunctive enclitic after *ci*; in other instances, where *ci* is wanting, *utsbacu* alone occurs), Dr. Hincks has already set aside Dr. Oppert's *yutsbacuni*.

It is an impossible form, which cannot be matched in Assyrian. "*Iṣbakuni* would be legitimate; and so would *iśabkuni*, or with *st* or *ss* in the place of *ṣ*; *yuṣabkuni* might pass also for conjugation III. [Pael]; but the substitution of *yu* for *i* before *ṣb*—such a form as *yupgaluni*—is unparalleled." And lastly, if the above arguments were not sufficient, the bilingual tablets conclusively settle the whole matter. Here, for example, we have a sentence which runs in Assyrian *daltu va sicuru cunnu*, "the door and the porch are founded," where *cunnu* (third plural Palel) answers to the Accadian *ib-tan-gubbu-s*, "they caused to be fixed" (third plural aorist causative). Another passage, in an inscription of Nebuchadnezzar (W. A. I., 54, 3, 19), affords an example of the Permansive used with the pronoun-suffix of the verb, and the infinitive and preposition: *ana ebisu Bit-Ili nasa-nni libb-i*, "to the building of Bit-Ili my heart urges me." Here the participle must have had *ya* (*nasu-a* or *nas-ya*), not -*ni*. These two instances by themselves are sufficient to disprove the opinion of Dr. Oppert, who seems to have forgotten that *in its origin* the Perfect (or Permansive) of the Semitic languages was nothing more than the participle, and that the arguments brought against its form in Assyrian apply equally well to Hebrew or Æthiopic.

As regards the confusion made by Dr. Oppert between Pael and the present of Kal,—a tense whose existence he denies,—no arguments have been brought forward against Dr. Hincks. An appeal can only be made to the inscriptions, where a distinction between the two parts of the verb is always maintained. *Isaccin* invariably has a present meaning. Dr. Oppert does indeed say that the present of Pael ought to have the second radical quadrupled. We have to do, however, with matters of fact, not of *à priori* fitness: and the Assyrians conceived that a sufficient distinction was made by a change of vowel. The whole question is set at rest by the bilingual tablets. On the one hand, a careful distinction is made between the aorist and the present Kal, the Accadian aorist being translated by the form *iscun*, the Accadian present by the form *isaccin* (e.g. *in-lal* ("he weighed")= *iscul, in-lal-e* ("he weighs")= *isaccal*): on the other hand, the Pael (with prefixed *u*) is generally set apart for the Accadian intensives, while the present and aorist in Pael itself are accurately noted down (e.g. *in-gin* ("he placed")= *yucin, in-gin-e* ("he places")=*yuca'an*). With respect to the *nuances* of meaning in the lengthened forms of the aorist and future, I do not mean to say that the form *isaccinu* contains as clear an idea of future time as the Latin *constituet*. It was set apart to express that conception with a kind of unconscious instinct; so that in the inscriptions wherever we should speak of future time the form *isaccinu* is almost invariably used. In the case of the perfect the instinct was not so clearly marked: we can only say that in the majority of instances the lengthened form of the aorist represents the perfect or the pluperfect.

Traces of the use of *waw consecutivum* are to be found in Assyrian, though the comparative rarity of the Permansive greatly restricts the use. Thus we have *Sina mussura-va ramanussun ittanallasa*.

Contracted forms.—The Assyrian verb frequently drops a short vowel. Just as in Pael (or other grammatical forms in which one of the radicals is doubled) where the reduplication of the letter leads to the lengthening of the preceding vowel, like the Arabic third conjugation, an *i* or *â* is frequently elided. Verbs with ע as second radical, often omit it; e.g. *sibi* by the side of *si-'ebi*. The same happens when ע is third radical before *u* and *a*; thus, *ismu*, "they heard," by the side of *isme'u* and *isma'a*. In verbs ע"א, *a* falls away before *i* with *hemza*, e.g. *ucin*, *ubi'*. So in verbs which begin with ע, the Assyrian drops this radical after *i*, while the Babylonian transposes the vowels, e.g. *ipsit* and *s'ipsit* (עפש); with *u* as preformative, ע becomes *u* also, and in Assyrian the two letters coalesce (thus *ulla'a*, "I ascend" (עלה), Babylonian *u'ulla'a*; so *utstsib* for *u'utstsib*). The same holds good of פ"י and פ"ה, e.g. *utstsi* for *u'utstsi*, pael of יצא. Verbs פ"ה compensate for the loss of ה by doubling the second radical. In Iphteal the short vowel after the second consonant may be suppressed, when an open syllable, e.g. *tastalmi* for *tastalami*, *listalmu* for *listalamu*, *taptikdi* for *taptikidi*. So, too, in Pael, where the loss of the vowel is accompanied by the loss of the double consonant (thus *tasalmu* for *tasallimu*, *muparca* for *muparrica*). In Iphtaal and Niphal the contractions are frequent; e.g. *ittalcu* for *ittallicu*, *istacnu* for *istaccanu*; *ippatka* for *ippattika*, *innabtav* for *innabitav*, *lissacna* for *lissacina*. In Shaphel they are rare, chiefly occurring when the first radical is a 'sibilant, as *ussis* or *uksis* for *usasis*, "he caused to fix"; but we also find *yusdhibbu* for *yusadhibbu*.[1]

Shaphel is chiefly distinguished by ellipse of the characteristic consonant. Just as this has become ה in Hebrew (as

[1] This, however, may be Shaphael, as the Assyrians possessed a root טבה by the side of טוב.

in the case of the third personal pronoun), and *a* in Arabic, Aramaic, and Æthiopic, so in Assyrian has *us* become first *uh* and then *u* in the concave verbs. Another assimilation of consonants takes place in Iphteal (and Iphtaal). When the first radical is *d*, *ts*, *z*, or *s*, the characteristic *t* is assimilated to these letters; thus we have *itstsabat* for *itstabat*, *izzacar* for *istacar*. Sometimes even *s* changes the *t* into *s*; e.g. *issacan* for *istacan*, *assarap* and even *asarap* for *astarap*.¹ So in Arabic *t* is assimilated with *d*, *ḍ*, *z*, *s*, *ts*, *dh*, *ḍh*, as first radical. In Niphal and verbs פ״נ *n* is regularly assimilated to the following letter (as in Hebrew, etc.), e.g. *iddin*, *ippakid*, *lissaoin*, *tabbanu*, *tadani* for *taddani*. The assimilation, however, is not always observed. If the first radical cannot be doubled, the characteristic letter is elided; in the Achæmenian period, however, the second radical was doubled, as *ibbus* (quoted by Dr. Oppert from Nakhsh-i-Rustam; see below).

After gutturals and nasals *t* may be changed into ט or ד, as *ikdharib*, *ikdhabi*, *igdamar*, *nimdagar*, *amdakhits* by the side of *amtakhits* (probably read *antakhits*).

THE STRONG VERB.

Kal.—I shall give the forms of the Permansive (where this is possible), the Present, and the Apocopated Aorist. The longer forms can be supplied from these in accordance with the rules already given.

¹ In these cases the *t* has been transposed (as in Hebrew, Arabic, etc., or in Assyrian defective verbs), and *ts* regularly becomes *s* (see p. 32). The assimilation is common in Æthiopic (e.g. *yĕssabar* for *yĕtsabar*). Compare Arabic *yatstsarra'ūna* for *yatatsarra'ūna*. For the Hebrew see Is. i. 16; Eccl. vii. 16, etc.

Verbs in Kal are either transitive or intransitive. The majority of those found in the inscriptions are transitive. As in Arabic (also in Hebrew and Aramaic), the second radical takes either one of the three primary vowels in the aorist. By far the largest majority of verbs have *u* (which has been confined to intransitives in Arabic).

Among those which take *i* are found *bi'elu, gadaru, dagalu, khalaku, casaru, casapu, cataru, nacasu, sacaru, sanaku, eribu, esibu, ekhiru, ecimu, enisu, etiku, padharu, pakadu, basamu, pataku, tsanaku, rakhatsu, ratsapu, sabalu, sam'e'u*.

Verbs in *i*, like those in *u*, are either transitive or intransitive (so with *i* in Arabic). Among verbs in *a* are *canadu, lamadu, makhatsu, makharu* ("to receive"), *palakhu, pasakhu, tsabatu, racabu, rasabu, tab'e'u*: mostly transitives (*a* denoting the passing-on of the action).

Many verbs admit both forms; e.g. *itsbut* and *itsbat, epus* and *epis*.

The first person singular of the aorist is often formed in Babylonian by *e*, especially when the vowel of the second radical is *i*; e.g. *esnik, escir*. The same was the case in vulgar Assyrian.

Verbs נ״פ also in Assyrian might undergo the same change: thus we find both *acul* and *ecul*, "I ate." Comp. *ekdhol, ekkâtél* in Hebrew, and see p. 33.

The first person plural is always *ni-*, except where the singular has *u*, when *nu* is used (e.g. *nubahi*, "we sought," in the Aphel).

The typical form of the infinitive is regarded in the tablets as *casadu*. Verbs ע״פ substituted *i* after the second radical, and dropped the *a* of the first. The *nomina verbi*, however, will be considered hereafter, as well as the participles. In verbs פ׳ע, the *a* of the first radical in the present Participle is dropped; thus, *ebisu* by the side of *cāsidu*.

Permansive.	Present.		Aorist.
Singular.			
1. sacnacu (sacnaq)	asaccin	ascun	arkhits atsbat
2 m. sacinta	tasaccin	tascun	tarkhits tatsbat
2 f. sacinti	tasaccini	tascuni	tarkhitsi tatsbati
3 m. sacin	isaccin	iscun	irkhits itsbat
3 f. sacnat	tasaccin	tascun	tarkhits tatsbat
Plural.			
1. sacinni	nisaccin	niscun	nirkhits nitsbat
2 m. sacintunu	tasaccinu	tascunu	tarkhitsu tatsbatu
2 f. sacintina	tasaccina	tascuna	tarkhitsa tatsbata
3 m. sacnu	isaccinu	iscunu	irkhitsu itsbatu
3 f. sacna	isaccina	iscuna	irkhitsa itsbata
Dual.			
3. sacnā	isaccinā	iscunū	irkhitsā itsbatā

The same verb sometimes takes indifferently more than one vowel after the second radical in the aorist, as *acsud* and *acsid*. Occasionally the difference of vowels distinguishes two separate verbs; e.g. *amkhar*, "I received," and *amkhur*, "I increased."

In the later inscriptions a feminine nominative is now and then used improperly with a masculine verb. Thus, Assur-bani-pal has *ikbi'* and *yusapri'* (for *takbi'* and *tusapri'*) with Istar. So in the law-tablet the Assyrian translator has used *isir* and *iktabi'* with *assatu*, "woman" (as well as *su* for *sa*, like הוּא and נַעַר in the Pentateuch). The same is the case in the Assyrian text of the legend of Sargon (W.A.I. iii. 4, 7). In the earliest inscriptions even the feminine of the third person of the Precative is lost. So in Amharic the feminine second and third plural have been lost.

IMPERATIVE.

SINGULAR.
2 m. sucun; rikhits; tsabat
2 f. sucini, sucni; rikhitsi, rikhtsi; tsabti

PLURAL.
2 m. sucinu, sucnu; rikhitsu, rikhtsu; tsabtu
2 f. sucina, sucna; rikhitsa, rikhtsa; tsabta

PRECATIVE.

SINGULAR.
1. luscun; lurkhits; lutsbat
2 m. lutascun; lutarkhits; lutatsbat
3 m. and f. liscun; lirkhits; litsbat

PLURAL.
3 m. liscunu; lirkhitsu; litsbatu
3 f. liscuna; lirkhitsa; litsbata

The first person singular of the Precative stands for *lŭdscun*. The second feminine singular would be, according to analogy, *lutascuni, lutarkhitsi, lutatsbati*; the second plural would be *lutascunu* (masculine), *lutascuna* (feminine), etc.

Both the Imperative and the Precative may take the augment of motion (*a*). In this case *sucun, rikhits*, and *tsabat* are generally contracted into *sucna, rikhtsa*, and *tsabta*.

Iphteal.—This conjugation is formed from Kal by the insertion of *t* after the first radical (as in the Arabic eighth conjugation), except in concave verbs, where it precedes the first radical; e.g. *itbuni, tebácu* (as in Hebrew, Aramaic, Æthiopic, and the fifth and sixth conjugations in Arabic).[1] The

---

[1] So, too, in the Aramaising form, *illicean*, "they went," at Behistun, for the regular *italicu*, contracted *itlicu*, in the conditional *itlicáni*, with the subjunctive enclitic added.

secondary conjugations formed by the insertion of *t* have an intensive force, and are for the most part intransitive. This arises out of the originally reflexive sense imparted by *t*. Its origin is to be sought in the pronominal root, pronounced with the dental, which has given rise to the characteristic of the feminine in the verb and the noun, as well as to the second personal pronoun. For the changes of letters see above, p. 71.

The Present and Aorist are distinguished, as in the Kal of concave verbs, by a difference of vowel in the last syllable: the aorist is *imtakhits* or *issasus* (for *istasus*), the present *istaccan* or *istacan*. The latter is distinguished from Iphtaal only by wanting the preformative *u*.

Verbs which have *s* in the aorist of Kal generally assimilate the vowel of *t* to that of the last syllable in the aorist; e.g. *iptikid* for *iptakid*. In verbs with ע for first radical *t* is followed by *e*; e.g. *etebir*, "he crossed." *Te* is sometimes wrongly expressed by *ti* and even *ta*. Another peculiarity of these verbs is that the second radical is sometimes doubled in the aorist, Iphteal being confused with Iphtaal through the presence of the *e*: e.g. present *etappas*, aorist *etibbus* and *etebus*, *etettika* (elsewhere *etattik*). Two verbs, *episu* and *eribu*, always have *s* in the aorist, *etebus* and *eterub* or *etarub*. If the last radical is increased by any addition, the vowel of the second radical is usually dropped, even in the present, where the double letter is thus lost; e.g. *etarba* for *etarraba*, "I am going down," *itstsabtu* for *itstabitu*, *tastacnu* for *tastaccanu*, *listalma* for *listalama*.

The tendency to nasalization which appears in the mimmation (rarely, in later inscriptions, changed to a nunnation, as in Assur-bani-pal, where for *in cirib Ninâ illikam-ma yusanna'a* we have a variant *illikan-ma*), or in the plural ending in *an*, has given rise to a lengthened form of the inserted *t*, viz. *tan*. Hence we get the present *attanakhkhar, ittanakhar* or *imdanakhar*, "he receives," *tattanakhkhar, ittanallac, itanarrar, iśśanakhkhar* (for *iśtanakhkhar*), *iśanammā* (for *iśtanammā*), *iktanarrab, iltanappar* and *istanappar, ikhtanabbata* (with the subjunctive augment), in the aorist *imtanallic, tattanigir, ittanassi, ikdhanabbi*. Where Iphteal has *te* (*ti*), Iphtaneal has *ten*, e.g. (in Babylonian) *erteniddi*. The form in *tan* seems to have been a vulgarism, and is chiefly met with in and after the time of Sargon.

The common verb *atnimmus*, "I departed," is well explained by Dr. Oppert (who wrongly reads it *atnummus*) as an Iphtaneal, standing for *atanimmus*. Another verb of the same signification is *attuśir*, an Ittaphal, with *u* for *a*, according to the rules of verbs 𐎊'𐎁.

For letter-changes see p. 71.

	Permansive.	Present.	Aorist.	
		SINGULAR.		
1.	kitnusac (kitnusacu)	astaccan, astacan, altacan	astacin, altacin;	aptikid
2 m.	[kitnusta]	tastaccan, etc.	tastacin;	taptikid
2 f.	[kitnusti]	tastaccani	tastacini;	taptikidi
3 m.	kitnus	istaccan	istacin;	iptikid
3 f.	kitnusat	tastaccan	tastacin;	taptikid
		PLURAL.		
1.	[kitnusni]	nistaccan	nistacin;	niptikid
2 m.	[kitnustunu]	tastaccanu	tastacinu;	taptikidu
2 f.	[kitnustina]	tastaccina	tastacina;	taptikida
3 m.	kitnusu	istaccinu	istacinu;	iptikidu
3 f.	kitnusa	istaccina	istacina;	iptikida

IMPERATIVE.	PRECATIVE.	PARTICIPLE.
	SINGULAR.	
2 m. sitcin	1. lustacan; [luptikid]	
2 f. sitcini	3. listacan; liptikid	mustacann, multacanu
	PLURAL.	
2 m. sitcinu	3 m. listacanu; liptikidn	mnptikudu
2 f. sitcina	3 f. listacana; liptikida	

Niphal.—The Assyrian Niphal agrees exactly with Hebrew, both in form and use. Arabic and Æthiopic have prefixed '*a*. Aramaic employs *eth* instead. Originally reflexive, as in *innabid*, "he fled," both in Hebrew and Assyrian Niphal has become the passive of Kal. The characteristic is probably the pronominal root which we find in the Aramaic *nektul*, *nektylun*, and which refers us to the demonstrative *annu*, etc. As in Hebrew, *n* regularly assimilates with the first radical. Exceptions, however, occur, chiefly in later times, *e.g.* Achæmenian *indin* for *iddin*.

Verbs פ״נ double the second radical, *s* not admitting reduplication.

PERMANSIVE.	PRESENT.	AORIST.
	SINGULAR.	
1. [nanzuzacn]	assacan	assacin
2 m. [nanzuzta]	tassacan	tassacin
2 f. [nanzuzti]	tassacani	tassacini
3 m. nanzuz	issacan	issacin
3 f. [nanzuzat]	tassacan	tassacin
	PLURAL.	
1. [nanzuzni]	nissacan	nassacin
2 m. [nanzuztunn]	tassacanu	tassacinn
2 f. [nanzuztina]	tassacana	tassacina
3 m. nanzuzu	issacanu	issacinu
3 f. [nanzuza]	issacana	issacina

The forms *nagarrur* and *nasallul* instanced by Dr. Oppert, do not belong to Niphal, but to Niphael. Another form of the aorist is *izzanun*.

IMPERATIVE.	PRECATIVE.	PARTICIPLE.
	SINGULAR.	
2 m. nascin	1. lussacin	
2 f. nascini	3. lissacin	mussacinu
	PLURAL.	
2 m. nascinu	3 m. lissacinu, lissacnu	
2 f. nascina	3 f. lissacina, lissacna	

Ittaphal.—This voice is but little used, and chiefly with quadriliterals.

According to Dr. Hincks the Permansive would be *nastecun*.

The Present is *attapalcat;* the Aorist *attapalcit,* for which we once find *ittapalcutu,* and in vulgar Assyrian even *ittapalaccita.*

The Precative is *littasgar;* the Participle *muttascanu.* Dr. Oppert believes the Imperative to have been *nitasgir.*

Pael.—Pael is distinguished from the Present of Kal by the preformative *u,* answering to Æthiopic *a,* Arabic 'i (in conjugations 7, 8, 9, 10, etc.).

Pael expresses intensity, and therefore doubles the second radical, giving emphasis to the idea which is longer dwelt upon. The same machinery produces the present with its idea of extension of time. The Assyrian form corresponds with Hebrew Piel, Aramaic Pael, Arabic *kattala,* Æthiopic *gabbara.*

From its intensive meaning comes the idea of causation. When Kal is intransitive, Pael becomes transitive.

The reduplication is neglected especially in the more ancient inscriptions. This is particularly the case, Dr. Oppert points out, with *kh*, *o*, *r*, and *s*. The reduplication in labials and dentals is sometimes replaced by a nasalization (as in Aramaic), *e.g.* in the Kal Presents *tanambu* for *tanabbu*, *imandad* for *imaddad*, *inandin* for *inaddin*.

There is no reduplication of *e*, *h*, and *'a*, though it always takes place in *kh* and *r*.

The Present and Aorist are distinguished by *a* and *i* after the second radical, as is stated in a grammatical tablet, where we have *yunaccar* and *yunaccir*, *yusanna* and *yusanni*.

Irregularly (as with Kal Present) *u* takes the place of *i* in the Aorist, as in *yuracum* (like *iraggum*). As in Iphteal, verbs with *i* in the Kal Aorist may take *i* after the second radical, thus, *yunicim*.

Permansive.	Present.	Aorist.
	SINGULAR.	
1. karradacu	usaccan	usaccin
2 m. [karradta (karratta)]	tusaccan	tusaccin
2 f. [karradti]	tusaccani, tusacni	tusaccini
3 m. karrad	yusaccan	yusaccin
3 f. karradat	tusaccan	tusaccin
	PLURAL.	
1. [karradni]	nusaccan	nusaccin
2 m. [karradtunu]	tusaccanu	tusaccinu
2 f. [karradtina]	tusaccana	tusaccina
3 m. karradu	yusaccanu	yusaccinu
3 f. karrada	yusaccana	yusaccina

Imperative.	Precative.	Participle.
	SINGULAR.	
2 m. succin (sucin), sullima	1. lusaccan	
2 f. succini	3. lusaccan, lusaccin	musaccinu
	PLURAL.	
2 m. succinu	3 m. lusaccanu	
2 f. succina	3 f. lusaccana	

Iphtaal.—Iphtaal is formed from Pael by the insertion of *t* after the first radical. Dr. Oppert calls it the middle voice of Pael, strengthening the latter conjugation: thus in Kal *halacu*, "to go," Pael *hallacu*, "to make go," Iphtaal *attallacu*, "to be driven to go," "*ambulare*."

An instance of Iphtaneal is the aorist *ultanpiru* (for *ustanappiru*), as distinguished from the present *ultanapparu*.

As in Iphteal, verbs with *i* in Kal aorist may substitute *te* (*ti*) for *a* after the dental, e.g. *yuptekid*. The same takes place with verbs י'פ; thus, *lutebus, lutibbus*.

Neither the Permansive nor the Imperative have been found.

	PRESENT.	AORIST.	PRECATIVE.	PARTICIPLE.
		SINGULAR.		
1.	ustaccan	ustaccin	1. lustaccan	mustaccinu
2 m.	tustaccan	tustaccin	3. lustaccan	
2 f.	tustaccani	tustaccini, tustacni		
3 m.	yustaccan	yustaccin	[IMPERATIVE. sutcin]	
3 f.	tustaccan	tustaccin		
		PLURAL.		
1.	nustaccan	nustaccin	3 m. lustaccanu	
2 m.	tustaccanu	tustaccinu	3 f. lustaccana	
2 f.	tustaccana	tustaccina		
3 m.	yustaccanu	yustaccinu		
3 f.	yustaccana	yustaccina		

Shaphel.—This is one of the most commonly-used conjugations in Assyrian, and is formed by a prothetic *s*. Like the Aramaic Shaphel, presupposed in Arabic *istaktala* (conjugation 10) and Æthiopic *ystagabbala*, Hebrew and Phœnician Hiphil, Arabic and Æthiopic *aktala*, Aramaic and Assyrian Aphel, the conjugation has a factitive meaning. I would refer it to the root which appears in the Arabic *shahâ*, "wish," attached to the verb, like *sa* in Arabic (from *saufa*, "in the end"), which is prefixed to the Imperfect to express futurity. As *s* has become *h* in Hebrew, etc., it must have been initial, so that the peculiarly Hebrew root עשה is excluded. A large number of roots in the various Semitic tongues, even in those which, like the Hebrew, have lost nearly every trace of Shaphel, are really Shaphel forms, *e.g.* שחר from חר, שכן from כון.

In verbs פ'ע, *a* after the characteristic *s* becomes *e;* e.g. *usebis, useli*. In the later inscriptions this change of consonant is sometimes transferred to the regular verbs, as in *usascin, tusasnin, musasnis;* just as *a* in Babylonian tends to become *e* (see p. 26); and as we get *uptekid*, etc., in Iphtaal and Iphteal.

The vowel of the characteristic may be dropped; e.g. *usis* and even *ulsis* for *usasis*.

For the Imperative see p. 58.

The Permansive has not been found. Dr. Hincks restores it as *satoan*.

	PRESENT.	AORIST.	IMPERATIVE.	PRECATIVE.	PARTICIPLE.
			SINGULAR.		
1.	usascan	usascin		1. lusascin	musascinu
2 m.	tusascan	tusascin	2 m. suscin		
2 f.	tusascani	tusascini	2 f. suscini		
3 m.	yusascan	yusascin		3. lusascan	
3 f.	tusascan	tusascin			
			PLURAL.		
1.	nusascan	nusascin			
2 m.	tusascanu	tusascinu	2 m. suscinu		
2 f.	tusascana	tusascina	2 f. suscina		musascinu
3 m.	yusascanu	yusascinu		3 m. lusascinu	
3 f.	yusascana	yusascina		3 f. lusascina	

Istaphal.—This conjugation corresponds to Aramaic Istaphal, Arabic Tenth conjugation, Æthiopic *ystagabbara*, Hebrew Hithpael, and has a desiderative signification.

Verbs פ"י have *e* after the dental instead of *a*, e.g. *ultebis*. This is imitated by other verbs in the Babylonian period; e.g. *ultesib* and *usteni'edu*.

The Permansive Dr. Hincks believes would be *satsecan*.

Present.	Aorist.	Participle.
	SINGULAR.	
1. ustascan, ultascan etc.	ustascin, ultascin etc.	mustascinu, multascinu

Imperative.		Precative.
	SINGULAR.	
2 m. sutiscin		1. lustascan
2 f. sutiscini		3. lustascan
	PLURAL.	
2 m. sutiscinu		3 m. lustascanu
2 f. sutiscina		3 f. lustascana

After the example of Iphteal, another form of Istaphal, without the preformative *u*, seems to have come into use in the later period of the language. Thus we find in the Achæmenian inscriptions *altabus* (a corrupt form) by the side of *ultebis*, and *istandhakhu* may be another instance from Shalmaneser; but this is rather an Iphtaneal from שׁכן.

Aphel.—This conjugation is confined, so far as I know, to the concave verbs, and will be treated of under them.

Itaphal.—Dr. Oppert quotes from the syllabarics *itatspur* as an example of this conjugation. The form ought to be *yutatspir; itatspur* will stand by the side of *altabus* above; but I should prefer to regard it as standing for the Ittaphal *ittatspur*.

Shaphael.—The same grammatical regularity that distinguishes Assyrian among the Semitic languages like Sanskrit among the Aryan languages, producing the secondary conjugations with every voice, has also displayed itself in the Causative conjugation. Kal and Pael, answering to the aorist and present tenses, were regarded as the primary voices; to each of these was attached a causative in (*u*)*sa*. Each of the four forms thus obtained had a Passive assigned to it, the Reflexive Niphal being set apart for the Passive of Kal, as otherwise standing outside the regular verbal scheme —and finally all were provided with a secondary conjugation in *t* and *tan*. Shaphael is rarely found in the strong verb, as *e.g.* in *yusnammir;* but it frequently takes the place of Shaphel in verbs ל"ה: thus *usdhibbu'*, *usmallu'*, *usrabbi'*. The Permansive may have had the form *sasaccan;* but it has not been found.

The Present is *usnammar*, the Aorist *usnammir*.

The vowel after *s* is regularly dropped on account of the weight of the following syllable.

The Imperative was probably *susucsin*. The Participle is *musnammiru*.

Istaphael.—Here we find *yusteni'edi* for Aorist, *ustamalta'* for Present. The other tenses have not been detected.

The Passives.—I have already given my reasons for not considering forms like *ilubusu* as Passives of Kal, but as examples of a Poel.

As examples of the Passive of Pael, we have for the Permansive *nussuku* third plural masculine, *nussuka* third plural feminine, *nummuru*, *summukhu*, etc. In the Present we find *yubullat*, in the Aorist *yubullit*. Judging from Arabic analogy, there was no Imperative. I can add nothing to what I have already said about the Passives of the remaining conjugations. The Passive of Shaphael ought to be *sunummur* or *sunammur* Permansive, *yusnummar* Present, and *yusnummir* Aorist. The Passive is never formed, as in Aramaic, by the dental. A solitary Aramaising form is *itpisu* for *etpisu*, "constituted," and here the dental is inserted after the first radical, while the word is only a *nomen verbi*. Traces of other conjugations, or rather *nomina verbi*, such as *papel*, *pealpel*, etc., will be found (see further on) under the head of the *nomina verbi*.

THE DEFECTIVE VERBS.

Verbs פ״נ.— These verbs follow the example of Niphal, assimilating the nasal when followed by any consonant except *h* or *n*, and the consonant is doubled. Before *n* and the vowels the first radical remains unchanged. *Nn* is never written *n;* thus we never find *inamar* for *innamar*, "it is seen."

The Aorist of Kal takes *u*, *a*, and *i* after the second radical.

Among those that have *u* are *na'amu, nabalu, nagagu, namaru, nasakhu, nasacu, napakhu, napaku, natsaru, nakabu, nakaru*.

Among those that have *i: nadanu, nakhatsu, nadhu, nacalu, nacamu, nacasu, nacaru, natsagu, nasagu, nasaku, nasaru*.

Among those that have *a: na'aru, naharu, nazalu, nazaru, nakhazu, nadhalu, napalu, natsabu, natsatsu, nakamu*.

The nasal is sometimes irregularly retained, more especially in the Achæmenian period. Thus we have *indin* for *iddin*, *mandattu* and *mandantu* for *maddattu*. It is possible, however, that the *n* was frequently not pronounced, though written, as in Arabic. Some few verbs always retain the *n*, e.g. *indhur*, as in Hebrew.

Before *b* or *p*, *n*, instead of being elided, may be changed into *m*; thus we find *ambi* and *abbi* ("I called"), *munambu* and *munabbu*. This has had a reflex action; *nabu'u* can replace the reduplication of the second radical by *mb*; e.g. *tanambu, nunambu*.

The Imperative Kal rejects the first radical, as in Hebrew, but replaces it by *u, i, a*, according to the vowel of the Aorist; thus *ugug, idin, ecil, apal*.

The principal forms are as follows:—

	PERMANSIVE.	PRESENT.	AORIST.	IMPERATIVE.	PARTICIPLE.
Kal.	namir	inammir[1]	immur	umur	namiru, namru
Iphteal.	nitmur	ittamar	ittamir	nitmir	muttamiru
Niphal.	nammur	innamar	innamir	nammir	munnamiru, munnamru
Ittaphal.	nattemur	ittammar	ittammir	nitammir	muttamaru
Pael.	nammar	yunammar	yunammir	nummir	munammiru
Iphtaal.	—	yuttammar	yuttammir	—	muttammiru
Shaphel.	sammar	yusammar	yusammir	summir	musammiru
Istaphal.	satnemar	yustammar	yustammir	suttimmir	mustammiru
Shaphael.	sanammar	yusnammar	yusnammir	sunummir	musnammiru
Istapael.	—	yustenammar	yustenammir	—	mustenammiru
Passive Pael.	nummur	yunummar	yunummir	—	—
Iphtaal.	yuttumkit	yuttummar	yuttummir	—	—
Shaphel.	sunumur / sunamur	yusummar	yussummir	—	—
Istaphal.	sutenumur	yustummar	yustummir	—	—
Shaphael.	sunummur / sunammur	yusnummar	yusnummir	—	—

Verbs פ׳א, פ׳ה, פ׳ו, פ׳י.—These verbs have some forms in common. Others are shared in by the last two. In other

---

[1] A false analogy with Niphal Present has produced forms like *inaccar*.

forms they all differ from one another. They constitute the most difficult part of Assyrian grammar; and it is here that Dr. Oppert and Dr. Hincks are in the most direct opposition. The following are the results obtainable from the inscriptions.

(1.) Verbs פ׳א and פ׳ה are identical, save in the third masculine. Regularly, however, the second radical of verbs פ׳ה is doubled, e.g. *alliq, illiq,* for *ahliq* and *ihliq;* but this doubling is often omitted in writing; thus we find *aliq, iliq, ipuq.* (2.) Verbs פ׳א and פ׳נ are used interchangeably; so in Hebrew אצב and נצב, etc., the syllabaries equate *namaru* with *amaru:* hence *umar* (Pael present) comes, not from *mamaru,* but from *amaru.* (3.) Verbs פ׳א and concave verbs have certain forms in common; the Pael of verbs פ׳א is often identical with the Aphel of concave verbs, and the Kal of the latter has the same form as the Kal of the former when written defectively (without reduplication). (4.) Verbs פ׳א and פ׳ע are confounded, especially in the Babylonian period: thus we have indifferently *acul* and *ecul, elih* and *alih* (see p. 33), so *usesib.* (5.) Verbs פ׳א and פ׳נ are liable to be confounded; the syllabaries, for instance, give both *aladu* and *uladu.* (6.) Verbs פ׳נ have the same forms in Kal as the (irregular) Pael of verbs פ׳א and the Aphel of concave verbs. (7.) The Pael of verbs פ׳ה and פ׳ע is the same; e.g. *u'ulla'a* and *ulla'a* from עלה, and *u'ullil* and *ullil* from הלל. (8.) As in Hebrew, verbs פ׳נ tend to become פ׳י; hence *ilitluv* (*ilidtuv*) by the side of *ulidu.*

It will be seen from this that Dr. Hincks is not right in asserting that verbs פ׳א have no forms in common with verbs פ׳נ, which are not also common to verbs פ׳י. Neither is Dr Oppert justified in the belief that Hebrew verbs פ׳י

become in Assyrian פ'א if they correspond to Arabic verbs in *u;* while if Arabic has *i*, Assyrian has the same. This is generally the case; but it has many exceptions. Dr. Oppert has not sufficiently distinguished between verbs פ'א and verbs פ'ה; the first have *ya* in the third person Aorist and Present, e.g. *yatsab*, "he creates;" the latter have *i* or *ih* with the second radical doubled. The Aorist Kal in *u*, again (as *ulid*), comes from a verb פ'י, not פ'א. The learned Doctor, moreover, has confounded verbs פ'ע and פ'א; as well as all these classes of verbs with concave verbs.

The participles *muridu, mulidu*, etc., which Dr. Oppert believes to belong to Kal, are really Pael participles, with the reduplication omitted, as in *mucinu* for *muccinu*.

Our chief difficulty as regards these verbs lies in the uncertainty of the first radical. Sometimes this was *a*, sometimes *e* (Babylonian), sometimes *u:* thus two roots were indifferently employed by the Assyrians, *atsu* and *utsu*. From the first we have *attatsi* (Ittaphal), from the second *attutsi*. But *h* and *i* are always carefully distinguished. In Shaphel, however, the first radical becomes *e*, whether originally *a*, *e*, or *i*.

It was only at a comparatively late period that the Semites came to distinguish between the various forms which a biliteral root might take. The servile letters were for the most part absolutely interchangeable. The sharp divisions of the Hebrew grammarians are the results of later reflection. Assyrian has hardly entered upon this discriminating stage: hence the same biliteral root appears under different forms which a grammar has to assign to different triliteral stems. From סב, for instance, we have forms which presuppose

טוב, and טבה; from כן forms which presuppose כנן, כן, יכן, וכן, אכן, נבן, and י.

Verbs פ׳א Kal :—

AORIST.		PRESENT.	IMPERATIVE AND PRECATIVE.
SINGULAR.			
1. asib, esib {acul/ecul}		asab	1. lisub, lusib
2 m. tasib	tacul	tasab	2 m. acul
2 f. tasibi		tasabi	2 f. aculi
3 m. yasib		yasab	
3 f. tasib	etc.	tasab	3. {lirur / lisub, lusib}
PLURAL.			
1. nasib		nasab	
2 m. tasibu		tasabu	2 m. aculu
2 f. tasiba		tasaba	2 f. acula
3 m. yasibu		yasabu	3 m. {lisubu / lusibu}
3 f. yasiba		yasaba	3 f. {lisuba / lusiba}[1]

PARTICIPLE—asibu.

Verbs פ׳ה Kal :—

SINGULAR.		
1. allic	allac	1. lillic
2 m. tallic	tallac	2 m. halic
2 f. tallici	tallaci	2 f. balci
3 m. illic	illac	3. lillic
3 f. tallic	tallac	
PLURAL.		
1. nallic	nallac	—
2 m. tallicu	tallacu	2 m. halcu
2 f. tallica	tallaca	2 f. balca
3 m. illicu	illacu	3 m. lillicu
3 f. illica[2]	illaca	3 f. lillica

PARTICIPLE—allicu.

[1] These Precative forms, lusib, etc., though ordinarily used, do not come from אשב, but from ישב. So the Pael yussib for yu'assib (cf. p. 57).
[2] Besides this usual form for verbs פ׳ה, we also find instances in which

Verbs פ״י Kal:—

Aorist.	Present.	Imperative and Precative.
SINGULAR.		
1. ulid	ulad	1. lulid, lusib
2 m. tulid	tulad	2 m. lid
2 f. tulidi	tuladi	2 f. lidi
3 m. yulid	yulad	3. lulid
3 f. tulid	tulad	
PLURAL.		
1. nulid	nulad	—
2 m. tulidu	tuladu	2 m. lidu
2 f. tulida	tulada	2 f. lida
3 m. yulidu	yuladu	3 m. lulidu
3 f. yulida [1]	yulada	3 f. lulida

PARTICIPLE—ulidu.

Verbs פ״י Kal:—

SINGULAR.		
1. inik	inak	1. linik
2 m. tinik	tinak	2 m. nik
2 f. tiniki	tinaki	2 f. niki
3 m. inik	inak	3. linik
3 f. tinik	tinak	
PLURAL.		
1. ninik	ninak	—
2 m. tiniku	tinaku	2 m. niku
2 f. tinika	tinaka	2 f. nika
3 m. iniku	inaku	3 m. liniku
3 f. inika	inaka	3 f. linika.

PARTICIPLE—iniku.

the initial letter is regarded as a strong radical, and the verb is accordingly conjugated regularly; e.g. *ahbid*, "I destroyed," *ahapta* for *ahbida*, *ihbid*, *uhabid*, for *uhabbid*, etc.

[1] Besides ילד, we meet with הלך conjugated both regularly and like *alacu*; e.g. *usahlid*, *ihaldu* (= *ihlidu*).

ASSYRIAN GRAMMAR.

The other conjugations of verbs פ״א :—

	PERMANSIVE.	PRESENT.	AORIST.	IMPERATIVE.	PARTICIPLE.
Iphteal.	tesub	itasab	itasib	itsib	mutasabu
Niphal.	[nāsub]	inasab	inasib	nasib	munasibu
Ittaphal.	—	ittesab	ittesib	—	muttesibu
Pael.	[assab]	yu'assab	yu'assib	ussib	mussibu
Iphtaal.	—	yutassab	yutassib	itasab	muttassabu
Shaphel.	sūsab	{yusasab / yusesab}	{yusasib / yuscsib}	susib	musesibu
Istaphal.	[satesab]	yustesab	yustesib	sutesib	mustesibu
Istataphal.	[satetesab]	yustetesab	yustetcsib	sutetesib	mustetesibu
Itaphal..	—	yutesab	yutesib	[utesib]	mutesibu
Pass. Pael	ussub	yu'ussab	yu'ussib	—	—
Pass. Istaphal.	sutesub	[yustusab]	[yustusib]	—	—

Verbs פ״ה :—

Iphteal.	—	itallac	itallic	itlic	mutallacu
Niphal.	[nalluc]	inallac	inallic	nallic	munallicu
Ittaphal.	—	ittallac	ittallic	—	muttallicu
Pael.	allac	yu'allac	yu'allic	hullic	mu'allicu
Iphtaal.	—	yutallac	yutallic	itallic	mutallicu
Shaphel.	[sallac]	yusallac	yusallic	sulic	musallicu
Istaphal.	[satallac]	yustallac	yustallic	sutallic	mustallicu
Passive Pael.	[ulluc]	[yu'ullac]	[yu'ullic]	—	—

In all the above cases the reduplication may be dropped, and often is dropped in the inscriptions. On the other hand, these verbs פ״ה may be conjugated like the strong verb.

Verbs פ״י :—

Iphteal.	telud	itulad	itulid	—	mutalidu
Niphal.	nulud	[inelad]	[inelid]	nulid	[munelidu]
Ittaphal.	—	ittulad	ittulud	—	muttelidu
Pael.	[ullad]	{yu'ullad / yullad}	{yu'ullid / yullid}	ullid	mullidu
Iphtaal.	—	yutullad	yutullid	—	muttelladu
Shaphel.	[sulad]	yuselad	yuselid	sulid	musalidu
Istaphal.	[sutelad]	yustelad	yustelid	sutelid	mustelidu

Verbs פ״י :—

	PERMANSIVE.	PRESENT.	AORIST.	IMPERATIVE.	PARTICIPLE.
Iphteal.	tenuk	itinak	itinik	itnik	mutiniku
Niphal.	[nenuk]	ininak	ininik	ninik	muuiniku
Ittaphal.	—	ittinak	ittinik	nitinik	muteniku
Pael.	[ennak]	{i'ennak / innak}	{i'ennik / innik}	unnik	mu'enniku
Iphtaal.	—	yuttennak	yuttennik	ittinnik	muttenniku
Shaphel.	[senak]	yusenak	yusenik	sunik	museniku
Istaphal.	[satinak]	yustenak	yustenik	sutenik	musteniku
Istataphal.	[satetinak]	yustotenak	yustetenik	sutetenik	musteteniku

It must never be forgotten that all this class of verbs (with the exception of פ״ה) are greatly confounded with one another, and had a tendency to adopt the same form borrowed from verbs פ״י. The Assyrians pronounced י as a vowel, and this served as a common meeting-point for the obscured sounds of the three primary vowels.[1] The same verb is sometimes conjugated as a פ״ו, sometimes as a פ״י, sometimes as a פ״א; just as in Hebrew we have טוב and יטב, etc.

Concave Verbs.— These are not so numerous in Assyrian as in the cognate languages. They are generally replaced by verbs פ״א, פ״ו, פ״נ, or more especially by *palel*. So in Hebrew the concave verbs substitute *polel* for *piel*.

In Kal the first radical can be doubled, as in Hebrew.[2] So, too, with verbs ע״ה, as *innar* for *inhar*.

In Pael, the Permansive generally has a Passive or neuter meaning, and changes *ayya* into *i*. The other tenses are formed as though from פ״ו.

---

[1] Even *h* sometimes represents *e;* thus, *buhi* (from *buh'u*) = בעה.
[2] The reduplicated forms really come from verbs פ״ה.

Niphal is formed as though from Palel.

Besides the participle active, Kal also possesses a participle passive, like Hebrew, though *u* has become *i*, as in Aramaic, e.g. *dicu*, "slain." This takes the same form as some parts of the Permansive Pael. Babylonian substitutes *e* for *i* in the first syllable, e.g. *nebi* for *nibi*.

Verbs א"ע, ו"ע, and י"ע are all conjugated in the same manner, except in Kal Aorist and Imperative. Palel and Iphtalel regularly appear in these verbs.

Intensive and Iterative forms, *Papel* and *Palpel*, are also formed from them; e.g. *babbaru, lallaru, gargaru, rakraku, khalkhallu*.

The Assyrians seem to have regarded in most cases the typical form as belonging to verbs פ"א; thus, the infinitive given in the syllabaries is *ta'aru*, not *turu* or *tavaru*.[1]

Kal :—

	PERMANSIVE.		AORIST.		PRESENT.
			SINGULAR.		
1.	camacu	ca'inacu	atur, attur	aciś	atar, attar
2 m.	camta	ca'inta	tatur, tattur	taciś	tatar, etc.
2 f.	camti	ca'inti	taturi, tatturi	taciśi	tatari
3 m.	ca'am	ca'in	itur, ittur	iciś	itar, idakki
3 f.	camat	ca'inat	tatur, tattur	taciś	tatar
			PLURAL.		
1.	camnu	ca'innu	nattur, natur	naciś	natar
2 m.	camtunu	ca'intunu	taturu, etc.	taciśu	tataru
2 f.	camtina	ca'intina	taturu	taciśa	tatara
3 m.	camu	ca'inu	ituru	iciśu	itaru
3 f.	cama	ca'ina	itura	iciśa	itara

[1] Strictly speaking, however, *ta'aru* stands for *tawaru*, like קָם for קוּם and קָם (see p. 27).

IMPERATIVE AND PRECATIVE.

SINGULAR.
1. luttur, lutur
2 m. duk, cin, tirra
2 f. duki, diki, eini
3. littur, litur.

PLURAL.
2 m. duku, cinu
2 f. ducā, cinā
3 m. litturu, lituru
3 f. litturu, lituru

PARTICIPLE ACTIVE—*ta'iru, ca'inu*.[1] PARTICIPLE PASSIVE—*tiru, cinu.*

In the other conjugations:—

	PERMANSIVE.	PRESENT.	AORIST.	IMPERATIVE.	PARTICIPLE.
Iphteal.	[citnacu] tebācu. "I come"	{ictan / itbā}	{ictin / itba'}	{citun / tebu}	muctinu
Niphalel.	[nacnun]	iccanan	{iccanin / izzanun}	nacniu	muccaninn
Ittaphalel.	[nactenun]	ittacnan	ittacnin	nitacnin	muttacnanu
Pael.	nibacu, nikha	{yu'acean / yuccan .}	{yu'uocin / yuccin}	[nccin]	muccinu
Iphtaal.	—	yuctan[2]	yuctin	—	mutaccinu
Palel.	cunnu, 3rd plural	yucnan	yucnin	ucniu	mucninn
Iphtalel.	—	ictenan	{ictenin / ittarru}	—	—
Shaphel.	[sacân]	yussean	{yusacen / yusacin}	sucun	musaccinu
Istaphal.	[satecan]	yustacan	yustacin	sutcun	mustacinu
Aphel.	—	yuca'an	yuciu	{cin / cun}	mucinu
Itaphal.	—	yuccan	yucein	—	muccinn
Shaphael.	[saccan]	yusaccan	yusaccin	snccun	musaccinu
Istapael.	[sateccan]	yustaccan	[yustaccin]	[suteccin]	mustaccinn
Pass. Shaphel.	sucun	yusucan	yusucin	—	—

The regular forms of the Iphteal and Iphtaal have been first given above. These are occasionally met with—e.g. *etud* from עוד, *astil* from סול, *ultil* from סול, *uctin* from

---

[1] So in Aramaic קָאֵם, Arabic *kā'imuñ.*

[2] The length of this syllable is sometimes denoted by doubling the final letter before the conditional suffix; e.g. *uctanna-su,* "I establish it."

כון;—but the usual forms are those in which the dental precedes the first radical: thus, *itbu*, "he went," *itcun*, "he established;" where the vowel of the last syllable is *u* in the Aorist, and *a* in the Present.

Verbs ל'א, ל'י, ל'ו, ל'ה, ע'י. These verbs, like the classes already spoken of, are confounded in Assyrian.

The final vowel of the Aorist in verbs ל'א, ל'י, is *i*; verbs ל'ע have *e*, e.g. *isme‘e*, often improperly written with *i*. When *u* is added, the two vowels often coalesce into *u*; e.g. *itbi‘u* and *ikbū*, *ismi‘u* and *ismū*. The last radical almost always coalesces with *a* following. The pronominal suffixes generally require *a* in the last syllable.

Hebrew verbs ל ה' are for the most part ל'י in Assyrian. These have *u* final in the Aorist. Such Hebrew verbs ל ה as are ל' in Assyrian follow verbs ל'א in having *i* in the Aorist, unless *u* is added, when *u* generally reappears: thus, *ikbi‘*, *ikbu‘u*. So, too, *a* is found when followed by the subjunctive augment *a*, or in the Present of the derived conjugations.

In the Imperative second singular verbs ל'א lose the last radical; e.g. *nas* (from נשא); but verbs ל ה (ל'ו, ל'י) and ל'ע have *i*, as *siti*, "drink" (from שתה). These verbs possess a Niphael as well as a Shaphael; thus, by the side of *illaki* we find *illakki*, "it was taken."

Permansive.	Aorist.		Present.
	SINGULAR.		
1. nasacu	abnu‘	akbi‘	agabbi‘
2 m. nasata	tabnu‘	takbi‘	tagabbi‘
2 f. nasati	tabni‘	takbi‘	tagabbi‘
3 m. nasu	ibnu‘	ikbi‘	igabbi‘
3 f. nasat	tabnu‘	takbi‘	tagabbi‘

ASSYRIAN GRAMMAR.

PERMANSIVE.	AORIST.		PRESENT.
	PLURAL.		
1. nasanu	nabnu'	nakbi'	nagabbi'
2 m. nasatunn	tabnn'	takbu'	tagabbn'
2 f. nasatina	tabna'	takba'	tagabbā'
3 m. nasu'n	ibnu'	ikbu'u'	igabbn'u'
3 f. nosā	ibna'	ikbā'	igabbā'

IMPERATIVE AND PRECATIVE.			PARTICIPLE.
SINGULAR.		PLURAL.	
1. lubnn' lnkbi'		2 m. banu'	banū', banitu
2 m. ban, bani, khidhi'		2 f. bana'	kabū', kabitu
2 f. banī' khidhī'		3 m. libnn'	
3 libnu' likbi'		3 f. libna'	

	PERMANSIVE.	PRESENT.	AORIST.	IMPERATIVE.	PARTICIPLE.
Iphteal.	[kitbu']	ikteba'	iktebi'	kitbi''	muktebū
Pael.	[kabba']	yukabba'	yukabbi'	kubbi'	mukabbū
Iphtaal.	—	yuktabba'	yuktabbi'	kitibbi'	muktabbū
Niphal.	nakbu'	ikkaba'	ikkabi'	nakbi'	mukkabu
Ittaphal.	[naktebu']	ittabna'	ittabni'	nitabni'	muttabnū
Niphael.	[nakabbu']	ikkabba'	ikkabbi'	[nakabbi']	mukkabbū
Shaphel.	[sakba']	yusakba'	yusakbi'	sukbu'	musakbū
Istaphal.	[satkeba']	yustckba'	yustekbi'	sutekbi'	mustckbū
Shaphael.	[sakabba']	yuskabba'	yuskabbi'	snkubbu'	muskabbū
Istapael.	[satkabba']	yustckabba'	yustckabbi'	[sutekabbi']	mustekabbū
Passive Pael.	kubbu'	yukubba'	yukubbn'	—	—
Pass. Shaphael.	sukubn'	yuskubba'	yuskubbi'	—	—

Verbs containing ע.—Most of the peculiarities of these have been already alluded to.

In verbs ע״פ, the first person singular, as well as the third person singular and plural in Kal, were represented in Assyrian by *e*; in Babylonian and Achœmenian *i* stands in the third person; the Babylonian, also, often used *e-i*. When preceded by *u*, *e* became *u*; the two *us* were then contracted into *ū* in Assyrian, though not in Babylonian, e.g. *ullā* Assyrian, *u'ulla* Babylonian.

The second radical may also be irregularly doubled in Niphal. This is only found in the Achæmenian period: the older inscriptions omit the characteristic altogether.

Verbs ע״ע have been already considered under concave verbs, from which they do not differ. The Babylonian inscriptions insert *e* in the Imperative, as *se'ebi*.

Verbs ע״ל do not differ from verbs י״ל.

Verbs ע״פ are declined in the following manner:—

Kal:—

PERMANSIVE.	AORIST.	PRESENT.	IMPERATIVE AND PRECATIVE.
	SINGULAR.		
1. [epsacu]	ebus, emid	epas, emad	1. libus
2 m. epista	tebus, temid	tepas, tebbas	2 m. ebus
2 f. episti	tebusi, temidi	tebasi	2 f. ebusi
3 m. epis	ebus, emid	ebas	3. libus
3 f. epsat	tebus, temid	tebas	
	PLURAL.		
1. episnu	nebus, nemid	nebas	
2 m. epistunu	tebusu, tomidu	tebasu	2 m. ebusu
2 f. epistina	tebusa, tomida	tebasa	2 f. ebusa
3 m. episu	ebusu, emidu	ebasu	3 m. libusu
3 f. episa	ebusa, emida	ebasa	3 f. libusa
	PARTICIPLE—ebisu.		

	PERMANSIVE.	PRESENT.	AORIST.	IMPERATIVE.	PARTICIPLE.
Iphteal.	etbus	etappas	etebus	etpis	mutepisu
Niphal.	[nebus]	i(b)bas	i(b)bis	ni(b)bis	munebisu
Ittaphal.	[netebus]	ettebas	ettebis	nitebis	mutebasu
Pael.	[ebbas]	yubbas	yubbis	ubbis	mubbisu
Iphtaal.	—	yutebbas	yutebbis	—	muttebbisu
Shaphel.	[sebas]	yusebas	yusebis	subis	musebisu
Istaphal.	[satebas]	yustebas	yustebis	suttebis	mustebisu

Verbs doubly defective.—These may be divided into four classes:—

(1.) פ״נ and ל״ה; as *nasu, nadu, nabu, nagu, naku, nadhu, naru, nasu.*

(2.) פא and ל'י; as *abu, adu, akhu, alu, anu, atu, apu, atsu, aru, alu, yasu, yaru, yanu.*

(3.) פ'י and ע'י; as *aibu, 'umu, 'udu, 'unu, uru.*

(4.) ע'י and ל'י; as *bavu (bu), davu, cavu, lavu, navu.*

In (4) the second radical generally becomes a consonant:[1] in the other cases the verbs are conjugated according to the rules already laid down; thus, *isi,* "I had," from נשא; *tsd, tsî, tsu'u, tsa'a,* Imperative of *atsu,* from which a syllabary gives us the following *nomina verbi: atsu, atsit, tsav, satsu'u* (Shaphel), *sutsu'u* (Passive Shaphel), *tetsitu* (Iphteal), *sutetsu'u* (Istaphal). So *ibbi,* "he called," from *nabu.*

Quadriliterals.—These are comparatively few in number in Assyrian. Dr. Oppert gives the following instances: *parsidu, palcitu, parzakhu, palsakhu, paskaru, khamzatu,* to which may be added *kharpasu, naskaru, sakhparu.* In the Aorist verbs with *u* (mostly transitives) have *iskhupir,* Present *iskhupar;* verbs with *a* (and *i*) (mostly intransitives) give *ipalcit,* for which the vulgar language had *ipalaccit* and *iplacit.*

For further details see p. 52. The conjugations will be:—

	Permansive.	Present.	Aorist.	Imperative.	Participle.
Kal (Palel).	palcit	{ipalcat / iskhupar}	{ipalcit / iskhupir}	palcit	mupalcitu
Iphtalel.	[pitlucut]	yuptalcat	yuptalcit	pitalcat	muptalcitu
Saphalel.	[saplacat]	yuspalcat	yuspalcit	supalcut	mupalcitu
Istaphalel.	[saptelcat]	yustapalcat	yustapalcit	sitpalcut	mustapalcitu
Niphalel.	[naplacut]	ippalcat	{ippalcit / ipparsud}	nipalcat	muppalcitu
Ittaphalel.	[naptelcut]	ittapalcat	ittapalcit	natepalcat	muttapalcitu
Niphalella.	—	ippalcatat	ippalcitit	—	muppalcittu

[1] Not always, however. Thus *bavu,* "to go," is always conjugated as if it were *bu;* e.g. *ibu,* "they went," *yustebā* or *yusteba'a,* "he caused to go."

THE PRONOMINAL SUFFIXES OF THE VERB.

These are identical with those of the cognate languages, the third person beginning with the original sibilant, as already explained (p. 12). They are as follows:—

SINGULAR.

1st pers.	-anni, -inni, -nni, -ni.
2nd m.	-acca, -icca, -cca, -ca, -c.
2nd f.	-acci, -icci, -cci, -ci.
3rd m.	-assu, -issu, -su, -s.
3rd f.	-assi, -assa, -ssa, -ssi, -sa, -si.

PLURAL.

1st pers.	-annini, -annu, -nini, -nu.
2nd m.	-accunu, -accun, -cunu, -cun.
2nd f.	-accina, -accin, -cina, -cin.
3rd m.	-assunut(u), -assunu, -assun, -sunut(u), -sunu, -sun.
3rd f.	-assinat(u), -assina, -assin, -sinat(u), -sina, -sin.

In the first person, the longer form -*anni* was used when the form of the verb ended in a consonant, and the double letter merely showed that the accent rested upon the penultimate. If the form terminated with a vowel, *ni* was properly used alone; e.g. *irucú-ni*, "they have given to me;" *ikbú-ni*, "they ordered me"; *yumahrá-ni*, "he urged me." The penultimate was long, and in order to show this a kind of Furtive Pathakh was introduced, producing *irucú-'inni*, a form that is frequently met with; e.g. *usasisú-'inni*, "they made me strong." *Inni* was sometimes used even after *a*, though here the correct form again was *ratsibá-nni*, "pierce me," where the double letter only marks the accent. In later inscriptions the language approached more nearly to the Hebrew pronunciation by substituting Pathakh for *i* (in -*inni*), and expressing in the writing the *hemza*: thus, in the Achæmenian period we find *litstsuru-h-anni*, "may they protect me," *itticru-h-anni*, "they were estranged from me." After *u*, *-nni* was never used, as *u* was known to be long of itself: if, therefore, particular stress had to be laid upon the enclitic, hemza was employed as shown above. Very rarely *u* was dropped after first becoming *w*; e.g. *yuraps'-inni*, "they enlarged for me." *U-a* became *wa*; accordingly, when the union-vowel *a* was used for the sake of emphasis, and hemza did not intervene to produce *u-h-inni* or *u-h-anni*, *u* was dropped altogether, so that we get *yusatlimanni*, "they conferred on me," for *usatlimwanni*. The union-vowel *a*, as in Hebrew and Æthiopic, is found with all the pronouns. It is the same vowel that we have in the accusative of the noun and the subjunctive aorist, and it well expresses the action of the verb passing on to the governed pronoun. Compare the union-vowel *â* in Æthiopic, which expresses the construct state both in the singular and the plural. Like the Æthiopic, the Assyrian has no separate form to express the dative of the pronoun.

With the second person feminine, *a* after *i* is dropped, so that we get *tucassipinni*, "thou didst reveal to me," *tucasinni*, "thou didst cover me," *tu'alinni*, "thou didst exalt me." This contraction of *ya* into *i* has met us before, as in *bitu* for *biyatu* (see p. 35).

Instead of the suffix *ani*, *yati* or *yasi* could be used as a substantive; e.g. *ikbû yati* (see p. 38).

In the second person the same rules hold good, except that the contracted forms of the pronouns (*ca*, *ci*, etc.) may be attached to consonants. The last vowel of the second person singular masculine, and masculine and feminine plural is sometimes omitted, as in *attápsac* for *attappisáca*, and the accent is thrown back upon the preceding syllable. In the vulgar language, instead of the suffix, the substantival *attunu* (*attina*) could be used in the accusative, e.g. *altapra attunu*, "I sent to you," where -*a* carried on the action of the verb to the pronoun.

In the third person singular and plural, again, the final case-vowel is frequently dropped (as in the *status constructus*, and in Hebrew, Aramaic and modern Arabic generally). Thus we find *usdtlimus* for *usatlimúsu*. This is especially the case, if the verb ends one sentence, and the next word begins with a vowel. In Babylonian, verbs ל"י might assimilate this final letter to *s* following; e.g. *indanassu-nu-ti* for *indanan-sunuti* (Palel), *tumašissunuti* for *tumaššinsunuti*, "thou knewest them."

The longer forms, *sunutu*, etc., are as often employed as the shorter ones. They are increased by the same suffix as that of the Æthiopic pronouns *wetu*, *yeti*, which forms abstract substantives in Assyrian (see below).[1] The nominative would be -*tu*, but, of course, when governed by the verb, we only find the oblique and accusative cases -*ti*, -*ta*, more generally the former. This is accounted for by the fact that the idea contained in the verb does not pass on to any new idea: the pronoun refers back to some preceding notion. Just as the genitive has -*i*, marking its priority to the noun in the *status constructus*, so is the priority contained in the personal pronoun suffix expressed by the same case-termination. These

---

[1] As the same suffix builds the plural, a double plural is the result. According to Philippi (Wesen u. Ursprung d. Status Constr., p. 26), this suffix is the demonstrative that we have in the third person feminine of the Imperfect, the Arabic demonstrative تِ .

longer forms, it must be observed, are used as accusative substantives, not as suffixes like *-sunu*, etc.

The final vowels might be dropped in *sunut*, etc., as in *-s* for *su* or *-ca*.

In the third person feminine singular, *si* is nearly as common as *sa*, *a* being weakened to *i* (like רֹאשׁ and *risu*, etc.), *-assi*, *-assa* stand for *-āsi*, *-āsa*, as in *pitassi*, "open for her," where the double letter only expresses the length of the final vowel (=*pitā-si*).¹

With the enclitic conjunction *va*, mimmation generally takes place to denote the accent: e.g. *icsuda-ssuv-va*, "they obtained him, and," *icsudu-sunutav-va*, "they obtained them, and."

With the pronoun-suffixes contractions in the verbs are frequent, *i* and *ā* being as often elided as retained; e.g. *isalmusu* for *isallimú-su*.

THE NOUNS.

As in the cognate languages, nouns substantive and adjective have in Assyrian the same form, and but two genders, masculine and feminine. There is no separate form for the comparative and superlative. Like Æthiopic and Aramaic, Assyrian possesses no article, which in Hebrew and Arabic is merely the demonstrative pronoun. In the Achæmenian period, however, an article was being introduced (see p. 5).

Assyrian has three numbers, Singular, Plural, and Dual; but the last is very little used. It preserves (like classical

---

¹ The strange form *cunu-si* in Assur-bani-pal's proclamation (S.H.A., 189)—*ludhab cunnusi*, "may it be well with you,"—must be a badly-engraved *ti*, as in *at-si-mus* for the usual *atnimmus* (see p. 76), unless the character has a value *tim*.

Arabic) the case-terminations of the primitive Semitic speech, -*u* (nominative), -*i* (genitive), -*a* (accusative). These have been lost in modern Arabic (though still used in Central Arabia), in Aramaic, and in Hebrew (which has but a few traces of them); while Æthiopic only preserves the accusative in -*a*. In Assyrian itself the suffixed pronouns are often found without the final vowel; and the Construct State is marked by the absence of the case-ending in the governing noun if in the singular; thus, *sarru*, "king," but *sar nisi*, "king of men." Besides the case-endings, as in the verbs, a final *m* might be added to the vowel, giving *nisum*, *nisim*, *nisam*. This is regarded in the syllabaries as the correct form, though in the inscriptions this *mimmation*, as it has been happily termed by Dr. Oppert, is frequently omitted. Dr. Oppert compares the Arabic *nunnation*, and refers to the mimmation traceable in Hebrew in the adverbial accusatives יוֹמָם, חִנָּם, אָמְנָם, רֵיקָם, פִּתְאֹם, compared with يَوْمًا, etc., where an obsolete plural can hardly be represented.[1] The origin of the mimmation is probably, as with accusatives and neuters in the Aryan languages, an attempt to give firmness to the final vowel, which produces an obscure closing of the syllable.

Before going further, it will be necessary to controvert Dr. Oppert's extremely misleading ascription of an "emphatic state" to the Assyrian noun. Olshausen has already objected that "the value of the nasalisation of the case-vowel in

---

[1] So יוֹמָם in Phœnician (Cit. 38) and Aramaic *yêmâm*, *îmâm*. Nöldeke (Gött. gel. Anz. June 7, 1871) objects that these words are as little accusative as לַיְלָה (Assyrian *lilatu*) or the Syriac *ai* in *lailai îmâm*, "day and night." Himyaritic, like Assyrian, possessed the mimmation.

Arabic, and of the *status emphaticus* in Aramaic, is not only altogether different, but totally opposed: the Arab nasalises the termination of the indeterminate word, the *status emphaticus* marks the determined word. The nasalisation is really part of the case-ending; the *status emphaticus* is first made possible through the loss of the latter. While it is conceivable that in Aramaic the termination *â* arose from the termination *â*, it is in the highest degree improbable, nay impossible, that *â* could also arise from *û* and *î*." The last sentence refers to Oppert's transliteration of all the case-endings by א; a procedure which throws Semitic philology into the greatest confusion, assumes the original identity of the case-terminations, which is philologically impossible, and in spite of Arabic derives them from the post-fixed article of the Aramaic. Oppert replies that as the Assyrian has no article, it cannot be compared with Arabic: its case-endings correspond to the Arabic noun without *tanwîn* preceded by the article, and to the Aramaic emphatic state. But the emphatic state in Aramaic is most probably a post-fixed article, consequently it can be compared with the Assyrian even less than Arabic. Moreover, under any circumstances, the Aramaic emphatic state has a different philological origin from the Assyrian case-endings, which can be compared only with the similar terminations in Arabic. Besides, the case-endings are used in Assyrian in cases where the article, as a general rule, would not be allowed (as with predicates). Dr. Oppert seems to separate the mimmation and the case-vowels: this cannot be done: the mimmation is but the older and more correct form belonging equally to verbs and nouns, which a later stage of language began to drop, though it was generally retained before the conjunction *va*. Dr. Oppert's view reduces itself to this: either the "emphatic state" in Assyrian means a post-fixed article, which is untrue, or it means that special emphasis was to be laid upon the words which have the case-endings—always added unless the noun is in the construct state—which is equally untrue.[1] The error is a serious one; it not only calls up misleading ideas, but it actually gives rise to mistakes, such as placing '*ilu* (with the case-vowel) by the side of *bucur* (in the *status constructus*) and the feminine *ilit* (also in the *status constructus*), the statement that "the emphatic state is sometimes reduced to the syllable -*an*" (again the *status constructus*), and the strange assertions that "the plural of feminines is always formed from the simple form of the singular. Thus the plural *rapsat* does not come from *rapasuti* [it ought to be *rapâsutu*], but from *rapsat*," and that "the plural of masculines is generally formed from the emphatic state, e.g. *gimri* from *gimir*, status emphatious *gimru*." It is like saying that *dominis* comes from *domino*.

Derivation of Nouns.—As in the other Semitic languages, a distinction may be made between primitive nouns, such as '*abu*, "father," '*ummu*, "mother," and derivative nouns. Properly, however, derivative nouns ought to be those which are formed by the addition of a new letter, *m, t*, etc.; the so-called verbal nouns arising simultaneously with the verb itself from the radical idea. The different forms of the verbs, modified by pronouns and formative letters, are more strictly derivative than many of the so-called derivative participial or infinitival nouns. We may assume a time in the history

---

[1] As in the case of the predicates mentioned above, or of substantives used as prepositions, e.g. *erti sarri*, "against the king."

of Semitic speech when the same combination of consonants might be used either as noun or verb:[1] gradually differences of meaning were introduced, firstly by means of *nuances* of vowel-sounds, or by reduplication of the radicals, and afterwards by additional elements. However, it will be convenient to adhere to the usual custom of Semitic grammars, and to treat of "verbal nouns" as derivatives.

With three radicals we have:—

From Kal—

(1.) *sacan*, nomen permanentis, to be distinguished from infinitive *sacân*; e.g. *zacaru* "monument," *casadu* "acquisition," *sadharu* "writing," *alapu* "ox," *tsalamu* "image," *naharu* "river"; as adjectives *karadu* "warlike," *gasaru* "bold."

(2.) *sacin*, nomen permanentis, to be distinguished from the nomen agentis *sâcin*; e.g. *zacipu* "cross," *amilu* "man"; adjectives *namiru* "bright," *malicu* "king," *cabidu* "heavy," *labiru* or *laberu* "old."

(3.) *sacun*, nomen permanentis, to be distinguished from *sacûn*, the nomen mutati; e.g. *batulu* "young man"; adjectives *marutsu* "difficult," *ru'uku* for *rahuku* "distant," *casusu* "servant."

(4.) *sicin*, a segholate; e.g. *sidhiru* "a writing," *sipicu* "a heap," *episu* "a work," *gimiru* "the whole," *cisid-tu* "spoils"; adjective *zikhiru* "small."

(5.) *sican*, nomen permanentis; e.g. *cisadu* "presence"; adjective *zicaru* "manly."

(6.) *sicun*, nomen mutati; e.g. *zicuru* "memorial," *cisudu* "a captive"; adjective *emuku* "deep."

(7.) *sucun*, nomen permanentis; e.g. *sulukhu* "citadel," *cupuru* "bitumen," *cududu* "gem."

(8.) *sucan*, nomen permanentis; *suparu* "measure," *khuratsu* "gold"; adjective *pumalu* "strong."

(9.) *sucin*, nomen permanentis;[2] e.g. *buridu* "a pie" (bird).

---

[1] Comparative grammar, however, shows that in Semitic the verb presupposes the noun; just as in Aryan the noun pre-supposes the verb.

[2] These three last forms are identical with the Hebrew קְטָל, קְטֹל, קְטִיל, formed after the infinitive, and therefore dissimilar from the forma-

(10.) *sacân*, nomen mutationis; e.g. *tsabâtu* "to take," *rakhâtsu* "to inundate," *paraccu* for *parâcu* "to rule," *canâsu* "submission."
(11.) *sicîn*, nomen mutationis; e.g. *nicîsu* "to cut off," *episu* "to make."
(12.) *sucûn*, nomen mutationis; e.g. *sumûru* "to keep."
(13.) *sâcin*, nomen agentis; e.g. *mâlicu* "ruling," *kâ'isu* "snaring," *dâciku* "governing," *âlicu* "going," *mâgiru* "loving."
(14.) *sacin*, nomen mutati; e.g. *dalîkhu* "troubled."
(15.) *sacun*, nomen mutati; e.g. *darûmu* "a dwelling."

From Pael (expressing intensiveness)—

(1.) *saccan*, nomen permanentis; e.g. *gammalu* "camel;" adjective *karradu* "warlike."
(2.) *siccan, sican*, nomen mutantis; e.g. *limmanu (limanu)* "injuring," *siearu* (for *siccaru*) "remembering."
(3.) *siccun, sicun*, nomen mutati; e.g. *limmunu (limunu)* "injured."
(4.) *siccin*, nomen permanentis; e.g. *citstsilli* "royal."

From Pael Passive—

(1.) *succan, sucan;* e.g. *'ummanu* "army."
(2.) *succun, sucun;* e.g. *gurunu (gurrunu)* "a heap," *supucu* "a heap," *cussu* "a throne"; *cutummu* "gilded"; and the infinitives *tsukhkhuru, sullumu,* etc.

From Palel—

(1.) *sacanan*, nomen permanentis; e.g. *adannu* "mighty."
(2.) *sacunun*, nomen mutati; e.g. *agurru* "cement."
(3.) *sicinin*, nomen mutationis; e.g. *cidinnu* "ordinance," *citirru* "cornice."
(4.) *sucunun*, nomen mutationis; e.g. *cudurru* "landmark"; *lulummu* "alliance."
(5.) *sacanin*, nomen permanentis; e.g. *namriru* "bright."

From Iphteal, Iphtaal—

(1.) *sitcun*, nomen permanentis; e.g. *kitrubu* "a meeting," *etubu* "witness"; adjective *pitkudu* "good"; also infinitives, as *sitlumu* "to perfect."

tion of *sacan, sacin,* and *sacun* from *sacnacu*. They express a permanent state *after change,* and therefore may perhaps be better termed *nomina mutati*.

(2.) *sitcun* (Iphtaal), nomen mutati; e.g. *citmusa* "stored."
(3.) *satcun*, nomen mutati; e.g. *latbusu* "covered," *latcu* "made king."
(4.) *sitcin*, nomen mutati; e.g. *etpisu* "made."
(5.) *sitcan*, nomen permanentis; e.g. *citmas(tu)* "a gathering;" adjective, *gitmalu* "benefactor."

From Shaphel—

(1.) *sascan*, nomen permanentis; e.g. *sapsaku* "opening," *satsū* "expulsion."

From Shaphel Passive—

(1.) *suscun*, nomen mutationis; e.g. *sumcutu* "a slaughter," *surbu* "greatness," and the usual infinitives *sulburu* "preservation," *sundulu* "protection," *susmuru* "guard," etc.

From Niphal—

(1.) *nascan*, nomen permanentis; e.g. *nabkharu* "collected," *naramu* "chosen," *namratsu* "difficult."
(2.) *nascán*, nomen mutationis; e.g. *napdhāru* "to defend."
(3.) *nascin*, nomen permanentis; e.g. *nabnitu* "offspring."
(4.) *niscin*, nomen mutati; e.g. *nemiku* "deep," "learned."
(5.) *niscan*, nomen mutati; e.g. *niclalu* "a completion."
(6.) *nuscan*, nomen mutati; e.g. *numkharu* "the receipt."
(7.) *nasacin*, nomen permanentis; e.g. *nadannu* "strengthened," *naparcu* "diminished."

From *papel* and *pilpel* we have *gigune* "defences" (גגן), *gigurū* "copulative" (גור), *dandannu*, "very powerful," *durdaru*, "great age." Verbs פ״א and פ״ן have curious derived forms which repeat the second radical; e.g. *liliccu* "a going," *lillidu* (pael) "a birth," *dadmi* "men" (אדם), *babilat* "bringing" (of water, יבל), *papakhu* "shrine" (אפח).

From defective verbs we get similar formations. In concave verbs, except in the participle active Kal, the vowel of the first radical was assimilated to that of the second; e.g. *ru'uku* for *ra'uku* (ראק, רחק), *miru* "offspring" for *ma'iru*. In

Pael we have a nomen mutati *saccin*; e.g. *mi'iru* "offspring" for *ma"iru*. Verbs with *s* for second radical often take *h* instead; thus we have *bahlatu* by the side of *belatu*. Verbs פ״נ, as in Hebrew, drop the first syllable in *sacin*; e.g. *sahu'u* "summit" (from נשא). So *sascan* appears as *sass'u* "spoil" (נשא). In verbs פ״י the initial radical was dropped in *sacan, sicin,* and *sicin, sucun, sacin* (but not *sacin*), and *siccin*; e.g. *radu* "servant" (ירד), *ridu, rittu* for *rid(a)tu* "foot," *rudu* "chariot," *littu* (for *lidtu*) "offspring," and *liditu, lidu* (but *ilittuv*), *li'idu* or *li'itu*. In other cases the initial vowel is always *a*; e.g. *ardatu* "service," *atsu* "a going." The same verbs give us also such forms as *lida'atu* (from the infinitive), *littutu* (palel). In Niphal the forms are *nullatu* "height" (*nuscan*) and *nebiru* "passage" (*niscin*). The Pael Passive is *ubburu* "ford," with the second radical doubled according to rule. In verbs ע״ע the second radical is doubled before a case-ending: otherwise only the first two radicals are expressed; e.g. *sar* but *sarru, lib* but *libbu, 'um* but *'ummu*. *Pilpel* generally becomes *papel* in Assyrian, as *kakkadu*=קְרְקֹד, *caccabu*=כּוֹכָב (כבכב). Verbs ל״ה assimilate their last vowel to the case-ending; thus *pu'u, pi'i, pa'a*.

Besides these inner and more primitive formations, we have also, as in the cognate languages, external formations created by the broken-down roots *m, t, n,* and an initial vowel.

The prefix *m* (see p. 59) denotes the instrument, action, or place; e.g. *mansazu* "a bulwark" ("anything fixed"), *marsitu* "a heritage," *mandattu* "tribute" ("what is given"), *miscunu* "dwelling," *midduku* "slaughter" (ארק),

where *a* has been weakened to *i*, as is often the case in Hebrew. Its use in forming the present participles of the verb has already been considered.

N is used both as prefix and as suffix. As a prefix it is to be referred to Niphal (see p. 77). As an affix it must be carefully distinguished from the plural, with which it may easily be confounded. The usual form is *ānu*, like Arabic *ánăn* for adjectives, or *án* and *ón* in Hebrew. Originally it would seem to have been *āmu* (comp. עֵרֹם and פִּרְיוֹם). In this case its origin would have been the same as that of the mimmation.[1] Besides *ānu*, we have also *inu* (and even *innu* for *inu*), more especially in adjectives. It builds abstracts and adjectives used as substantives: e.g. *lisānu* "tongue," *kirbānu* "an offering," *bunanu* "image," *almanatu* "widow," *ristānu* "first-born," *sildhānu* "king," *elinitu* "high," *terdinnu* "a descending." -*Unu*, as in Hebrew, is rare: we find *dilunu* by the side of *dilutu*, and *agunu* "crown," by the side of *agu*.

T inserted has already been noticed. Of a different origin is *t* affixed to build abstracts, which must be referred to the same source as the feminine termination. This is always *utu*, as in *malcutu* "kingdom," *sarrutu* "royalty," *belutu* "lordship," *ristanutu* "headship." These feminine abstracts must be distinguished from the masculine plurals in *utu;* and they never admit the plural. There is also another rare feminine

[1] Possibly, however, considering the long *ā*, it is a plural form, used to express an abstract singular, like neuter plurals in Aryan languages. This is borne out by forms like *saniyānu*, "for the second time." In Hebrew *án* has been changed into *ón* (Ewald, Gramm., § 341, who refers it to the demonstrative *an(nu)*); so '*anochi* for *anacu*, etc. Compare the feminine abstracts in -*utu* by the side of the plurals in -*utu*. The plural -*ānu*, it must be remembered, was indifferently masculine or feminine.

abstract formation in -*ti* from -*dti;* e.g. *amarti* "a body," *tukulti* (*tuklat*) "help." It is difficult to say whether this irregular formation is the oblique case of the ordinary feminine in -*tu*, or whether it is a plural, the masculine termination in -*i* being affixed to the feminine termination, as in the plurals in -*tan*, to be considered later.

T prefixed is common, and is derived from the secondary conjugations, like תִגְמֹל in Hebrew, or the Arabic *takattulūn, takātulūn.* It refers us to a period when strong verbs, as well as concave verbs, might prefix the dental. The forms with *t* prefixed are *tasmeatu* "hearing," *tamkhatsu* and *takhatsu* "battle," *talucu* (*tallucu*) "a going," *talidtu* "birth," *tamirtu* (*tammirtu*) "sight," *takhlupu* "a coping."

With *e* (*i, u*) initial, *ta* becomes *te;* e.g. *tenisetu* "mankind," *terdinnu* "descent." As in Hebrew, the forms thus produced are abstracts. *Tu* even is found, e.g. *tupukatu* "race" (iphtaal), compared with *piteku* and *pitku, tukumatu* or *tukmatu* "opposition," from קוּם.

Roots increased by prefixed vowels are rare; though, not as in Hebrew, preserved only in such old words as יִצְחָק, etc. The original vowel seems to have been *a;* this was weakened to *i* and *e*, and even to *u*. Thus we find *alcacat* and *ilcacat* "stories," *aplusu* "weight," *askuppu* "doorpost," *acalutu* by the side of *calutu; ipdhiru* "ransom" (פטר); *edakhu* by the side of *dakhu* "king"; *ebillu* by the side of *belu; utuhut* "desire" (תַּאֲוָה), *urinni* "ostrich-hens" (רְנָנִים), *uta'ama* and *ita'imu* "lawgiver." The length of the first syllable is shown by the fact that it may be doubled before a defective root, as in *immiru* "youngling," by the side of *miru* and *emartu*. As in Hebrew and Arabic, intense active qualities are thus denoted. The origin of the prefixed vowel is obscure. It may be compared with Aphel (Hiphil, etc.), and so may be set by the side of *sascan* and *suscun*: on the other hand, as initial *s* passes into *h*, it may be referred to the third person pronoun, in which case *u* will be the original vowel. Perhaps this may throw light on the origin of the third person of the imperfect, where *i-* will stand for *u-* (= *su*) (see p. 61).[1]

Gentile nouns are formed like the Arabic relatives in *iyyûn* by *ai* (*aya*), e.g. *Accadai* "the Accadians," *Aramai* "the Aramæans." So -*i* in Hebrew, -*ai* in Aramaic, -*i* in Æthiopic for derived adjectives, and -*âwî* and -*ây* for gentilic nouns.

A few rare forms, *pilpal* (e.g. *mulmulu* "heavy-armed," *laklaku* "stock," *girgirru* "roaring water") and *peawel* (Arabic Twelfth conjugation) (e.g. *adudillu*), are also met with (see p. 107).

Quadriliterals are occasionally found, as well as a few quinqueliterals. Generally the former are produced by the insertion of *r* or *l*, and more rarely *n*, into the root; e.g. *sikhuparu* "overthrow," *kharpasu* "vehemence," *asaridu* "eldest," *palcitu* "trespass." Sometimes a dental has this function, as in *ipparsu* by the side of *ipparsidu* or *ipparsudu*. One of the superfluous letters, especially an *r*, is often assimilated by the Assyrian, as in *annabu* (Hebrew and Arabic ארנבת) "hare," *itstsuru* "bird" (Hebrew צפור, Arabic *tsâfir*, '*atsfûr*). Another way of forming these words is by repeating at the end one of the radicals, more usually the

---

[1] The length of the syllable precludes us from ranking it with the merely euphonic *ŏ* in the numerals (see further on).

first, as in *khamilukhkhi* "stores," *gablubu* "roof" by the side of *gablu*. The initial is also repeated, as in *gungulipu* "hump," with *n* inserted as a fulcrum-letter. So in *seseru* "hero," by the side of *serru*, and in *saskhartu* "small," by the side of *sukharu'u* and *tsikhirutu*: in *sassaru* an assimilation has taken place. Many of these increased roots double the last letter before the case-ending, as in verbs ע״ע; e.g. *barzillu* "iron," *khabatsillatu* "lily."

Primitive roots must be left to the lexicographer. In these the Assyrian approaches most nearly to the Hebrew. Its vocabulary was very large, and the syllabaries enable us to compare together certain roots and forms which throw light upon the phonology of the primitive Semitic language as well as of the Assyrian. Thus *l* and *r* are interchanged in *ayalu* and *ayaru* "man," "hero" (איל); and *abru* (=*abaru*), *namaru*, *amaru*, *acaru* and *aduru* are all given as synonymous. With this correspondence of *c* and *d* compare the synonymes *acasu* and *atasu*. So, again, we have *nadu'u*, *adu'u*, and *aru'u* ("clear") (compare *irin*=*idin*); and *askhu* joined with *asru* "place." *G* and *c* are interchanged, as in *acu* "crown," by the side of *agu* and *egu*, or in *daragu*, *durgu* "road" (דֶּרֶךְ), or in *dugaku* "king," by the side of *daciku* and *dakhu*. The interchange of *a* and *e* is frequent; and *t* and *d* are interchanged in *atamu*, *atmu*, "man," by the side of *adamu*, *admu* (the converse takes place in *nadanu*=נתן). *Kalu'u* and *kamu'u* or *camu'u*, "burn," may be compared; and *p* and *q* are interchanged in the root *asluq* and *aslup*, "I pulled out."

The noun may have its meaning rendered more specific by the reduplication of the first radical, or the prefixing of the pronoun *a* (see p. 110), as in *dadmu* and *admu*, "man"

(אדם), from *damu* "blood," "relation," "child." The tablets also afford us a number of synonymous forms from the same root: thus, *mar* "youngling," is equivalent to *mir, ma'aru, immiru, mi'iru, mu'uru; beltu* ("lordship") to *bahilatu, be'lilu, ebiltu*, and *bilatu; tsikkhirutu* ("small") to *sassaru, ikhru'utu, saśkhartu, sisseru, tsikhirutu, śukharu'u* (where the interchange of *ś* and *ts* is to be noticed); *assatu* to *issu* ("woman"); *malucu* and *malicu* are identical in meaning; and *biltu* or *bilatu*, and *tsikhritu* or *tsikhirtu*, may be indifferently used.

The most interesting point connected with this part of the subject is the Turanian origin of many Semitic words, more especially of the so-called biliteral roots (see p. 9). Besides the many instances given in the syllabaries in which Accadian words in the one column are Semitised in the other column,—e.g. *muq = muccu, nanga* ("town") = *nagu'u, kakkul* = *kakkullu, gurus* ("hero") = *gurusu, lamma* ("monster") = *lamassu* (? Talmud. לכם), *śa = śa'amu* ("blue"), *dī = denu* ("judge"), *śilim = sulmu, ab = abtu, sik = sikku, surru = surru'u* ("beginning"), *ingar = iccaru* ("foundation"), *sab = sabbu, al* = *allu, ge = citu* ("abyss"), *śangu = śangu'u, piśan* ("branch") = *piśannu, cir = ci'iru, mitsi = manśu'u, sek = sakummatu* ("height"), *sab = za'abu, mar = marru, cur* ("land") = *cu'uru, mat* ("country") = *ma'atu, gur* ("return") = *gurru*,—we find the prototypes of many words hitherto known as Semitic in the Accadian language.

Instances may be found in the above list, *śa'amu* (שהם). *denu, ge* (גיא), *surru* (Æthiopic *sārara*), *ingar* (נקר), *gur* (גרר, גור); to which we may add *id* "hand" (יד), *sar*

"king," apparently *pa* "speech" (פֶּי),[1] *khul* "sick" (חלה),
gun "inclosure" (גן), *uru* "city" (עיר, as in *Jerusalem*; the
Assyrian is *âlu*, אהל), *cin* "work" and *gin* "make" (כון),
whence *gina* is translated *cinu* "constituted," *bat* "open"
(perhaps Assyrian *pitu'u*, פתח), *sabar* "bronze" (Assyrian
siparru, Arabic *tsifr, tsufr, atsfarra*), and many others. In some
cases the loan-word has been further modified in accordance
with the rules of Semitic grammar. Thus, the Accadian *kharra*
"man," gives rise to the Assyrian *khairu*, whence we get the
usual word for "wife," *khiratu, khirtu*, with the feminine
termination attached. The Assyrian especially has been
indebted to the Accadian vocabulary, and one of the chief
difficulties of decipherment arises from our ignorance of the
meaning of the numerous words so derived, which are not to
be found in any of the other Semitic tongues. Thus one of
the commonest Assyrian adjectives is *dannu* "strong," from
Accadian *dan*; and *matu* "country," has a similar Turanian
origin (*ma* or *mada*). A converse interchange of words seems
also to have taken place in those prehistoric times when
Turanian and Semite bordered one upon the other: thus,
surru, in the list given above, may really have been Semitic;
gabiri, one of the many Accadian words for "mountain,"
appears clearly to be Arabic *jebelün*, and the ungrammatical
title of the Proto-Chaldean kings *ciprat irba* was borrowed
from the Semitic *cipratu irbai* or *irbittu*, "the four races"
(of Syria).

Number and Gender.—The Assyrian, like the cognate languages, possessed three numbers, Singular, Dual, and Plural.

[1] So, just as *ca-ca* "mouth-mouth," meant "face," *pânu* or *pâtu*,
פנים, etc., has the same signification in Semitic.

The Dual is rarely used, and is restricted, as in Hebrew, to pairs like *uznā* "ears."[1] Similarly, in modern Arabic the dual has been lost almost entirely in verbs, pronouns, and adjectives; and only three words in Syriac possess it. In Æthiopic it does not exist at all. It is, however, older than the plural: the primitive savage, with his narrow wants and small stock of language, had neither need nor capacity of speaking of more than two persons. Gradually as isolated life gave way to nomade life, and the power of counting numbers was developed, the plural—which originally expressed merely the indefinite number that all beyond two seemed to the feeble mind of the savage to be—came more and more into use, until civilization finally dropped the dual altogether. The dual is usually denoted in the inscriptions by the addition of the symbol of "two": it was sounded as *ā*. This corresponds to Arabic *-āni*, Hebrew *-aim*, Aramaic *-ain*, the final consonant being dropped, as generally in the plural. Examples of the dual are: *uzna'a* (and in Babylonian *uzūna'a*) "the ears," *katā* "the hands," *birkā* "the knees," *ina'a* "the eyes," *sepā* "the feet." There is no distinction of gender.

The Plural is formed in several ways. The oldest is that which terminates in *-ānu*, *-āni*, *-ān*, which is found in a comparatively small number of substantives, some of which also form their plural in other ways: e.g. *pa'anu* and *pa'atu*,

---

[1] The adjective in agreement is always found in the plural, consequently a case like *sa katā-su atsmā*, "whose hands are strong," shows that we are dealing with a Permansive. The participle of the derived conjugations may, however, take the dual: thus, *ukukh Dunanu S'amaĥgunu munirridhu* and a variant *munirridā*, "I carried off D. (and) S'. the opposers."

matânu, *matâtu* and *matti*. It is noticeable that this termination is not confined to the masculine. We find it in the feminine *emukânu* ("deep powers"), *risânu* ("heads"), *khaltsânu* ("strongholds"), just as in Hebrew some feminines like מִלָּה make their plural in יִם, or in Aramaic the absolute form of the feminine plural is in -*in*. Often the oblique case -*âni* stands for -*ânu*, from analogy with the common plural-ending -*i*; thus we find *duppa'ani* "tablets," *khaltsa'ani* "fortresses," *kharsa'ani* "woods," used as nominatives. The contracted form -*ân* is occasionally used even when not *in regimine*. As in the cognate languages, -*ân* in Babylonian could be weakened to -*in*. Thus in Khammurabi's inscription we find *cilalin* instead of the usual *cilallan* "omnia."

An was irregularly added to the feminine singular to express a *collection* of anything (Arabic *nomina abundantiæ*). Thus from the feminine *ebirtu* "a crossing," we have the plural *ebirtân* ("where crossings are made," "a ford"), *cilatân* "all," *pardhutân* "the preceding," *akhratân* (instead of the ordinary *akhrat* and *akharitu*) "the remainder," "the future." Adjectives which have this form are used absolutely as substantives, or rather adverbially, generally following the verb, and omitting the preposition *ana* (like *he local* in Hebrew). Compare the plural of the numerals from 2 to 10 in Samaritan in ־ֹתִי.

An old and very rare form of the plural is that which reduplicates the root. Thus by the side of *agi* or *age* "crowns," we have *agagi*. It is probable that this plural is of Turanian origin; I have found no true Semitic radix in which it occurs.

Another old form is that which is preserved to us in *satunu*, *sunu*, etc., which seems to have been partly suggested by false analogy with the case-endings of the singular, partly due to the original long *ū* of the third person pronoun. Instances of this Arabicising plural in nouns are to be found in *dilunu* by the side of *dilutu* "door-posts," and *datunu*, which seems of Accadian origin.

Another masculine plural is in *-utu*, *-uti*, *-ut*, like the Hebrew masculines in יוֹת, which should be distinguished from the feminine plural. It is employed especially by words derived from verbs לְ"הֹ, or which otherwise end with a vowel. It is used by all adjectives, and by the *nomina mutantis* of all the conjugations. Examples are *zicrutu* "males," *nacluti* "complete," *hunut takhazi* "materials of war."

The most common masculine plural, however, was formed by *-e* or *-i*, like the construct masculine plural in Hebrew. It is an instance of the omission of the final nasal similar to that which allowed the mimmation to be dropped. In monosyllabic nouns this plural did not differ in form from the second case of the singular, though an attempt to distinguish it was often made by writing *e* instead of *i*, especially in Babylonian. Indeed the length of the syllable in the case quoted from the Hebrew, and the fact that the plural had been weakened from *ām* (*ān*), would tend to show that there was properly a real difference in pronunciation between the plural-ending and the short vowel of the case-termination. In dissyllables, however, where the accent is on the first syllable, and the second syllable is not long, the two forms were distinguished by dropping the vowel of the second radical in the singular, and laying the accent on the first syllable, while the plural retained the vowel of the second radical, and placed the accent upon it, which is frequently marked by doubling the third radical; e.g. *nakri* "enemy," *nakiri* "enemies"; *nakhli* "valley," *nakhalli* "valleys." Examples of this kind of plural in monosyllables are *su'uri maruti* "young oxen," *nisi labiruti* "ancient men," *succi naoluti* "complete houses," *yume mahduti* "many days." Many masculine substantives took both the earlier and the later plural ending: thus we have *sarrānu* and *sarri*, *khaltsanu* and *khaltsi*.

The termination of the feminine plural was twofold. Usually we find -*ātu*, -*āti* or -*āte*, *āt*; e.g. *elātum* "high," *ummanātu* "armies," *khirātu* "wives" (so distinguished from the singular *khirātu* or *khirtu*), *dannāti* "strong," *tsirāte* "supreme," *khutarāte* "rods," *idāt* "forces." This -*ātu* answers to the Æthiopic -*āt* (*āta*), Aramaic -*āth* (in construct), Arabic *ātūn*, Hebrew *ōth*. Besides this termination of the feminine plural, we also meet with another in -*etu* or -*itu*, -*ete* or -*ite*. Some nouns take both terminations; many, however, are confined to the rarer form, as *esreti* "sacred places," *ruke'eti* "distant parts," *khidheti* "sinners," *anneti* "these." Dr. Hincks conjectures that the latter form was used only in the case of adjectives used as substantives. It is an instance of *a* being weakened to *i* or *e*, which we find in -*an* and elsewhere. It is mostly to be found in Babylonian inscriptions, and may perhaps be ascribed to an Aramaic influence.

Many words, as in the other Semitic dialects, admitted of both plurals, being of common gender. Thus we have *pa'anu* and *pa'atu*, *babi* and *babātu* ("gates").

It is often uncertain what plural an Assyrian noun took, owing to the employment in the inscriptions of the monogram for multitude in place of the final syllable, which all readers were supposed to be capable of supplying. Sometimes, however, the proper plural was added to this symbol, and sometimes the symbol was not expressed at all.

The Assyrian, like the cognate tongues, possessed but two genders, the masculine and the feminine. The neuter is a refinement upon primitive language, which endowed nature with the life and gender of the subject. The feminine was weaker than the masculine: hence abstracts, in which the notion of life was necessarily harder to conceive than in the case of material objects, were considered as feminines. In this way is to be explained the substitution of a feminine singular with a collective signification for a plural; e.g. *libnatu* "bricks." Many feminine substantives have no distinctive termination, and their gender can only be known from their meaning, from their plurals, or from their being joined with feminine adjectives. Such are *ummu* "mother," *ummanu* "army," *katu* "hand," *usnu* "ear," *khaltsu* "fortress," *lisanu* "tongue."

Those that have a distinctive suffix are of three kinds. Firstly, there are the feminine abstracts in *-ūtu*, as *sarrūtu* "kingdom," which are carefully to be distinguished from the masculine plurals in *-utu*, and which do not admit the plural. Secondly, there is the general feminine termination *-ătu, -ăti, -ăta*, which may be shortened into *-tu, -ti, -ta*, where possible. Thus besides *khirătu* we may have *khirtu*, besides *belătu, beltu*. Triliterals, in which the second syllable is not long, can drop either this or the vowel of the feminine-ending: thus, "life" may be either *napsatu* or *napistu*, "fear" may be *pulkhatu* or *pulukhtu*. Surd roots do not allow this omission of the *-â*, as the final radical must be doubled: thus from *sar* "king," we may only have *sarrâtu* "queen." A third mode of forming the feminine singular is by *-îtu*, weakened from *-âtu;* e.g. *elinitu* "high." According to Dr. Hincks, this form is never used in the case of *nomina agentis* or with surd roots. The same rules that apply to the omission of the vowel of *-âtu* apply also here, except that surds always have *-âtu*. Thus we have *binitu* and *bintu* "daughter," *saplitu* and *sapiltu* "low," *makhritu* and *makhirtu* "former," *tsikhritu* and *tsikhir:u* "small." Words ע״ל admit only this form, as *elitu* "high"; just as from *dannu* we can only have *dannatu*. Otherwise both forms are indiscriminately used, e.g. *ilitu* and *ilâtu* "goddess," *belitu* and *belâtu* "lady."[1]

The addition of the feminine-terminations often causes a change in the last radical. *N, d, dh,* are regularly assimilated, as in *limuttu* "injuring" for *limuntu, libittu* "brickwork" for *libintu, cabittu* "heavy" for *cabidtu*. So *s, z, ś,* and *ts* were generally changed to *l*. Thus we have *mikhiltu* "fortified," besides *mikhitstu* and *mikhtsatu, marustu* and *marultu* "difficult" (where *ts* has become *s*, as in *risti* for *ritsti*), *lubustu* and *lubultu* "clothing."

In one or two instances the feminine termination seems to have been contracted to *a'*, as in Hebrew, Aramaic, and Arabic. Thus Dr. Hincks quotes the variant *sukalula* for *sukalulat* from Assur-nazir-pal.

[1] This indiscriminate use of *a* and *i* in the feminine noun is analogous to the indifferent employment of *sa* and *si* for the feminine relative pronoun.

The origin of the feminine termination would take us back to the personal pronoun. The Assyrian, like Æthiopic, classical Arabic, Phœnician, and Sinaitic, preserves the archaic *āt(u)*, which also appears in the Hebrew הָ and the construct state, and in the Aramaic construct and emphatic states. In Berber the third personal pronoun is *netta* "he," *netteth* "she," plural *nuthni* (masculine), *nuthnet* (feminine), and the accusative verbal suffix of the third person is -*ith*, -*it*, plural -*ithen*. So the demonstratives are *wayyi* "this" (masculine), *theyyi* (feminine), *winna* "that" (masculine), and *thinna, thidhek* or *idhek* (feminine). In Coptic *nethof*= "he," *nethos*="she," *nethóu*="they." The Assyrian enclitic -*tu*, -*ti*, which belongs to the pronouns (*sunutu, yati*, etc.), and is met with again in the Æthiopic *wĕtu, yĕti, ĕmuntu*, and, with the plural-ending affixed, *wĕtomu, wĕtón*, cannot be separated from the feminine abstract suffix -*utu*, or the ordinary feminine termination -*ătu, -ĭtu*. These forms, accordingly, will be like *iste*, an emphatic reduplication of the demonstrative. We have already seen that the primitive Semitic recognized but one root for all the three persons (see p. 41).

The original plural-ending seems to have been -*āmū*, as found in old Arabic *humū, antumū, kataltumū;* Æthiopic *hōmū, wĕtōmū, antĕmū, nagarcymmū;* Aramaic *himmo, himmón;* Hebrew הֵמָּה, יְמוֹ, etc. Arabic has shortened the final vowel, according to its general rule (e.g. *ană* "I," *hunnă, kataltŭ, kataltă* by the side of Æthiopic *gabaroŭ*, etc.). So has Assyrian, as in *sunŭ* by the side of *sunutu, khaltsănŭ* by the side of *khaltsānŭm*. *Am* has been changed to *ăn* in Assyrian, Æthiopic, Himyaritic, and Berber (just as the mimmation becomes nunnation). So, too, in the Syriac *anakhnan, hynan,* "we." This change takes place in Assyrian even between two vowels, as in *khaltsânu, sunu*. *Am, an,* are weakened to *im, in,* in Hebrew and Aramaic; though the original form seems to be preserved in Hebrew כִּנָּם "gnats." The Arabic *-ind* would display the same weakening; *ûnd* appears to be the result of a false parallelism with the singular case-endings, as though the nunnation were the same as the plural sign, and cannot be compared with the verbal *-ûnd* (with which compare Syriac *nəkdh'lûnd-chon, nəkdh'lûnāi(hi),* etc.). The dropping of the consonant in the Assyrian plurals *sucei,* etc., or in the Hebrew construct, is parallel with the loss of the mimmation, or with the Assyrian verb-forms *sacnu, sacna, iscunu, iscuna,* for *sacnunu, sacnanu, iscununu, iscunanu.* The Assyrian dual in *â,* compared with the plural in *-i,* seems to have lost a final *m,*[1] which is retained in Hebrew *-dim,* Aramaic *-din,* Arabic *-âni* and *-aini,* Syriac *en.* The original dual was probably *-â'amu,* expressing by its long-continued reduplication of the pure primary vowel the reduplication of the object. So the Botocudos of Brazil extend *ouatou* "stream," into *ouatou-ou-ou-ou* "ocean," with the Chavantes *rom-o-wodi*="I go a long way," but *rom-o-o-o-o-wodi*="I go an exceedingly long way," in Madagascar *ratchi*="bad," *ra-a-atchi* "very bad," and still more analogously among the Aponegicrans 6=*itawuna,* 7=*itawu-û-una* (Tylor, "Primitive Culture," vol. i. pp. 196, 197). Similarly, according to Schott, "six" in the Ural-Altaic languages is expressed by a modification of "three." Now *a+a*=either *â* or the gunated *ai* (p. 35). In Hebrew we

[1] In Arabic *n* falls away in the dual before the pronoun-suffixes.

find *Dothain* becoming *Dothân*. The plural would have been formed upon the dual, with a contraction of the vowel-sound, as the idea to be expressed by the plural was less definite than that expressed by the dual. The *m* final, inclosing and strengthening the vowel, is to be compared with the mimmation, or with the accusative and neuter in Aryan nouns. We cannot follow the analogy of these, however, in holding that the plural -*m* was attached to the case-endings of the singular, or ever had a separate existence pronominal or otherwise. Here, as elsewhere, Semitic and Aryan procedure was contradictory. A double set of case-endings would have been unmeaning. The form in -*ân* must be explained differently, as above. The plural imperfect follows in its vowel-endings, not the cases, but the contrasted pronouns *sunu* and *sina* (*sana*). The feminine plural -*âtu* or -*a'atu*, Hebrew -*ôth* (for -*âwath*=-*âmath*), is formed from the plural -*âm*, which indifferently denoted both genders, by the addition of the feminine termination, exactly as in the singular. *Ât* stands for -*âmat* or -*âwat*, *m* and *v* being interchangeable in Assyrian. (So *amaru*= אוֹר, *ma*= ו, etc.)

The forms *ebirtân*, etc., are of later growth, in which the plural termination has been attached to the feminine, instead of the converse. The same irregular formation appears in the Æthiopic *wĕtômû*, *wĕtôn*. This is another point in which Assyrian and Æthiopic grammar curiously agree. The Æthiopic forms are even more exactly paralleled by the Assyrian demonstrative plural *satunu*, *satina*. For a Samaritan comparison see p. 116.

The Cases.—These are like the Arabic : -*û* nominative, -*î* genitive, -*â* accusative. Very frequently a final *m* is added, lengthening the preceding vowel, similar to the nunnation in Arabic. The mimmation, as Dr. Oppert has happily termed it, becomes rarer in the later Assyrian inscriptions. The case-terminations are attached both to the singular and to the plural, to the masculine and to the feminine. They cause certain alterations in the vowels of many forms; and these are as follows. Whenever a long vowel precedes the last letter, or when the word is a monosyllable (provided it be not derived from a surd root), or when the last vowel, though short, is preceded by more than one consonant (as in *sitcun, musascin, niscin*), no change takes place. Thus we have *'ummanâtu* (construct *'ummanât*), *mutu* "man" (construct *mut*), *kitrubu* "midst" (construct *kitrub*). When, however, a root ends in a weak letter, the latter is assimilated to the case-vowel. Thus, from *atsi* "going-out" (feminine *atsitu*), we have *atsu'u*. From *agu* "crown," Accadian *ega*, we get *agu'u, agi'i* or *age'e, aga'a*. So, again, we find *pu'u, pi'i, pa'a*.

In surd roots the construct form is a monosyllable. The case-ending, however, doubles the last consonant; e.g. *sar, sarru; lib, libbu; 'um, 'ummu*. This is really a Palel form of a biliteral; like the Palel triliterals *agammu* "lake" (*agam*), *cidinnu* "ordinance" (*cidin*), etc.

The vowel of the second radical is always omitted before the case-ending in *sacan* (but not in *sacân*), *sicin, sucun,*[1] *sicun*, and in augmented forms like *mustacin*, where the second radical stands between two vowels, the latter of which

---

[1] In Babylonian, however, instead of *'uznâ*, the usual dual form, we have *'uznâ-su* (W.A.S., I. 51, 1, 1, 4). As it occurs at the end of the line, the retention of *u* seems due to the pause and the naturally long syllable *â*.

is short. Thus we have *kardu* (*karad*), *gimru* (*gimir*), *pulkhu* (*pulukh*), *limnu* (*limun*), *muntakhtsu* (*muntakhits*). It is generally omitted also (especially in Babylonian) in *sacin*, as well as in *sacun*, *sican*, and *siccan*: e.g. *namru* (*namir*), *labru* (Babylonian, but *labiru*, and more archaically *laberu* in Assyrian), *martsu* (*maruts*), *zicru* and *zicaru* (*zicar*), *gisru* (*gissar*). Dr. Hincks believed that a liquid as third radical preserved a preceding *á*; hence he would explain *pumalu* "powerful," and *badhalu* by the side of *badhluti* (from *badhil*) "interrupted."

The Construct State.—This is formed, as in Hebrew, by shortening the first word, and so bringing the two words so closely into connexion one with the other, that they may be pronounced in the same breath. The first word is subordinated to the second, which is the source from which the determined idea of the first word is derived. Just as in Arabic *tenwin* is dropped, or in Hebrew the vowels contracted, so in Assyrian the case-ending of the first word falls away. Thus, instead of *sarru sarri*, we have *sar sarri*, "king of kings," *susub napsati*, "the preservation of life." The determining word has the case-ending -*i*, as in Arabic, as expressing a weakened conception of the direction towards which the mind of the speaker is looking (in this case the direction is that of derivation, origination). The *status constructus* may be replaced, as it often is, by the relative *sa*, when the first word—except in some rare instances from analogy with the *status constructus*[1]—retains its case-ending; e.g. *sarru sa Assuri*, "king of Assyria": the second word

[1] In this case the first word is in the *status constructus* before the whole sentence following. According to Philippi, *sa*, in such instances, retains its original demonstrative meaning, and is not a relative.

has either -*u* or -*i*. So in Phœnician, ש is sometimes substituted for the *status constructus*, and in Hebrew we may compare the proper name *Methu-sa-el* "man of God." D is used in the same way in Himyaritic, *de* in Syriac, *di* in Aramaic, *sa* in Æthiopic. The union-vowel (*â*, in pronouns *i*) in the so-called *status constructus* of the Æthiopic cannot be identified with the *ya* in Amharic, which was originally the demonstrative *sĕya*.[1]

The case-endings have been already compared with those of the other Semitic languages (p. 15, *note*). They form one of the most striking likenesses between Assyrian and Arabic. The name is unfortunate, as their use does not correspond to that of the cases in the Aryan tongues. The subject-termination was always -*u* or -*um*, which, accordingly, invariably appears in the syllabaries as the typical form of the word. The case-terminations, though short in Arabic and Assyrian, were originally long. This is shown in Assyrian by the mimmation, and by such forms as *icṣu'u* by the side of *icṣu* ("a door") in the syllabaries. So in Arabic, we find the pausal -*â*; and both languages have a tendency to shorten a final vowel (see p. 121). On the other hand, Hebrew has long vowels וֹ, ִי, הָ, and this language does not lengthen final short vowels. So, again, the Æthiopic -*â* of the accusative occasionally appears as -*hâ*. In this way, too, must be explained the long vowel of the Assyrian feminine abstracts in -*û-tu*. The origin of this -*û* must be assigned to the same instinct that set apart *u* in the pronouns to denote the stronger masculine. The subject, being absolute, was

[1] Forms like *Penuel*, etc., in Hebrew (p. 15, *note*) go back to the Arabic, which herein separates itself from Assyrian.

naturally regarded as stronger than a determined case. The accusative ought rather to be called the augment of motion. It expresses the direction to something, or the object to which the idea has travelled. This is best exemplified in the Hebrew use of *he local*. The idea of motion was suggested, it would seem, to the primitive Semite by dwelling upon the pure deep sound of -*ā* or -*hā*, by which the word was lengthened and extended, as it were, beyond itself. This accusative case, needed as soon as a verb appears to distinguish verbal from nominal government, is the oldest Semitic case, and naturally, therefore, the "nearest" vowel.

A, as always in Semitic—in the Assyrian *sa* and *si*, *risu* and ראש ex. gr.—is weakened into *i*; hence the so-called genitive -*i*, intermediate between the subject and the direct object, and expressing a weakened kind of motion or direction. This is well exemplified in such Assyrian phrases as answer to the Hebrew *he local*, in which the preposition is omitted, and where, instead of -*a*, we have the weakened -*i*; e.g. *takhazi* "to battle," instead of *ana takhaza*. From the substantive these terminations (primarily strengthened by the mimmation) were transferred to the verbs, without losing their meaning.

The Pronominal Suffixes.—These are as follows :—

SINGULAR.
1st pers. -*ya*, -*a*, -*i*
2nd pers. -*ca*, -*c* (masc.), -*ci* (fem.)
3rd pers. -*su*, -*s* (masc.), *sa*, *si* (fem.)

PLURAL.
1st pers. -*ni*
2nd pers. -*cunu*, -*cun* (masc.), [-*cina*, *cin* (fem.)]
3rd pers. -*sunu*, -*sun* (masc.), -*sina*, *sin* (fem.)

The second person feminine plural has not been found.

The second and third persons masculine singular, after an unaccented *u*, are shortened to *c* and *s*: e.g. *napistu-s* "his life." After an accented *u*, a second *u* is generally inserted, as *tsiru'u-a* "upon me," *yanu'u-a* "I (am) not," or else the consonant of the pronoun is doubled, as *yanucca* "thou (art) not," *yanussu* "he (is not)," *tsirussun* "upon them," *katussu* "his hand," *kibitucca* "(it is) thy will," *panucci* "before thee," *kirbussa* "within it." This reduplication does not take place after the feminine formative *t*, except in a monosyllable.

The suffixes can be attached either to the case-endings of the noun, or to the construct state. In the first instance they are purely adjectival, in the second the third personal pronoun is regarded as a substantive. The apparent construct state with the pronoun suffixes of the first and second persons is really euphonic. The suffixes of the third person are more usually attached to the construct; the converse holds good of the suffixes of the first and second persons. Euphony comes into play here: four short syllables cannot stand together, so that we may have either *kiriboa* or *kirbica*, just as we may have *tukmatu* or *tukumtu*.

The suffix of the first person singular is -*a*, or more generally -*ya*, when the root terminates in a vowel, or has the case-endings, especially after *i*; e.g. *abu-a* "my father," *galli-ya* "my servants." *I-a* (=*yá*) might become *ai* in Assyrian (see p. 35); hence we find *gabrai* "my rivals." After a consonant -*i* is used; e.g. *ab-i* "my father," *usman-i* "my army," *bint-i* "my daughter," *kat-i* "my hand," *raman-i* "myself," *assat-i* "my wife." Surd roots doubled their final letter, as *'umm-i* "my mother." Sometimes, in the Babylonian inscriptions, *-a* takes the place of *-i*, as in *ab-a* "my father," *be'el-a* "my lord." With the dual *i* is employed: e.g. *katâ-i* "my hands."

When the noun ends in *d, dh, t, s, ṭ, z, ts*, the third person suffix becomes *ṡu, ṡa*, etc., e.g. *khirit-ṡu* "its ditch" (for *khirit-su*), *bit-ṡu* "his house." Still more frequently, the last letter of the noun is assimilated to the *s* of the suffix; e.g. *khiriṡ-ṡu, biṡ-ṡu, rupuṡ-ṡu* "its breadth" (from *rupus*), *libnaṡ-ṡu* (from *libnat*). As elsewhere, the reduplication may be dropped, so that we get *khiriṡu, biṡu, rupuṡu, rakhaṡu* (by the side of *rakhtṡi-ṡu*) "his flood," etc.

The plural of masculine nouns attaches the suffix to the plural-ending *-i*; e.g. *kharri-ṡu* "its hollows." Following this analogy, the plural in *-ânu* annexed the pronoun to the oblique case; e.g. *sarrâni-ṡu* "his kings," instead of *sarrânu-ṡu*. Compare in Arabic the insertion of *ı* after a word ending in *jezma*, in the case of *watsla* (when the next word begins with an *elif conjunctionis*). Sometimes the pronoun was affixed to the construct *-ân*: in this case the nasal was according to rule assimilated to the next letter; thus *gabrâ-ṡu* (for *gabrâs-ṡu*) "his rivals," *risâ-ṡu* (for *risâs-ṡu*) "his heads."

In the later period of the language *attu*, answering to the Hebrew אֵת, Aramaic *âth*, Arabic *'iyyâ*, and used in the same way, makes its appearance, with the personal suffixes attached superfluously. The inscriptions mostly afford examples of the first person only: e.g. *attu'u-a abû-a* "to me (was) my father," *sir-ya attû-a* "my own race" ("my race (which is) mine," "mon père a moi"), in Hebrew אֹתִי.[1]

[1] Assur-bani-pal uses *attū* exactly as in Hebrew to mark the accusative; thus, *as la iptallakhu abi-ya va attû-a*, "who revere not my fathers and me."

We find also *attû-ni, attû-cunu*; and the other persons might be restored, *attû-ca, attû-ci, attû-su,* etc. See p. 15.

THE NUMERALS.

These have two forms, masculine and feminine, as in the other Semitic tongues, and show the same peculiarity of using the masculine of the numerals from 3 to 10 with feminine nouns and the feminine of the numerals with masculine nouns. Originally the numerals seem to have been abstract substantives, like τριάς, and could take either a masculine or a feminine form. The feminine was most commonly employed, and so became associated with nouns of the predominant masculine gender. In Æthiopic (and vulgar Arabic) the feminine is almost exclusively used.

The forms of the Semitic numerals early became fossilised, and hence are almost identical in the various dialects. Notwithstanding this, the Assyrian cardinal-numbers are more closely connected with the Hebrew than with those of the cognate languages. *Estin* "one" is found in the Hebrew עִשְׁתֵּי; there are no traces of the Æthiopic *cal'a* "two"; and the numeral for "six," like Hebrew, omits the dental, which appears in Arabic and Æthiopic, while the Aramaic consonantal changes in תְּרֵין, etc., find no place in Assyrian.

The cardinals are as follows.—

Masculine.	Feminine.	Hebrew.
1. akhadu, khad-u or khidu, edu, estin	ikhit, ikhtu (for ikhidtu)	אֶחָד, אַחַת
2. sane'e, san'u, sin'u	sanctu	שְׁנַיִם, שְׁתַּיִם
3. salsutu, salsatu	salsu	שְׁלֹשָׁה, שָׁלֹשׁ

Masculine.	Feminine.	Hebrew.
4. irbittu, riba'atu	arba'i, irba'i	אַרְבַּע, אַרְבָּעָה
5. khamistu, khamiltu	khamsa, khansa	חָמֵשׁ, חֲמִשָּׁה
6. sisatu	sissu, sis	שֵׁשׁ, שִׁשָּׁה
7. sibittu, sibitu	sib'u, riba	שֶׁבַע, שִׁבְעָה
8. [samnatu]	samna	שְׁמֹנֶה, שְׁמֹנָה
9. [tisittu]	[tis'u]	תֵּשַׁע, תִּשְׁעָה
10. esirtu, esrit, eserit	esir, esru	עֶשֶׂר, עֲשָׂרָה
15. khamisserit (for khamis esrit)		חֲמֵשׁ עֶשְׂרֵה

20. esra'a (Hebrew עֶשְׂרִים); 30. sclassa'a; 40. irbahā; 50. khansa'a; 60. sisa'a, sussu; 70. sibba'a; 80. [samna'a]; 90. [tissa'a]; 100. mih (Hebrew מֵאָה); 1000. alapu (אֶלֶף).

The words in brackets have not yet been found in the inscriptions. Generally the cardinals are denoted by symbols; "one" is an upright wedge, "two" two wedges, and so on. "Ten" is expressed by <; 11 by <|; 20 by <<, and so on.

The masculine numeral *estin* is important as throwing light upon the Hebrew עַשְׁתֵּי in 11, which does not appear in the cognate languages. Besides *akhadu*, a theme *khad* seems to exist, which shows itself in the adverb *edis* "only," *edis-su* "by himself." We also have instances in which the Accadian *id* "one" is used, apparently with the value of *khad* or *ed*, as both masculine and feminine, singular and plural. Now *kh* and *e* are interchangeable (see pp. 28, 29) in Assyrian, especially in the case of foreign words, and the Semite often tried to represent the rough Turanian vocalisation at the beginning of an Accadian vocable by the guttural

---

[1] *Sh* in Æthiopic.

kh (as in *Idiklat*, חרקל).[1] *Id* or *kat* in Accadian meant "hand" primarily, so that we are taken back to the time when the savage signified "one" by holding up his hand. As in Hebrew and Arabic, *irba'* interchanges with *reba'*. The form *khamisserit* shows that the Assyrian could contract its numerals like vulgar Arabic, or New-Syriac.[2]

The origin of the Semitic cardinal numbers is a matter of some difficulty. Ewald and others, struck by the superficial resemblance of one or two, *shêsh, sheba'*, etc., to the corresponding Aryan numerals, have imagined common roots. But this proceeds upon the assumption of the common parentage of the two families of speech; and even were this granted, we should have no Grimm's Law upon which to base our comparisons. Moreover, there are several numerals which are confessedly unlike in the two classes of languages; and the resemblances in the case of those which are most like are not greater than between *shêsh* and the Basque *sei*, or *irba* and the Mongol *durban*. Nothing, again, is more usual among savage tribes than to adopt different roots at different times to express the same numerals. Thus in English we have "first," "second," "ace," "tray":[3] and among the Semitic languages themselves, the only trace which Æthiopic presents of the ordinary numeral for "two" is in the words *sanuy* and *sânet*, while it has taken another root, *cal'a* "to divide," to express the idea of duality. The same holds good of *estin* and *'ashtê*. The whole theory, however, has been disposed of by an analysis of the Aryan numerals, which

[1] See my paper on Accadian in the Journal of Philology, vol. iii., No. 5 (1870), p. 39.
[2] Nöldeke, Neusyr. Gramm., p. 152.
[3] Cf. Tylor, Primitive Culture, vol. i., pp. 231, 233.

demonstrates that the original forms of the numbers were widely different from those required to bring them into relationship with the Semitic. Thus "six" (which a similar analysis applied to the Semitic languages shows was primarily *shadash* in them) had originally a guttural at the beginning of the word, now preserved only in the Zend *kshwas*. Professor Goldstücker, taking this word as the starting-point of his investigations, has obtained the following results from an analysis of the numerals. "One" is the demonstrative pronoun "he"; 2 is "diversity" (διά, *dis-*, *zer-*); 3 = "that which goes beyond" (root *tar*, whence *trans*, *through*, etc.); 4 = "and three," *i.e.* "1+3" (*cha-tur*); 5 = "coming after" (*pan-chan*, *quinque*); 6 = "four," *i.e.* "(2) and 4" (*kshwas* for *ktwar*); 7 = "following" (*saptan*, ἕπω, etc.); 8 = "two fours" (dual *ashṭau*, ὀκτώ, with prosthetic *à*, *o*); 9 = "that which comes after" (same root as *navas*, *novus*); 10 = "2+8" (*da-san*, *de-cem*).

These results are in full accordance with the facts presented by the Turanian and Allophylian languages generally, and, in short, by all those modern savage dialects which still bear on their surface, unobscured by decay, the primitive machinery of language and calculation. Analogy would lead us to infer that the Semitic tongues formed no exception to this mode of forming numbers, which, so far as it can be analysed, is found to be universal. Calculation is an art slowly acquired; many modern savages cannot count beyond "two" or "three," and we find that this was the case with the ancestors of the highly-gifted Aryan race itself. Once acquired, however, calculation is continually needed: no words are more used than those which denote the numerals;

and consequently no words are more liable to be contracted, changed, and, in short, to undergo all the phenomena of phonetic decay. If we apply this test to the Semitic tongues, we shall find that they fully submit to it. Not to speak of instances like *khamisserit*, or vulgar Arabic *sette* "six," a more pertinent example would be *shésh* for *shadash*. The Aramaic *tĕrên* shows how an often-repeated word could change its primitive form, and the Æthiopic *cal'a* and Assyrian *estin* remind us of the possibility of co-existing roots. Then another element has to be taken into consideration. We have seen how many words, not to speak of an alphabet, the Semites could borrow from their Turanian neighbours, more especially words like *sabar* "copper" which signified objects communicated by the civilized Accadian to the rude Bedouin tribes. Now the Accadians had attained a high degree of knowledge of arithmetic and astrology; the great libraries of Huru and Senkereh, formed in the sixteenth century B.C., contained tablets of square and cube roots, a developed sexagesimal system, observations of eclipses, and a symbolic numeration. We may therefore expect to find among Semitic loan-words Turanian numerals. Comparative instances among other nations warrant, I think, the following analysis of the Semitic numerals.

Akhadu, found in Assyrian in *akhadi—akhadi* "the one— the other," has already in historic times undergone contraction in the feminine *ikhitu*, *akhat* for *ikhidtu*. The stronger masculine *a* has been weakened into the feminine *-i*, and this has affected both vowels, according to the vowel-harmony of all savage people. Now by the side of *akhad* we have Aramaic and Targumic *khad*, and Assyrian *ed(u)* and

khad, represented by the Accadian '*id* (and *kat*) " one " or
" hand." It is difficult not to see here a Semitic modification
of the Turanian numeral, with the prosthetic demonstrative
vowel prefixed in some cases. The other synonyme of "one"
which is found in Assyrian and Hebrew is more difficult to
resolve. *Estin* (or with the case-ending *estinnu*) compared
with *ashtê*, has *n* servile, like *terdinnu*, etc. Hence we get
estu as the original word, curiously like the preposition *estu*.
Now this we shall see is from the Accadian *es* "house,"[1]
whence Assyrian *esu'u*, *essu*, "house," "door," '*ussu*, *estu*,
"foundation."[2] Can it be also the origin of *estin*, as the
"foundation" or root of all numbers? In *sh'nai* we are
again met by an easily-recognized contraction in the feminine.
This numeral also presents us with an undoubted instance of
the prosthetic vowel in the Arabic '*ithnatain*;[3] while Aramaic
has extended the change of *s* into *t* to a change of *n* into *r*,
and has irregularly formed the plural of the feminine (*tar-tain*) by adding the plural-ending to the feminine-termination
(like Assyrian forms in -*tân*). *Sh'naim* is clearly "the two

[1] The Accadian *es* is itself resolvable into *s* "house" (literally " the hollow ") and *is* or *is* " heap," like *mes* " many," from *me* " multitude," and *is* " heap."

[2] The same borrowed root has produced the Hebrew אשיש and Arabic '*assun* (?). An Accadian synonyme of *Anu* is *Susru*, which is translated *ususu* " the founder," *ru* and *ra* being formatives in Accadian, as in *zana* and *zanaru* " high," *ticu*, *cicura*, and *zigaru* " heaven," *sa* and *sara*, " king," *dudhdhu* and *dadhru* " the deviser " (a title of the Babylonian Sargon).

[3] This prosthetic vowel meets us in most of the numerals, and is not to be confounded with the nominal vowel-prefix (p. 110). It is the demonstrative breathing prefixed in vulgar pronunciation to facilitate the pronunciation of common words. So, according to Wetzstein, the Bedouin pronounces *kabalatûn* ordinarily as *k'bâlet*, when in the Annexion as *arkâbet*; and compare Greek forms like ὀπέλλω, ἀμέργω, 'Οβριδρεως, Ὄλυμπος (root *dip*) or the Romance *estar*, etc. (Curtius, Grundzüge d. Griech. Etymol., pp. 650-5).

folds," from שָׁנָה "to bend" or "fold." *Shalosh* has become *sôs-t* in Amharic, and Coptic gives us *somn(t)*, which reminds us of *sh'moneh* "eight." The root has been supposed to be שַׁלְשֵׁל: compare *sulu* "a heap," "multitude." *Arba'* or *reba'* may have the prosthetic *a*: in this case the root may be רָבָע "to grow" or "increase." As, however, the Coptic *'ftu* "four" is plainly 5—1, from *tu* "five" and *wa* "one," so may *arba'* be the remains of some kind of similar composition. *Khamis* has lost its initial guttural in the Amharic *aumis-t*, and has changed it into *s* in the Berber *summus*. Assyrian shows the varying forms *khamiltu* and *khansa*. Here the final sibilant would be original, as well as a medial *m*; the initial was probably a strong guttural, successively weakened to *kh*, *s*, and *au*. This conducts us to קָמַץ "the fist," "five" being expressed in most languages by some word meaning "hand" (with its five fingers).[1] The next two or three numbers after 5 would be, according to the analogy of other languages, compounded out of two preceding numerals; and accordingly we find the names of 6, 7, and 8 all beginning with *s*. This raises the presumption that we may here find either *sh'nai* or *shalosh*. Most of the Allophylian tongues, however, form 6 not by means of 2, but of 1 or more generally 3; and the fact that the Semitic dialects give *three* successive numerals with an initial *s*, excludes the employment of *sh'nai*. Moreover, the most natural way of forming "six" was by saying "three-three." We have already seen that the more primitive form of *shêsh* was *shadash*, as in Arabic and Æthiopic, or Berber *sedis*, Amharic

[1] So the Malay *lima* "hand" =5; the Zulus call 5 *edesanta* "finish hand;" with the Tamanacs of the Orinoco *amgnaitóne* "whole hand" is 5.

sedis-t. Coptic has reduced the original word to *soü*. If *shalshal* were the primary form of *shalosh*, repeated to express number, like the plurals of Allophylian languages, the only part of the word used in composition would be *shal*. *D* and *l* were interchangeable in old Semitic (as in דוּשׁ and לוּשׁ, רעד and רעל); hence *sad-sad*, contracted into *sadas* "six." To distinguish it from 3, the dental was retained in 6, the labial in 3.[1] If our theory be right, we ought to detect "four" in the termination of the name of 7. And this we do in *sheba'* "seven," where the final *ba'* unmistakably refers us to *arba'*. *R* throughout the Semitic tongues has a tendency to interchange with *s* on the one side, and a long vowel on the other. Both of these may be shortened, as in Assyrian *š* for *s*, and *Dîmasku* by the side of דרמשק (see p. 111). The *l* of *sal(as)* had already been assimilated to *r* and its representatives. In Coptic, 7 is *shasf* for *shasft*, in which *'ftu* "four" is recognizable by the side of *shas* (*shalas*) "three." This is better than to make *shasf*=6+1, especially as 6 is *soü*. *Sh'moneh* again discovers *sal(as)*: it ought to be compounded with *khamis*. Now the consonants of *sh'moneh*, besides the fluctuations of the initial between *š* and *s*, shown also by the other numerals, are not quite fixed, even in the historic period. In Markhes van "the 8th month" (in Assyrian *arakh samna*), the word has been shortened to שׁוּן; and in Berber (*tem*) the final nasal has been lost altogether, the sibilant becoming *t* as in *thanat* "two." *Khamis*, we saw above, has lost the guttural in Amharic, and *kh* is very frequently dropped in Assyrian, or replaced by a vocalic *e*

---

[1] So in Accadian *essa*=3, *as*=6; and, according to Professor Schott, 6 in the Ural-Altaic languages is expressed by a modification of 3.

(see p. 29). The final ה of the masculine shows that the word was originally generally pronounced with a final *t;* hence we may expect some change in the *s*. *S* became *l* (through *r*) in Assyrian, and a comparison of *terén* or *p'šant'rin* and the Æthiopic *dent* (for *delt*) would seem to show that *l* and *r* once, before a dental, regularly became *n*. That this was the case with the numerals is made likely by the Coptic *somnt* "three," which would stand for *solst* (*ol* passing into *-om*, or rather *ou*, before *n*); and just as *somnt = solst*, so would *shmen(t) = shmes(t)*, *m* being preserved by the intervening vowel. *Shal*, as we saw before, would have already become *sho*. Following still the analogy of other languages, 9 ought to be 10—1. In *tésha'* we have, I believe, *khad* (*ed*) or *est*(*u*), more probably *est*(*u*). *Ėsa'* points to a long initial syllable, such as *e*. This gives us the first two radicals of *eser* "ten." *R*, especially when final, has an intimate relation to *e* in the Semitic languages; Arabic grammarians explain *e* by *r* combined with a guttural. Hence *ésa'* may well stand for *eser*. The last word is from אסר (whence the Assyrian god Ussuru) "to bind together," referring to the combination of the two hands. *Méah* is obscure: it has been derived from *maim* "water," or from the Arabic *ma'i* "to be wide." Its origin, however, is best explained by the Accadian *mih*, which is interpreted "assembly" (*kâlu*), "mass" (*tamtsu*), and "herd" (*ramoutu*). *Eleph* is "a head of cattle."

The only ordinals hitherto found in the inscriptions are *ristânu* "first" (Hebrew *rishón*) and *salsa* "third," formed like the ordinals in Hebrew (*shénî*, etc.). Dr. Oppert restores the other Assyrian ordinals, *sana*, *rib'a*, *khansa*, etc.

A formation in *yānu* similar to *ristānu* was used to express relations of time: thus *saniyānu* "the second time," *salsiyānu* "the third time."

Fractions were formed as in Hebrew (*khomesh*, etc.) and Arabic by the form *sucun* or *sucnu*. Thus we find *sunnu* "one half," *sulsu* "a third," *sumunu* "an eighth," *sussu* "a sixth." *Sussu* is also used for "a sixtieth," whence the *sóssos* of Berosus, which we may translate "a minute." Dr. Oppert restores the other fractions *rub'u* "a fourth," *khunsu* "a fifth," *sub'u* "a seventh," *tus'u* "a ninth," *'usru* "a tenth." The Babylonians expressed their fractions with a denominator of 60. Thus 20, 40 = 20 $\frac{40}{60}$ = 20 $\frac{2}{3}$. This discovery is due to Dr. Oppert. Besides *sulsu*, the Assyrians also used *sussānu* for "a third," from the Accadian *sussana*. *Sinibu* was $\frac{2}{3}$, from the Accadian *sanabi* ("forty"), and *parapu* was $\frac{5}{6}$, apparently also Accadian, though *kigusili* seems to have been the usual term for the fraction in that language. *Sussu*, meaning 60, was also Accadian. *Baru* or *māsu* was $\frac{1}{2}$. According to Abydenus a *sarus* = 3600 years, a *nerus* = 600, and a *sossus* = 60. In the inscriptions a *ner* is denoted by a wedge (= 60) followed by the symbol of 10. All this notation, together with the symbols which expressed it, was derived from the Accadians.

Among the indefinite numerals may be reckoned *mahdutu* "much" (מְאֹד), *calu, cullat,* "all" (כֹּל), *gabbu* "all," *gimru* "the whole" (גָּמַר), *cabittu* "much" (כָּבֵד).

"Repetition" is expressed by *sanutu* (*sanitu* in Achæmenian, e.g. *saniti salsa* "the third time") and *rubbu*. "Anew" is generally *ana essuti*.

The measures of length were $\frac{1}{3}$ inch = $\frac{1}{60}$ of an *'ammu,* 6 'ammi ("cubits")=1 canu (קָנֶה), 2 cani=1 sa or ribu, 60 sa=1 sus, 30 sussi=1 kasbu or "day's journey." Time was divided into 6 kasbu(mi) of the day and 6 of the night, a kasbu being = 2 hours. The year contained 12 months of 30 days each, together with an intercalary Ve-Adar. At the end of certain cycles there were also a second Nisan and a second Elul. According to the lunar division, the 7th, 14th, 19th, 21st, and 28th were days of "rest" (sulum), on which certain works were forbidden; and the two lunations were divided each into three periods of 5 days, the 19th ending the first period of the 2nd lunation.

The tonnage of ships was reckoned by the *gurru;* thus we have ships of 15 and 60 *gurri.*

According to Dr. Hincks, the *iku* was $=4\frac{3}{10}$ grains, 30 *iki* =1 *cibu* (129 grs.), 60 *cibi*=1 *maneh* (*mana*), 60 *manehs*= 1 heavy talent (*bilatu*) (950,040 grs.). Half a talent, or a light talent (of 30 manehs), was the *biru* or *tsiptu* (479,520 grs.). The talent was according to the standard either of Assyria ("the royal talent" or "the talent of the country") or of Carchemish. Money was weighed, and there was a different talent for gold and for silver.

For measures of capacity the Assyrians possessed the *lagit* or *log* of 3 standards, which contained respectively 10, 9, and 8 subdivisions called *ka*. Land and grain were equally measured by this *lagit* (*tuv*), whose fractional parts are given as the *baru* (or "half"), the *aru*, and the *arrat*. The *arrat* was also a measure divided into the "*baru* of wood," and the "*baru* of stone," and the latter into *ka*.

THE PREPOSITIONS.

These are generally shortened roots; and, not being part of the stock of the primitive Semitic speech, naturally differ in the different dialects, which have set apart various substantives more or less stereotyped to express the relations of the several parts of a sentence.

In Assyrian the simple prepositions are:— *ana* "to," "for"; *ina* "in," "by," "with" (instrumental); *inna*, "in"; *innannu*, "from"; *itti* "along with;" *ultu* or *istu* "from"; *adi* "up to"; *ela* "over"; *eli* "upon"; *elan* or *illan* "beyond"; *assu* "in," "by," "on account of"; *cuv* "instead of"; *ullanū* "before"; *ullanumma* "upon"; *'illamu* "before"; *tiq* "behind," "from," "of"; *pan* "before"; *sa* "of"; *baliv*, *balu*, "without"; *ema* "around," "over"; *elat* "except"; *dikhi* "opposite"; *nir* "below," "near," "against"; *erti* "against"; *sepu* "below"; *'ulli* "among"; *mikhrit* "among"; *ci-la* "without"; *saptu, cibit*, "by the help of"; *sikharti* "throughout"; *nemidu* "towards"; *arci* "after"; *tsir* "against," "upon"; *illu* "upon"; *birid* and *cirib, kirib*, "within"; *akhar* "behind"; *makhri* "before"; *ci* and *ci pi* "according to (the mouth)"; *cima, tuma*, "like"; *limet, li*, "near"; *sar (im)* "from"; *ana sar* "to." Most of these are still used as mere substantives, as *sepu* "foot," *nir* "foot," *mikhrit* "presence," *tiku* "rear," some being adjectives, as *tsiru* "supreme," "above," and one, *sa*, the relative. *Itti, ci, adi,* and *eli* agree with the Hebrew; but Ewald's explanation of the final -*i* from the final ה of the root will not hold, as the Assyrian in that case would be -*u*. It can hardly be the plural, again, but, as in *arci*, will be a case-ending, like *li* and *bi* in Arabic.[1] '*Adi* stands for *edi*, like *agu* and *egu*. *Cum* is *cumu* "heap." '*Assu* is rare, and is apparently of Accadian origin. '*Ina* and '*ana*, with their lengthened forms *inna* and '*anna* (?), are objective cases of the old nouns '*inu* and '*anu*, '*ina* being identical with the Hebrew עֵין from עָנָה.[2] In *ultu* or *istu* the case-ending is abnormally retained (so *assu*). *Ultu* is formed from the Pael, *istu* from the Kal, of אֵשׁ, אֵשׁ, perhaps = שִׁי, like אוֹת, *tu* being the feminine suffix.[3] *Ulli*, *ullânu* are rather from the Pael of עָלָה, than from the pronoun '*ullu*; so also '*illamu* (for *elamu*) and *elat*. *Neru* is properly "yoke," *sepu* "foot," *saptu* "lip." As in the cognate languages, *ci* is generally used instead of *cima*; we also find sometimes *li*, *an*, *el*, and *it* (see p. 10). Before a vowel the final vowel of the preposition is rarely elided, as in *ult-ulla* ("from that" =) "from old time," *ad-ussi* "to the foundations."

Atta, the Hebrew אַתְּ, with the accusative of the pronoun, is found only in the later period, and bears witness to the Aramaising of the language.

The compound prepositions are numerous. Thus we meet with *ina cirib* "in the midst of"; *ina libbi* "in the midst of"; *ana itti* "to be with"; *ultu pani* "from before"; *ultu cirib*, *ultu libbi*, "from the midst of"; *ina pan* "from before"; *ina suki* "in front of"; *ina bibil*, *ina biblat*, *bibil*,

---

[1] This is borne out by the existence of other cases like *balu*, *saptu*, '*ana*, *ela*, *ema* (= עִם), etc., and the occurrence of the mimmation in *baliv*. So, too, words like *tigulti*, when used as a compound preposition with '*ina*, show the same fact. Cf., on the contrary, Philippi, Wesen u. Urspr. d. Stat. Const., p. 107.

[2] According to Philippi, '*ina* is a weakened '*ana* from the demonstrative root '*an*(*nu*).

[3] See, however, p. 135, in which case *istu* would = *estu* from עֶשׁ, like *assu* perhaps (p. 9).

biblat, "in the midst of"; *ina khatstsi* "in the time, presence of"; *ina nirib, nirib*, "near"; *ina eli* "above"; *ina la* "for want of"; *ana la* "not to be"; *ina tsat* "after"; *ana erti* "to the presence of"; *ana sar* "to"; *lapan, lapani*, "from," "before"; *ina anni* "at this (time)"; *ina adi dhemi* "by command of."

Lapani is hardly identical with the Hebrew לִפְנֵי, as the preposition is *li*, not *la;* and we cannot assume a change of vowel, such as we have in Hebrew *lô* (= *la-hu;* so Æthiopic *la*). *Li*, however, is contracted from *limet, limu* (לוה). From the same root comes *lamu* "a clay-tablet," and in this way I would explain *lam* or *lav* in an inscription of Assurizir-pal, where we read *lav samsi napakhi* "close upon sunrise." From this *lav* we get *lā* in *lapan*.

THE INTERJECTIONS.

Of these I have only noticed *'a* "O," and *ninu* "behold," *ninu-su* "behold him." We may add also *adu* "now," "thus."

THE ADVERBS.

These, like the prepositions, are fossilised noun-cases. Generally the accusative is the case used, as in Æthiopic and Arabic. Thus we have *belā* "copiously," *bazza* "as rubbish," *palcā* "amply," and most adverbs of place and time. The (original) mimmation is also found (as in Hebrew and Arabic). Dr. Oppert quotes *cusvam* "in a covert manner," *rub'am* "greatly," *cainam* "strongly." Rarely the second case is employed instead of the third; e.g. *batstsi* "in ruin," *makhri* "before," *arci* "afterwards." The mimmation is also found here; e.g. *labirim(ma)* "of old (and)," "through decay (and)," by the side of *labaris*.

The most common mode of forming the adverb in Assyrian is by the termination *is*. Dr. Oppert has happily explained this by the contracted third personal pronoun attached to the second case, which is here used as though a preposition had preceded. This actually appears in some rare cases, e.g. *ana daris* (see further on). Analogous are the Æthiopic adverbs formed by the third pronoun suffix, like *kadim-û* "first," *cant-û* "in vain." Dr. Oppert refers also to the Hebrew בְּכָל. Everywhere the inscriptions offer us words like *rabis* "greatly," *essis* "strongly," *namris* "brightly," *abubis* "like a whirlwind," *naclis* "completely," *elis* "above," *saplis* "below," *cacabis* "like a star." Sometimes the adverbial termination is attached to the plural in *-an*; thus *tilanis* "in heaps," *khursanis* "completely," *sadanis* "like mountains." In the last case, as often elsewhere, the adverbs preserve old forms which have been lost in the noun.

The most common adverbs of place and time are as follows:—*Umma* "thus," "that"; *as-umma, ya-umma,* and *umma ... la,* "never"; *umma assu* "because"; *allu, alla, alla-sa,* "then," "afterwards"; *sa, ci-sa,* "when"; *eninna* "again"; *arci* "afterwards"; *adi* "till"; *sis* "as of old"; *tsatis* "in future"; *ina yumi suma* "at that time"; *makhri, panama* "formerly"; *matema* "in times past"; *lu-mahdu, lu-mad,* "much"; *sanumma, sanamma,* "in a foreign land," "elsewhere"; *cihdm* "thus"; *calama* "of all kinds"; *enuva* "at that time," "when"; *ultu ulla* and *ulldna* "from that time," "from of old"; *udina* "at the same time."

Alla and *alla-sa* are only found in the Achæmenian period. So also is *'aganna* (from *'aga*) "here."

Lumadu (so *sanumma*) is like the Arabic adverbs which end with *-u*.

THE CONJUNCTIONS.

U and *vâ* "and" ("et"), *vâ* "and" ("que"); *û* "or"; *mâ* "for," "and"; *ai* "not" (with the imperative or precative); *lu* "whether," "thus" (verbal prefix of past time); *ci, ct,* "when," "while," "if"; *sa* "when," "because," "that"; *la* "not"; *ul* "not" (only with verbs, except in the Achæmenian period);[1] *inu* "behold," "now"; *ma* "also"; *mâ* "that" (for *umma*); *ina matima* "in any case"; *sa matima* "of what place?"; *im* "if"; *im matima* "if at all"; *adi-sa, adi-eli-sa,* "in so far as"; *assu* "when"; *summa* "thus," "when"; *ci* "as"; *libbu-sa* "just as."

Adi-eli-sa and *libbu-sa* belong to the Achæmenian inscriptions.

After verbs *a* is sometimes found instead of *vâ*, especially if the vowel *u* has gone before (see p. 27).

---

[1] The two negatives are derived from the demonstrative *'ullu, 'ulla*. The first half of the word, being the more emphatic and full of meaning, was appropriated to the verbs, and (as in Hebrew) had a prohibitive force; the second part of the word was conjoined with the noun, where the negative was less clearly brought out.

THE SYNTAX.

Speaking generally, the syntax of the Assyrian language agrees with that of the other Semitic dialects.

OF THE NOUN.

In the oldest inscriptions, and in a large proportion of those belonging to the later Assyrian period, the case-endings are for the most part carefully observed, *-u* as nominative, *-i* as genitive, and *-a* as accusative. Even in later Assyrian, however, *-u* is sometimes used for the accusative, and even *-a* for the nominative; *e.g.* Assur-banipal has *libba-sunu* nominative. So in Egyptian Arabic *-iñ* is found in the accusative, and *-añ* in the nominative, and *-i* for all cases in the *status constructus*. Similarly the Bedouins use *-i* and *-a* to prevent the concourse of consonants, and use *-a* for all the cases before plural-suffixes. *Tanwin* occurs in poetry when it cannot be used in prose. Compare Italian *loro* from *illorum*, and the Persian animate plural *-ān* originally a genitive.

The mimmation, especially frequent in Babylonian, was purely euphonic, and descended from a period in which none of the cases ended in an open vowel.

In the Babylonian the cases are all confused more or less with one another, and have ceased to express fully their flexional meaning. We even find *bit sarru* "house of the king," *dumku* in the accusative, *libba* in the nominative.

The accusative follows a verb. The genitive is used after a governing noun or a preposition, which is merely an old worn substantive.

The *status constructus* is carefully observed. Before a governed noun the case-ending is dropped. Cases like *rabbi bitu* are plural. Only expressions which have come to be used as compound prepositions are excepted; e.g. *ina tukulti* for *ina tuklat* (like *eli, adi*).[1] But even this exception does not occur in the oldest period. Anomalies, like *bucurti Anuv* "eldest daughter of Anu," are exceedingly rare. Conversely, when several short syllables come together, the *status constructus* is found after a preposition without a genitive; thus, *ana gürünit* by the side of *ana gurunte* (but see p. 30). The short final i was peculiarly liable to be lost in pronunciation as its case-meaning became weakened. A word is sometimes defectively written when the next word begins with the same vowel, the two really coalescing, as is probably the case in *bucurti Anuv* above.

The old plural-termination -*ān* very frequently retained the case-ending -*i* in the *status constructus*, partly from a confusion with the contracted, but more usual, plural in -*i*, and partly because -*i* is a weakening of -*a*, the original mark of the object. It must be remembered that the case-endings are older than the *status constructus*, hence we may find them sometimes anomalously retained when the *status constructus* had come to imply the loss of them in the first noun, as in Hebrew *yod compaginis*, or the Ethiopic accusative-ending -*a*. Compare too the pronoun-suffixes.

The first noun may be used without the case-endings before an adjective, when the latter is employed as a substantive:

---

[1] This short *i* had so far lost its original flexional signification as to be regarded as simply euphonic (see p. 153). It must also be remembered that in many cases the *i* is a mark of the plural, and that the euphonic *i* is only found after (ă)*tu*.

e.g. *ipparsu asar la-hári* "they fled to (a place of the unfruitful=) the desert," *dhudat la-hári paskáti* "crooked desert morasses."

The *nomen agentis* is used like any other substantive when *in regimine*.

The adjective always follows the substantive, both having the case-terminations; e.g. *sarru rabbu* "the great king."

When the substantive has a pronoun suffixed, the adjective still retains the case-ending; e.g. *kat-su dannatu* "his strong hand."

Abstracts are rare; hence a substantive expressing the possessor or subject is followed by another substantive expressing the attribute; e.g. *bel-khiddi* ("the lord of the rebellion"=) "a rebel"; *bel ade* ("lord of homage"=) "a subject"; *nis rucubi* ("the man of chariots"=) "the charioteers"; *er sarruti-su sa Arrame* "his royal city of Arramu."

These compounds have often become so closely united, that when the plural is required, it is sufficient to attach the plural-termination to the second part of the compound only. They may be still further compounded by prefixing the negative particle, as *Surri la-bel-cuśśu* "Surri, a usurper."

The adjective agrees with the gender of its substantive. Sometimes, however, the substantive is of two genders; e.g. *babátu rabbatu* and *babi rabbi* "the great gates." Where the substantive has not the feminine-ending in the singular, the gender can only be determined by the accompanying adjective, which must always have the appropriate termination.

The adjective in certain rare cases may precede its noun: in this case the case-endings are dropped; thus *halicet idi gamarri* "marching bands of troops." Really, however, it is here a substantive in the *status constructus*. If the noun is dual, the adjective is plural: e.g. *halicut idâ-su* "his marching bands."

To supply the want of abstract adjectives a substantive in the genitive is often found; as *hunut simi mahdi* ("furniture of great price" =) "costly furniture."

There are no special forms for the comparative or superlative. They are expressed by the positive with *istu* and *ina*: e.g. *rabu ina ili Uramazda* "Ormuzd is the greatest of the gods" ("great among the gods is Ormuzd"). The superlative may also be represented by a repetition of the adjective; e.g. *bilat mahda-mahda* "tribute very abundant," *asar dandanti* "a very strong place" (see p. 107).

Two substantives may be placed in apposition (the substantive verb being omitted) so as to qualify one another. In this case both have the case-endings: e.g. *bilutu Assur* "the lordship of Assyria" ("Assyria as a lordship"), *pulkhu adiru melam Assur* "exceeding fear of the attack of Assur," *abni khipisti sad Khamani pil-su usatritsa* "stones dug from Mount Amanus, the choice of it, I arranged."

A few nouns are collective in signification, (1) those which denote an individual out of a class, as *rucubu* for *rucubi* "chariots"; (2) feminine abstracts as *libittu* (*libintu*) "bricks"; and (3) measures and other arithmetical terms, as *esri mana* "20 manehs."

Nisu ("man") in the sense of "every one" is often used in this collective way; e.g. *nis sa mat Sukhi ana mat Assuri la illicuni*," none of the Sukhi had gone to Assyria."

The plural is used as in Hebrew to express extension of

space or time and their parts, e.g. *mie* "water," *pani* "face," *cirbi* "the interior" (as a permanent state).

The genitive often expresses the object as well as the subject; e.g. *zicir sumi-su* "the memory of his name," *sallat eri* "the spoil from the cities."

Geographical names replace apposition by the genitive; e.g. *mat Dimaski* "the land of Damascus." When the *status constructus* is replaced by *sa* ("of"), the first noun retains the case-endings: thus *kharitsa sa er-ya* "the ditch of my city." Rarely a feminine plural after a preposition may have the case-ending *-i* before the following noun (as though it had become a compound preposition); e.g. *ana taprāti cissat nisi* "for the delight of multitudes of men." Compare *yod compaginis* in Hebrew.

As in *ipparsu asar* "they fled to a place," an accusative of motion may follow the verb without a preposition; this is regularly the accusative, but the second case is sometimes found instead (as in the *status constructus*); e.g. *takhazi itsa* "he went forth to battle."

The later Aramaising stage of the language is marked by an increasing use of prepositions; thus *ana* becomes, like Aramaic ל, a mark of the accusative; e.g. at Behistun *aducu ana Gumātav* "I had killed Gomates."

Just as the prepositions are old accusative cases, standing for the most part in the *status constructus*, so substantives may be used absolutely as accusatives of limitation: e.g. *illicu resut* "they went ahead," by the side of *sa ana resuti suluov*.

OF THE NUMERALS.

As in the other Semitic languages, the cardinals from 3 to

10 use the masculine with feminine nouns, and the feminine terminations with masculine nouns; e.g. *ciprâtu irba'i* "the four regions," *elip khamis gurri* "a ship of 5 tons." This rule is rarely transgressed, as in *tupukatu irbittu* "the 4 races."

The cardinal (in the plural) may be placed before a following noun in the genitive in the place of the ordinal; the second noun being in the singular; e.g. *ina salsi garri-ya* "in my third campaign."

The plural masculine follows all the numerals (except in the case of arithmetical terms, measures, etc., when the singular is used) (so 2 Kings ii. 16); e.g. *esritu alpi* "20 oxen"; but *esri mana* "20 manehs."

The measures are often preceded by the preposition *ina*, followed by the sign of unity: e.g. CC *in* I. *ammi* "200 cubits," which Dr. Oppert has well explained as meaning 200×1 ("by 1").

In dates, first comes the day, then the month, then the year, each followed by the numeral, and preceded in many cases by *ina*.

"About" with a numeral is expressed by *istu*; thus *ina elippi sa ina khuli istu* XX. *i(dh)dhulâ-ni ina er Kharidi nahra Purat lu etebir*, "in ships, which on the sand about 20 in number were drawn up in Kharid, the Euphrates I crossed."

OF THE PRONOUNS.

The personal pronouns are used by themselves to express the substantive verb; e.g. *anacu sarru* "I (am) the king," *summa ina mati-ya sunu* "when they (were) in my country."

Occasionally the personal pronouns are found attached to

a noun in the sense of the demonstratives, though really in apposition; e.g. *ina cîse babi sināti* " in the niches of these gates" (literally "gates even them"), *khuśpa-sū eli sa ina yumi pani usarbi* "that masonry above what (it was) in former days I enlarged." So *usamkhar-ca cāta* "I capture thee, even thee."

The third personal pronouns singular and plural may stand at the beginning of a sentence absolutely, to call attention to the subject of the clause: as *sū ci pi'i annimma istanappara umma* " he, according to my dictation, sent word that;" *sū asaridu cabtu* "he, the glorious chief;" *sū Khazaki'ahu pulkhi melammé belluti-ya iśkhupu-su* "him Hezekiah, the fears of the approach of my lordship overwhelmed him;" *sū Elamū ala . . . sanamma ebus-su* "he, the Elamite another city built." So also *yāti*.

The possessive pronouns with the substantive verb are replaced by the personal pronouns with *eli* preceded by *ana* and *ina*.

When it is required to give emphasis to the third personal pronoun plural, a substantive form *sunuti* or *sunut* (*sināti, sinat*) is used, which is not attached as a suffix to the verb, and accordingly sometimes stands before it; e.g. *usalic sunuti* "I made them go," *sinati birid sallat-sazati ultil* " them within the image-gallery I placed," *paldhut sunuti icsud* "he took them alive," *tsabi sunuti . . . uratti* " the soldiers, even them (=those soldiers), I threw down," where the emphasis is laid upon the object. *Sāsunu* sometimes takes the place of *sunuti;* e.g. *sāsunu adi nisi-sunu . . . aslula* "them and their men I carried off." So *sāsu* and *sāsa* in the singular.

The verbal suffixes may be either in the dative or the

accusative: e.g. *usaldidu-ni* "they caused to be brought to me," *ana ebisu · Bit-Saggadhu nasa-nni libb-i* "my heart is raising me to build Bit-Saggadhu."

The pronominal suffixes may be regarded as independent nouns requiring the *status constructus*, or as simple adjectives.[1] Euphony has much to do in determining this question, and the suffixes of the first and second persons are generally used with the case-endings (the accusative excepted). Speaking generally, the second case-ending is very rarely dropped. The masculine plural in *-ut* is employed without the case-endings of the nominative and accusative, monosyllabic roots excepted. The singular *ut* drops the case-endings of the nominative and accusative, and if the second syllable is long (as in *cidinnut*), of the genitive also. The feminine plural (*âtu*) always retains all three case-endings, unless the first two syllables are short, or the last radical is doubled, when the accusative case-ending may be omitted. *Itu, etu,* also retain all the case-endings. So does the feminine singular (*âtu*), except in the case of monosyllables and roots derived from verbs y'y, which always drop *-u,* generally *-a,* and very often *-i*. The plural in *ân* always drops the terminations; monosyllables excepted, which retain *-i*. Ordinary triliterals retain *-i,* generally drop *-u* (which, if retained, is lengthened), and always drop *-a,* unless the noun is used as a preposition, when *a* is lengthened in Assyrian (e.g. *cibitassu,*

---

[1] Rather, perhaps, in apposition. It is not quite correct to say that the pronoun suffixes of the first and second persons are independent nouns, and the apparent *status constructus,* whenever used with them, is due to the euphonic law which forbids three short syllables to come together, or else is the result of contraction, as in *ab-â = abw-a* or *aba-a*. As in other languages, *u* and *a* have generally been weakened to the so-called connecting vowel *-i*.

but Babylonian *œrba-su*). The participle, however, retains the terminations. If the word is a quadriliteral, the case-ending may be kept, as *asur-sin* and *asurru-sin*. Monosyllabic roots more usually retain the case-endings, which may be lengthened; and roots ע'ע almost invariably do so.

When two nouns are so closely united as to form but one idea, the personal suffix is attached to the second noun; e.g. *kharudh sarruti-ya* "the sceptre of my kingdom" (="my royal sceptre"). This takes place even when the nouns are in apposition, as *papakha beluti-ya* "the shrine of my lordship."

The pronominal suffix is frequently added pleonastically to the verb at the end of the sentence; and sometimes the singular (expressing "the whole of it") refers to subjects which are in the plural; thus *sallut-su va camut-su ana er-ya Asur ubla-su* "his spoils and his treasures to my city Asur I brought it (=them)," *hunut takhasi-sunu ecim-su* "their materials of war I took them (it)."

The demonstrative pronouns always follow their substantive, which generally retains the case-endings.

The relative ordinarily requires the noun following as well as the verb to have a pronominal suffix attached: e.g. *Yahudu sa asar-su ru'ku* "Judah, whose situation (is) remote" (lit. "of which its situation (is) remote").

In this way the oblique cases of the relative are formed, as *sa ina abli-su* "upon whose son."

The relative pronoun may be omitted, as in Hebrew or English; e.g. *sarru . . . tanambu zicir-su* "the king (whose) memory thou proclaimest;" *miri eri nirmaq va namkhar siparri . . . bilata va madatta issa'a amkhar* "works of iron, a tray (?) and an offering of copper . . . the tribute and gifts (which) he brought I receive;" *itti kari ab-i iouru* " with the castle (which) my father had made;" *assu khultuv obusu* " on account of the wickedness (which) he had done."

The relative is frequently used absolutely at the beginning of a sentence, as *sa ana natsir citte va misari-su . . . inambuinni ili rabi* " as regards which (city) for the protection of its treaties and laws . . . the great gods proclaim me." Hence its adverbial use, as *sa . . . ina cussi sarruti rabis usibu* " when on my royal throne pompously I had sat."

The other pronouns may be used in the same absolute way; e.g. *annute cappi-sunu ritti-sunu ubattiq* " as regards some their hands (and) their feet I chopped off."

The relative generally follows its antecedent, thus interpolating a parenthesis between the latter and the verb which goes with it; e.g. *Sa-duri danānu epsētu sa ili rabbi isimuinni isme'e* " Sa-duris the mighty works, which the great gods established for me, heard of."

In the Achæmenian period we find the relative when used as a sign of the genitive standing before its governing noun; thus, *sa Cambusiya aga-su akhu-su* " the brother of this Cambyses " (lit. " as regards which Cambyses, him, his brother," where the addition of the demonstrative shows what a purely genitival mark *sa* had become). This use is traceable to the absolute employment of the relative at the beginning of a sentence ; *e.g.* in Sargon's inscription *sa Ambarissi malic-sunu damikte Sarru-cinu imsu* " as regards whom Ambaris their king has the prosperity of Sargon despised." So in Æthiopic and rarely in Arabic and later Hebrew.

The personal and demonstrative pronouns are often included

in the relative; in the vulgar dialect this may even take place when *sa* is used for the genitive: e.g. IV. *mana caspi ina sa Gargamis* "4 manehs of silver according to (the maneh) of Carchemish."

The indeterminate relative is sometimes omitted in the subordinate clause, even when it is placed first; e.g. *ikhkhira abdhu amattu sa pi'i-su ustennā* "(whoever) evades (his) pledge, the truth of his mouth changes."

When there is no definite antecedent, the third personal pronoun is very often used in the singular in the sense of "people"; e.g. *usalic-su* with variant *usalic-sunuti, usalmi-s* "I caused the people to approach," *edis pani-su ipparsid* "alone before them he fled." So also *si*; e.g. *ana bit cili la isarrac-si* "to the store-house he does not (=shall not) deliver them" (*i.e.* columns and other palace-decorations).

In the Achæmenian period the loose use of the genitive with *sa* allowed a personal pronoun to be placed before its antecedent pleonastically; e.g. *la Barsiya anacu abil-su sa Curas* "I (am) not Bardes, the son of Cyrus."

The later inscriptions occasionally use the third personal pronoun masculine for the feminine; e.g. *dicta mahád-su adduo, sirtare-sa* "her many soldiers I slew, her pavilions," etc. So in the Law-tablet *inaddu-su* "they place her." Conversely *sa* is used incorrectly for *su* before *a* following; e.g. *damkatu epusus-sa aspuru ittakhta-su insi* (for *imsi*) "the benefits (which) I had done him (and) had sent to his aid he despised."

Occasionally the pronoun is omitted after the verb; e.g. *yusannā' yāti* "he repeated (it) to me."

OF THE VERBS.

The third person masculine is sometimes used for the feminine (but not until the later days of the Assyrian Empire); e.g. *Istar . . . ana ummani-ya sutta yusapri-va ci'dm icbi-sunut* " Istar . . . to my soldiers a dream disclosed and thus said to them." So on the Law-tablet *ictabi* is used with *assatu* ("woman"), but as *su* is also found for *sa* or *si*, the translation from the Accadian was probably made by a person who was but imperfectly acquainted with the Assyrian language. Dr. Oppert well compares the want of a third person feminine in the precative; e.g. *si limut u anacu lubludh* "let her die and may I live."

On the other hand, in the second person plural there is a tendency to substitute the feminine for the masculine form: thus, Tiglath-Pileser I. says of "the great gods" (*ili rabi*) *aga'a tsira tuppira-su* "the supreme crown ye have entrusted to him." This is especially the case in the Imperative; e.g. *halca* "go ye," *khula* "rejoice," and even *duca'ah* "smite," all with masculine subjects. The last instance, however, would suggest another explanation of this anomaly, that the final *a* is the subjunctive-augment, like הָ Cohortative in Hebrew. In this case the preceding *u* will have coalesced with *a* into *d* or *ah*, as in *issa'a=issa-va* (*issa-ua*) or *aba=abu-a* (*abwa*).[1] This actually happens in *sima'a* by the side of *sime* "hear thou." In this way we may explain the ungrammatical use of the second person imperative with the relative at Behistun, in *mannu atta sarru sa bela'a arci-ya*

---

[1] Cf. *yuraps-inni* for *yurapsu-inni* (=*yurappisu-inni*). See p. 27.

"whoever thou (art), O king, who rulest (goes on ruling) after me."

If the first nominative be feminine, the second masculine, the verb, though in the plural, is generally feminine; e.g. *si va ili abi-sa tabbu'u sum-i* "she and the gods her fathers proclaimed my name."

When a singular noun has a collective signification, it may be followed by a plural verb; thus *lillicu-s suppu-ca* "may thy speech come to him."

The Imperfect of the other dialects has been split up into four tenses (as in Æthiopic into two): the Aorist, which is the one most commonly found in the historical inscriptions; the Pluperfect (often used, however, for perfect and aorist); the Present; and the Future. The Perfect, originally a present participle, has a permansive signification (see pp. 52, 62). Thus *bilata ascun* "tribute I established"; *sa Asur . . . kati yusatmikhu* "which Asur had caused my hand to hold"; *an sunne usun-su isaoanu-va libba-su imallicu* "to his two ears shall he put (it) and his heart shall rule"; *ina uppi tarappits* "in the dust dost thou lie down."

The subjunctive is used (1) when the accusative follows the verb, (2) is found in conditional sentences, and (3) is often attached to roots which contain *l* or *r*; e.g. *yutsalla'a beluti-ya* "he submitted to my lordship"; *icnusa ana neri-ya* "he submitted to my yoke"; *sa epusa* "which I had made"; *aslula* "I carried off"; *aspura* "I sent."

In many cases, however, the final *a* is the conjunction, for *va*. See p. 27.

After a conditional particle a Pluperfect generally follows; e.g. *sa amkhuru-si* "when I had invoked her."

The Hortative sense of the Subjunctive augment is confined to the Precative and Imperative; e.g. *lillica* "may he go," *sullima* "accomplish."

The Conditional Suffix is generally attached to the Perfect, and follows the relative and such particles as *ci* ("when") expressed or understood; e.g. *sa Asuru va Ussuru . . . ikisu-ni* "which Asur and Ussuru had entrapped" (at any time); more rarely it is attached to the Precative, as *ana yāsi va sirritti-ya ciribta dhabita licrubu-ni* "to myself and my seed may they give good fealty." Here the prayer depends upon the unknown conditions of future time. Occasionally the suffix is found with the Permansive, as in *ci utsbacu-ni* "while I was stopping." When *sa* is expressed, the pronominal suffix of the verb is inserted before the subjunctive-enclitic; e.g. *sa nisini . . . Pitru ikabu-su-ni* "which the men . . . call Pethor," *sa abilu-sina-ni* "which (countries) I have conquered."

When the future occurs by itself in a conditional sentence and after a relative, it expresses the certainty of the event which is looked forward to; e.g. *ci bitu-rabu ilabbiru-va innakhu* "when this palace shall grow old and decay" (as it certainly will), *ci takabbu'u umma* "if thou shalt say at all" (="whenever thou shalt say").

The Present is often, as in other languages, used for the Future and Imperative: e.g. *umpici la tasaddiri impuci la takabbi* "*umpici* (rubies) thou dost not write, *impuci* dost not say" (*i.e.* do not write and say), *tanadhala ana epis sassi asar panu-ci sacnu tebaou anacu* "thou shalt carry off to make spoil, (to) the place (which) before thee is set I will come," where the subjunctive augment after the Present in the sense of the Future or Imperative and the emphatic position of the pronoun are to be noticed.

The Imperative may also be used for the Future; e.g. *bukhkhir umman-ca dica'a caras-ca Bab-il* " select thy army, strike thy camp, O Babel" (for "thou shalt select," etc.).

In comparisons the aorist is used as an iterative present (as in Greek), what happens at any time being conceived to have already taken place on some definite occasion; e.g. *cima Ramanu isgum* " as the Air-god pours."

The substantive verb is usually omitted: *e.g.* in the Law-tablet *ul assati atta* (for *atti*) "thou art not my wife." When *existence* has to be expressed, in place of *yahu*, *basu* is generally used (e.g. *mal basu* or *mala basu* "as many as exist"), which Dr. Oppert has acutely compared with the Æthiopic *bisi* "men." *Isu* (𒄑). is also used in the same sense: e.g. *sanin su la isu* "a rival to him there was not"; but more commonly this verb includes the idea of possession, as *isi* "may I have" (*ai isi naciri mugalliti* "may I not have enemies multiplied").

The Infinitive, as a verbal noun, may have either the verbal or the nominal side brought most prominently forward. More usually the former is the case, the infinitive governing an accusative like the verb, and therefore retaining the case-endings; e.g. *ana sadada madata* "to bring tribute," *ana episu Bit-Saggadha* "to the building of Bit-Saggadh," *ana pakadav cal dadmi* "to preside over all men." To the same use must be referred the absolute employment of the infinitive in negative sentences; e.g. *ina la bana* "in the doing of nothing" (*i.e.* while I had leisure), *adi la basi'e* "until there were no more" ("up to the not being"), *ana la tsabate* "not to be taken," where it answers to the gerundive; *ana la tsibate-su* "that he might not take it," *ana la casad-i ina mati-su* "in order that I might not get to my country" (where the *construct Infinitive* is used). Often, however, the Infinitive is employed like any other noun in the *status constructus* without the case-endings, as *ana epis ramani-su* "to the working of himself," *epis buhri* "the making of snares."

Much of the same nature is the employment of the abstracts in *t* servile with a relative and a verb; e.g. *ina ta'aiarti sa alie* "(it was) at (my) return that I went."

Not unlike the use of *waw consecutive* (see p. 69) is the use of *va* to join a Pluperfect and an Aorist, in the place of a conditional clause; e.g. *itsbatūni-va emuru* "when they had taken they saw." The Permansive may take the place of the aorist, *va* becoming a true *waw consecutive*; e.g. *itsbatūni-va ... tebuni* "when they had taken they are continually coming."

As in the other Semitic languages, the idea of intensity or continuation is expressed by attaching to the verb, as object, a verbal noun formed from the same root, like the Infinitive Absolute in Hebrew; e.g. *dicta-sun aduo* "their slayables I slew," *khirit-su akhri* "its ditch I dug," *sipic ... aspuo* "a heap I heaped up," *amsukh misikhta* "I measured its dimension," *ikhtanabbata khubut nisi sa Assur* "he is ever wasting the wasting of the men of Assyria," *ilbinu libitta* "they made bricks." Sometimes the noun is accompanied by *ana* ("for"); e.g. *batuli-sun va batulâte-sun ana sagaltu asgul* "their boys and maidens I dishonoured"; sometimes by *cima* ("as"); e.g. *Bit-Amucāni cima dai'asti ades bukhar nisi-su* "Bit-Amucani, like a threshing-floor, I threshed the glory of its men."

The position of the verbal noun is generally before its verb: when continuance is implied, however, it stands after the verb (as in Hebrew), and the verb sometimes has the subjunctive augment. Herein the Assyrian marks itself off from Arabic, which regularly places the Infinitive when it expresses intensity after the verb, and attaches itself to Hebrew and Syriac. The Æthiopic usage agrees throughout with the Assyrian.

A verbal noun in *m*-, without the case-endings, may be used to express an adverb; thus *marab urabbi* " greatly I enlarged." It may also be used to express a participial clause; e.g. *utsabbita mutstsa-sun* " I captured the exit of them (=them as they were going out)."

A compound verb is often formed by שכן with a substantive attached; e.g. *takhaza ascun* " I made battle " = " I fought," *hapicta-sunu lu ascun* " I effected their overthrow " = " I overthrew them."

Two verbs in the same tense may be joined together without a conjunction to express a compound idea; e.g. *irdu'u illicu kakkar tsummi* " they descended, they went (to) dry ground," for " they came down to;" *illic enakh* " it went on decaying." So *'alacu* is used with *labaris* to form a compound idea: *labaris illic* " it became old."

The Participle present active is generally used as a noun, in the *status constructus*; e.g. *da'is matani naciri* " the trampler upon hostile lands," *semat ikribi* " hearer of prayers," *alic pani-ya* " going before me."

It may, however, preserve its full verbal character, and in this case it retains the case-endings; e.g. *la palikhu zicri beli* " not worshipping the memories of the lords."

Occasionally it is used as a finite verb, as in the proper names *Musallim-Ussur* "Ussur (is) a completer," *Mutaggil-Nabiuv* "Nebo (is) an auxiliary," *cullat aibi mupariru* "all enemies he (is) crushing."

Often it bears a relative signification; e.g. *munaccar sidhri-ya . . . Asur . . . nacris liziz-śu* "the defacer of my writing (=if any one defaces) may Asur in a hostile manner constrain."

The passive participle sometimes has the meaning of "able to be —," "ought to be—"; especially the Pael participles of concave verbs; e.g. *dicu* "what can be slain," *la niba* "what cannot be counted," *pu'u ussuru* "a mouth that should be bound."

The participle may be used in the singular as a collective noun, and so take a plural verb; e.g. *itti dagil pan Asuri* "with those who trusted in Asur" (literally "him trusting in Asur"), *racibu-sin dicu* "their charioteers were being slain," *nisi asib garbi-su . . . illicu* "the people dwelling within it went," *lamaśśi û alapi sa abni . . . natsiru kibśi musallimu tallacti* "colossi and bulls of stone guarding the treasures (and) completing the corridors."

The indeterminate third person is expressed by the third person plural, as *sa ina lisan Akharri Bit-Khilâni isaś-śu* "which in the tongue of the West Bit-Khilani they name," *ana mat Nizir sa mat Lullu-Cinipa ikabu-su-ni akdhirib* "to Nizir, which they call Lullu-Cinipa, I drew near." In a conditional clause the particle may be omitted, as *lû ana siga yusetstsu'u* "or (if any one) expose to harm."

This third person plural is also used impersonally (like צָרַר in Hebrew); e.g. *kharsânu sakûtu epis buhri-sunu ikbi'uni-su* "it had been ordered him to make snares in the thick woods" (literally "the thick woods (for) the making of their snares they had appointed unto him"), where the double accusative must be noticed. The singular may be employed in the same way; e.g. *allacu khandhu . . . illicav-va* "by a long journey (one) came and," *yusapri'* "(one) revealed."

All transitive verbs in Shaphel and Shaphael take two accusatives; e.g. *dura daliv palri Samsi-utsani Babili usaśkhir* "a high wall round the fords of the Rising Sun of Babylon I built." Many intransitive verbs may take an accusative of cognate meaning; e.g. *illica urukh mu'uti* "he went the path of death."

Verbs of motion may take an accusative of direction without a preposition; e.g. *illicu ritsut-su* "they went (to) his help," *sacut Ninua . . . utir asru-ssa* "the laws of Nineveh I restored its (=their) place," *cisittu sad caspi . . . alic* "(to) the acquisition of the silver mountain I went."

Verbs of *filling, giving, finding*, etc., take two accusatives; e.g. *Assuru . . . malcut Lasanan yumallu'u katassu* "Assur has filled his hand with the kingdom of the world," *sa Maruduc bel-a yumallu'u gatu-a* "with whom Merodach my lord has filled my hand," *dahtu imkhar sunuti* "the gifts he received them," XXII. *er-khaltsi . . . iddin-su* "22 fortresses he gave him," *sa itstsuru mubar-su la ibah* "which (mountain) a bird (for) its crossing finds not," *Bit-Saggadhu va Bit-Zida sannan ustetesser esret-i* "Bit-Saggadhu and Bit-Zida (to) restore I directed my direction" (literally "I caused Bit-Saggadhu and Bit-Zida to direct my course to restore," where *sannan* for *sannana* is the accusative of direction). The last instance will show how general the use of two accusatives is when one of them expresses an idea cognate to that of the verb: e.g. *sa masaq Ilu'u-biahdi khammahi itsrupu* "who had burned the skin of Ilu'u-biahdi with heat," *sa limniv va aibi itsannu imat mūti* "which repel the injurious and wicked (by) the fear of death."

As in all languages, the Assyrian affords instances of *constructio prægnans*, especially with צבת (" to seize ") used as a verb of motion, as *dur-su itsbat* "he fled to his fortress," *ana casad-i ana mat Madai* "for my getting to Media."

The derived conjugations sometimes change the meaning of Kal; thus Dr. Oppert instances from שׁמע the Istaphal participle *mustismə'u* "he who governs" (= " causes to hear himself"), and from כשׁר (" to possess") the Pael *cassadu* "make to approach." So in Niphal פלס "to weigh," but נפלס "to be favourable"; תגל "to serve," but נתגל " to trust."

With compound nouns, when the governing word is in the singular, and the genitive in the plural, the verb follows the number of the latter; e.g. *sabil-cudurri iscunu-su* "the magistrates (dwellers of boundaries) appointed it."

This is universally the case with *cal, cala, cullat,* and *gimir,* when followed by plural genitives (or, in the case of *cala,* nominatives); e.g. *sa cala simi u etsi kharrusu* "where all plants and trees were cultivated."

OF THE PARTICLES.

Originally the case-endings, the meaning of the verb, and the position of the noun, expressed those modifications of space, time, and relation which a later period of language more closely denoted by prepositions. Thus we find in the inscriptions the second case used occasionally without a preposition to express motion to a place (see p. 150).

The idea of "change," "result," "object," is expressed by *ana* with the accusative; e.g. *ana tulle u simmi itur* "it became (crossed over to) heaps and ruins," *or su ana essuti abni* "that city anew (for a change) I built," *ana susub napsati-sun ipparsidu* "to save their lives they fled."

For the Achæmenian (Aramaising) use of *ana* to denote the accusative, see p. 3.

The following idiom with *ana* is noticeable: *me va tehuta baladh napistiv-sunu ana pi'i yusacir* "water and sea-water (to) preserve their lives their mouths drank" (literally "water and sea-water, the preservation of their lives, to their mouths it drank," where *yussocir* is used impersonally).

Ina frequently denotes the instrument, like the Hebrew בְּ; e.g. *ina katti ramani-su* "by his own hands"; *ina epiri icatamu* "with dust shall cover."

It also bears the signification "into" with certain verbs; e.g. *ina neribi-sun . . . erub* "into their lowlands I descended."

The use of *ina* and *ana* with כָּשַׁד "to take," "occupy," is noticeable. Thus we have *ana la casad-i ina mati-su* "that I might not find myself in his country" (by the side of *ana casad ina matati satina*), and *ana casad-i ana mat Madai*, "on my getting to Media."

In one passage of Sennacherib (Grotefend's Cyl., l. 50) the preposition is actually placed after its noun: *abni sadi danni itti nahra ibbā acsi* "with strong mountain-stones the clear stream I concealed." Probably it shows the influence of the Accadian. We may compare such sub-Semitic dialects as that of Harar, in which the substantive regularly takes a postposition, and in which the determining word is actually placed before the determined.

Ultu is used to express "(exacting punishment) from"; e.g. *ultu Assuri tirra ducte abi* "from Assyria bring back the slaughter of (thy) father," *i.e.* revenge thy father's death upon Assyria.

Ultu is sometimes used adverbially for "after that" "from the time when" (with *yumi sa* "the day whereon" understood); e.g. *ultu bit-rabu . . . ana ribat sarruti-ya usaclilu* "after that I had caused the palace to be finished for the greatness of my sovereignty," *istu ibna-nni Maruduc ana sarruti* "from the time when Merodach created me for sovereignty."

Adi "up to," comes to have a conjunctive signification as denoting how far the objects pointed out extended; e.g. *nisi adi maruti-sunu* "men and children" (= "up to their children"), *sarrani matat Nairi adi sa niraruti-sunu illicuni* "the kings of the countries of Nairi, including (those) who (to) their aid had gone."

Itti may be used in the sense of "(revolting) from" (= "breaking with") or "against"; e.g. (*S'uti*) *itti-ya yuspalcit* "(the S'uti) from me he alienated," *icciru itti-ya* "they revolted against me," *idinu deni itti Urtaci* "they gave judgment against Urtaci."

As in Hebrew, a preposition which has been employed in the first member of a clause may be dropped in the second; e.g. *er suatu ana la tsabate va dur-su la ratsapi* "this city not to be occupied and for its wall not to be built."

The following idiomatic use of *sa* and *assu* with the infinitive, which has been well explained by Mr. Norris, is noticeable, "*sa limnu la bane paniv* " that the evil-doers may not make head" (literally "on account of the evil-doer the not making head"), and *assuv aibi la bane paniv*, where our idiom "to make head" curiously coincides with the Assyrian.

The adverbs in -*is* may pleonastically be preceded by *ana*, thus confirming Dr. Oppert's conjecture as to their origin; e.g. *ana daris likkura* "to futurity be it proclaimed," *ana daris yucinnu* "for ever they established," *isallu'u an nahris* "they rolled as in a river."

The negative *la* is put before a noun (substantive or adjective) to form a negative compound, as *la-mami* "the want of water," *la-magiri* "disobedient," *la-khaddu* "unerring."

Ul is put only before verbs, but it does not possess the prohibitive force of אַל in Hebrew. In the Achæmenian period *ul* has come to be used like *la* with all words; thus *ul anacu, ul sir-ya.*

The negative particle of prohibition or deprecation is *ai*, which in Æthiopic ('*i*) is the common negative, from אִין (Æthiopic *yn*). It is rare in Hebrew, and found only in a few compounds. Instances in Assyrian are *ai ipparou'u idd-sa* "may its defences not be broken," *ai isi naciri* "may I not have enemies." Compounded with the indefinite *umma* at the beginning of a sentence, with *ul* or *nin* following immediately before the verb, it signifies "no one whatever" (as *aiumma ina bibbi-sunu asar-su ul yumassi'i-va susub-su ul idi* " no one among them touched its site, and undertook its settlement"). Hence, the force of the negation lying in the second negative, *aiumma* has come to have a purely indefinite sense when used alone; e.g. *lu aklu* .. *lu aiumma* "whether a chief or any one whatever."

The substantive verb with the negative may be expressed by the substantive *yānu* "not-being" (𒁹𒀭), the different persons being denoted by pronominal suffixes; e.g. *manma yānu* "any one there (was) not," *yanu-a* "I (am) not."

The conjunction after a verb takes the form of the enclitic *-vā* (like the Latin *que*); e.g. *sa bitrabi sātu tuvlū-sa ul ibsi-va tsukhkhurat subat-sa* "of that palace its mound was not, and its site was small," *urukh Accadi itsbatuniv-va ana Babila tebuni* "the path of Accad they had taken, and to Babylon had come." The short enclitic throws the accent back upon the last syllable of the verb, which is therefore lengthened, and accordingly has often a second *v*. A preceding *b* may become *v*, as in *eruv-va* for *erub-va*.

The enclitic is sometimes contracted into *a* simply (for *va*), just as *abu-a* may become *ab-a*; e.g. *alpi tsini bilata va madata issa-a amkhar* "oxen, sheep, tribute, and offering he brought, and I received." This contraction may take place even after a consonant, especially a liquid, and may readily be mistaken for the subjunctive suffix (see p. 56, *note*): e.g. *remi paldhute yutsabbit-a ana er-su Asur yubl-a* "the wild bulls alive he took, and to his city Asur brought, and," *asar-sa usarda'a* "its place I deepened, and."

With substantives and clauses *ū* is used, also *vā* (only after vowels).

The conjunction is sometimes omitted both with nouns and verbs; e.g. *ili istari sātunu* "those gods (and) goddesses," *same irsiti* "heaven and earth," *appal aggur in isati asrup* "I overthrew, demolished (and) burned with fire"; *ina akhi 'apli imri-a* " amongst the brethren (or) sons of my family," *sû cisu-su ... yuptatekhu akhai* "he (and) his sword-bearer cut open one another."

When a verb is followed by a substantive so that they form but one idea, *vâ* may irregularly be placed after the latter; thus *attitsi ina giri-ya-va asukhra Azi'il* "I turned aside in my course and outflanked Aziel."

The same happens even if the first clause has only a substantive verb understood, but not expressed; e.g. *sa cimasâsu-va icciru* "who was like him and had revolted."

In the Achæmenian period *vâ* is ungrammatically found between two nouns; thus *mati saniti-va lisanu sanituv* "other lands and another tongue."

-*Va* may sometimes take the place of *yusannâ'* "he repeated," as in *isasi-va umma* "he told thus," where some verb like *ikbi'* "he said" is understood after the enclitic.

Lû is prefixed to verbs to denote past time (like *kad* in Arabic); e.g. *lû allic* "I went." If the first syllable of the verb is *u* or *yu*, the two vowels coalesce into one; e.g. *lusardi*.

In Babylonian and Achæmenian it is joined with nouns; e.g. *anacu lu sarru* "I (am) the king."

Lû also signifies "whether" or "either"—"or," and as such is found before nouns and clauses; e.g. *lû nuturda lû itû lû aiumma ... lû ana ila yusasracu lû ana ziga yusetstsu'u* "whether *nuturda* or *itu* or any one ... either to a god shall give or to harm shall expose."

Lû (Aramaic לוי, Arabic *lau*) is like *limeti, li* (Aramaic לות "at") from לוה "to adhere," hence "immediately," "union," "if."

The indefinite *umma* (as in *aiumma, manumma*, etc.)

(Arabic *anna*) in later inscriptions introduces a quotation with the meaning "thus," "that"; e.g. (*Istar*) *ikbi-sunut umma* "Istar told them that."

Im "if" is frequently followed by *matima* ("in any case") with the indefinite pronoun ("any one") sometimes understood before the verb. Occasionally we find *im* omitted, and only *matima* used. In the Law-tablet we have *ana matima* in imitation of the Accadian original; *ana matima mut libbi-su ikhuśśu* "in every case a man has full power over his child."

The conditional particle (*ci* or *im*) is not unfrequently understood, though the enclitic -*ni* is generally added; e.g. *yutsu-ni ner-ya itsbut* "(when) he came out, he took my yoke." Even the conditional augment (*ni*) may be omitted; e.g. *sa lā agru'u-su igranni* "who (when) I did not make war with him made war with me."

In one passage *ci* seems to mean simply "then," "accordingly,"—*Umma-khaldāsu emuci-su cī yupakhkhir*, "Umma-khaldasu then gathered his forces."

Summa "thus" occasionally takes the place of *im*; e.g. *summa assatu mut-su . . . iktabi* "if a wife (to) her husband say" (literally "thus," with "if" omitted).

Yumu "day" may be used absolutely, without a preposition, with "when" (*sa*) following omitted; as *yumu annitu emuru* "the day he had seen that dream."

The preposition which denotes the instrument may also be omitted; as *katā ū sepā biritav barzilli iddi* "(his) hands and feet (in) fetters of iron he laid."

PROSODY.

The order of the sentence is most commonly subject, object, and verb at the end (as in Aramaic). But the object very frequently follows the verb, especially when it has a suffix, and sometimes even the subject. Often a noun with a preposition comes after the verb, but its usual place is after the object or subject. The genitive circumlocution with *sa* is in some few instances placed at the beginning of the sentence with the subject following. Conditional and relative words always begin the sentence. Relative sentences are usually intercalated between the subject or object and the verb. The pronoun *sunuti* or *sunut* regularly ends the clause.

A dislocated word like *isme-va* in *isme-va cisitti eri-su Cudur-Nakhundu nis Elamu imkut-su khattuv* " Kudur-Nakhundu the Elamite heard of the capture of his cities, and fear overwhelmed him," is due to the blunder of the illiterate engraver, who inserted the word in the wrong place.

The Assyrians, like other nations, had their poetry; but little of this has been preserved to us, the religious hymns which we possess being literal translations of Accadian originals.* From the following purely Assyrian specimen of psalmody, however, it will be seen that Assyrian poetry corresponds to Hebrew; it was characterized by the same parallelism, and affected the same play upon words.

FIRST STANZA.

(1) *Ilu Ussur bel 'a-ba-ri | sa su-par-su dan-nu-su*
(2) *ana Sarru-cinu sarra gasra | sar Assuri*
(3) *ner-ebid Babili | sar Sumiri u Accadi*
(4) *ba-nu-u cu-me-es | si-bu-ut padh-si-i'u*
(5) *lis-ba-a bu-h-a-ri.*

* Cf. Lenormant: "Essai de Commentaire des Fragments de Bérose," Frgt. xx.

O Ussur, lord of the wise, to whom (is) beauty (and) power [of whom (is) his beauty (and) his power],
For Sargon mighty king, king of Assyria,
High-Priest (yoke-servant) of Babylon, king of Sumiri and Accad,
Build thy store-house, the dwelling of his treasure,
    May he be sated with (its) beauties!

SECOND STANZA.

(1) *ina ci-riṡ Bit Ris-Sallimi | u Bit S'er-ra*
(2) *cin pal-su | cin-ni irtsiti su-te-si-ra*
(3) *sul-li-ma tsi-in-di-su | su-ut-lim-su s-mu-kan la-sa-na-an*
(4) *dun-nu zic-ru-ti | galli-su su-udh-bi-va*
    (5) *li-na-ar ga-ri-su.*

In the midst of the Temple of the Head of Peace and Bit-S'erra (*i.e.* in peace and good fortune)
Establish his course of life: the stability of the land direct;
Make perfect his harnessed horses; confer on him the powers of the world,
Even greatness (and) renown; his servants make good, and
    May he curse his foes!

Here the double parallelism is very exact. Notice, too, the lively change of subject, and the semi-rhyme at the end of each stanza. The play upon *cin* and *cinni* plainly refers to the name of *Sarru-cinu*.

Before concluding, it will be well to select one or two inscriptions for analytical translation.* The first that I shall take is an Invocation to Beltis (W.A.I., II. pl. 66, No. 2):—

I. (1) *A-na(el) Beltis bel-lat matāti*[1] *a-si-bat*[2] *Bit-Mas-mas* D.P. (*el*) *Assur-bani-'abla sar mat Assuri rubu pa-lukh-sa* (2) *ner-ebdu*[3] *bi-nu-ut*[4] *katā-sa*[5] *sa ina ci-be-ti-sa rabitav*[6] *ina kit-ru-ub*[7] *takh-kha-zi*[8]

I. (1) Ad Beltim dominam terrarum, habitantem Bit-Merodach, Assurbani-pal rex terrae Assyriae princeps adorans-eam (2) pontifex creatura manuum-ejus, qui secundum jussa-ejus magna in vicinitate praelii

* The figures in parentheses refer to the lines in the inscriptions; the superior figures refer to the analyses on pp. 175, 176, 177.

ic-ci-śu[9] (3) kakka-du[10] D.P. Teumman sar mat Nuv-va-(ci)[11] u D.P.
Um-man-i-gas D.P. Tam-ma-ri-tav
D.P. Pa-h-e D.P. Um-man-al-das
(4) sa arci D.P. Teumman ebu-su[12]
sarru-ut[13] mat Nuv-va-(ci) ina tu-
gulti-sa rabbi-tav ka-ti[14] acsud śu-
nu-ti-va (5) ina D.P. pidni[15] sadadi[16]
ru-du[17] sarru-ti-ya atsbat-śu-nu-ti
u ina zic-ri[18] sa cabtu-ti ina cul-lat
matati (6) illicu'u-va gab-ri ul isu'u
ina yumi-su cidal bit D.P. Istari
bellati-ya ina pi-e-li[19] es-ci[20] (7) si-
cit-ta-su[21] u-sar-bi' a-na sat-ti D.P.
Beltis cidala su-a-tav pan ma-khir-
si (8) uc-ci'[22] ya-a-ti D.P. Assur-
bani-abla pa-lakh[23] 'il-u-ti-ci raba-
ti baladh[24] yumi sadadi (9) dhub
lib-bi itti sim-ma itallacu Bit-Mas-
mas lu-lab-bi-ra sepā-ya.

decapitavit (3) caput Teummani
regis terræ Elamidis; et Umman-
igas Tammaritu Pahe Umman-
aldasim (4) qui post Teumman
fecerat regnum terræ Elamidis
auxilio ejus magno manu-meâ vici
eos, et (5) in jugo immenso curru
regali-meo cepi eos; et in famâ
gloriæ in omnibus terris (6) ive-
runt * et rivales non fuerunt. In
die-eâ aram templi Astartis dominæ-
meæ ex cælatione-laboratâ cœlavi
(7) sculpturam-ejus. Auxi (eam) ad
voluptatem Beltis. Aram hanc
ante præsentiam-ejus (8) sacravi.
Meipsum Sardanapalum adorantem
divinitatem - tuam magnam vita
dierum longarum, (9) bonitas cordis,
cum stabilitate consequuntur. Bit
Merodach diu-maneat sub-me.

I next select a short private contract of the year 676 B.C.
(W.A.I., III. 47, 5):—

II. (1) $\begin{Bmatrix} bilat \\ ticun \end{Bmatrix}$[1] eri saki[2] (2) sa
ana 'ilati Istari sa er 'Arb'-'il (3)
sa D.P. Man-nu-ci-'arb'-'il[3] (4) ina
pan D.P. Maruduc-akhe-sallim (5)
ina arkhi Ab id-dan-an[4] (6) sum-ma
la-a id-di-ni[5] (7) a-na III. ribata-
su-nu[6] i-rab-bi-'u (8) ina arkhi
S'ivan yumi XI. (9) lim-mu D.P.
Bam-ba-a (10) pan D.P. Istar-bab-
cam-es (11) pan D.P. Ku-u-a D.P.
Sarru-ikbi' (12) pan D.P. Dumku-
pan-sarri (13) pan D.P. Nabiuv-
rub-abli.

II. (1) Talenta ferri optimi, (2)
quæ (sunt) danda deæ Astarti urbis
Arbelæ, (3) quæ Mannu-ci-Arbela
(4) in præsentiâ Merodach-akhe-
sallim (5) in mense Ab (Julio)
tradit, (6) si non reddiderunt (ea)
(7) quadrantibus usuris augere-
faciunt. (8) In mense Maio die XI.
(9) eponymo Bambâ (10) teste
(ante) Istar-bab-cames (11) teste
Kûa (et) Sarru-ikbi (12) teste
Dumku-pan-sarri (13) teste Nebo-
rub-bal.

* The story of my conquest of them has become famous everywhere.

My next selection is Sennacherib's private will (W.A.I., III., 16, 3):—

III. (1) D.P. *S'in-akhi-er-ba sar cis-sa-ti*[1] (2) *sar mat As-suri esiri khuratsi tu-lat karni* (3) (*gil*) *khuratsi a-gi esiri itti sa-a-ti* (4) *du-ma-ki*[2] *an-nu-te sa tu-lat-su-nu* (5) *abna ibba ina abna (likh-khal) abna za-dhu*[3] | (6) I. (*bar*)[4] *ma-na* II. (*bar*) *sibi*[5] (*dhu*) *si sakal-su-nu*[6] (7) *ana* D.P. *Assur-akhi-iddin abla-ya sa arcu* (8) D.P. *Assur-ebil-mucin-'abla sum-su* (9) *na-bu-u ci-i ru-hi-a* (10) *a-din cisat-ta*[7] *Bit* D.P. *A-muk* (11) [D.P. ...]-*iriq-erba ca-nu-ur-a'-ni*[8] D.P. *Nabi*.

III. (1) Sennacherib rex legionum (2) rex terræ Assyriæ armillas æreas, cumulos eboria, (3) poculum (?) aureum, coronas (et) armillas eum his, (4) bonas-res illas, quarum (sunt) cumuli-earum, (5) crystallum præter lapidem ... (et) lapidem aviarium: (6) I. (et) dimidinm minorum, II. (et) dimidium *sibi* secundum pondus-eorum (7) Essarhaddoni filio-meo, qui postea (8) Assur-ehil-mucin-pal nomini ejus (9) nomi-natus est secundum voluntatem-meam, (10) dedi, thesaurum templi Amuki (11) (et) . . . iriq-erba, citharistarum (?) Nebonis.

ANALYSES.

I. [1] *bellat matâti;* status constructus, feminine plural in genitive (dependent) case: *l* doubled after *e* as in the verbs יפ״ע. *Matu* (= *madtu* for *medâtu*) is of Accadian origin, *ma-da* "country" or "people."

[2] *asibat;* feminine status constructus, nomen agentis, from אשב.

[3] *ner-ebdu;* literally "yoke-servant," an Accadian compound (*ninit* or *seccanacu*), in which the first character was probably non-phonetic.

[4] *binût* from בנה, abstract feminine singular, status constructus.

[5] *katâ*, dual from *katu*, probably from לקח. *Kat* or *kattakh*, however, signified "hand" in Accadian, as well as *id*, which has lost the initial guttural. Comp. Talmud. קתא "handle" (like יד החרב).

[6] *rabitav*, feminine of *rabu*, with mimmation.

[7] *kitrub*, form *sitcun*, nomen permanentis of Iphteal from קרב.

[8] *takhkhazi*, also written *tukhazi*, for *tamkhazi*, nomen permanentis of Tiphel from מחץ, Heb. מחץ.

[9] *iccisu*, third person singular Perfect of נכס. Here the Pluperfect sense is almost lost.

[10] *kakkadu*, Hebrew קדקד. Assyrian assimilates the second radical to the first in Palpel, giving us instead Pappel or Papel: so *caccabu* "star."

¹¹ *Num* in Accadian meant "high" (Elamite *khapar*), translated by the Semitic *elamu* from עלה (עלו).

¹² *ebusu* or *epusu*, third singular Pluperfect after the relative. Schrader compares عبس ("to be strong").

¹³ *sarrut* or *šarrut*, abstract singular, status constructus, from שׂרר or סרר.

¹⁴ *kat-i* "my hand."

¹⁵ *iz-sa* (Accadian) is explained *pidnu*. Literally the Accadian would be "wood-work."

¹⁶ *sadadu* in Accadian is *bu* or *bu-da* "long." Mr. Smith translates "war-chariot." Compare Arabic *sadāʻ*.

¹⁷ *rudu* from ירד. *Sarruti-ya* is in apposition.

¹⁸ *zicru* form *sicin*.

¹⁹ *pelu* from פעל, passive participle, like *nibu* or *nebu* (of concave verbs) "worked" so "choice."

²⁰ *esciʻ* is of uncertain meaning. It ought to be a quadriliteral אשכה, but is more probably a Babylonian form (*e* for *a*, like Hebrew Niphal Imperative) from שׂכה.

²¹ *sicitta*, accusative for *sicinta* from שׂכן, literally "that which is made."

²² *ucciʻ* singular aorist of נכה, "strike down," in the sense of "found" (so נכה שׁרשׁ).

²³ *palakh* (and *palukh* above), nomen permanentis in status constructus, from the same root as *pulukhtu* "fear."

²⁴ *baladh*, or in Assyrian generally *paladh*, = פלט. It often happens that a root which in early Assyrian has initial *p*, but in Babylonian (and frequently in later Assyrian also) *b*, answers to a Hebrew radical with פ ; so *bakharu* or *pakharu* is פחר.

II. ¹ *ticun* was apparently the Accadian word, for which Assyrian substituted *biltu*, *bilat*, from יבל.

² *saku* was a Turanian loan-word, *sak* in Accadian being "head," "high." Hence also *sakummatu* "highlands."

³ *Mannu-ci-Arbʻil* "who (is) like Arbela," though *ci* may be *itti* "with." *Maruduc-akhe-sallim* "Merodach pacifies brothers," *sallim* being third singular Permansive.

⁴ *iddanan*, third singular Present Palel of *nadanu*.

⁵ *iddini*, for *iddinu*, is an instance of the vulgar pronunciation. It shows the same tendency as that which changed *-ūnuv* to *-ūniv*.

⁶ *ribata*, literally "increase," like Kal Present *irabbi'u*. We find besides 2 per cent., 4 per cent., etc. The Accadian is *śu*.

III. ¹ *cissāti*, plural genitive of *cissatu*, *cistu*, masculine *cissu*; Targumic כנש (Hebrew כנס), *n* being assimilated before *s* in Assyrian (see p. 31).

² *dumaki* plural of form *sucan*, generally *dumki* (*dumku*), "good fortune," etc.: also *dumuku*.

³ *abnu zadhu* is explained in a syllabary to be '*abn itstsuri* "birdstone."

⁴ *baru* "half," was probably so sounded in Assyrian; but it was a loan-word from the Accadians, in whose language *bar*="another," "second."

⁵ *cibi* is written *dhu*, which is explained to be *cibu*. This has no connexion with the Hebrew *kab*, but denotes "body," or "mass," from כבה, as in *cibe littūti* "heap of tributes," *cibu* "the person" (of a man), *cibe śiparri* "masses of copper."

⁶ For *sakal* we have the Accadian equivalent *lal* written (as an ideograph).

⁷ *cisatta* for *cisadta*.

⁸ *canurāni*, plural of *canuru*, which may be connected with כנור, form *sacun*. For the case-ending before the genitive, see p. 147.

The Latin translations given above are intended to answer to the Assyrian word for word. I subjoin an English version:—

(I.) To Beltis, queen of the world, dwelling in Bit-Merodach, Assur-bani-pal, king of Assyria, the prince who worships her, the high-priest, the creation of her hands, who, according to her high bidding in the meeting of battle, has cut off the head of Teumman, King of Elam; and Umman-igas, Tammaritu, Pahe, and Umman-aldas, who after Teumman received the kingdom of Elam, by her powerful help I conquered, and in the mighty yoke of my royal chariot I captured; and my conquest of them has become famous in all lands, for they had no equals. At that time, I carved the sculptured work of the altar of the temple of Istar with choice carvings. I made it great for the pleasure of Beltis. This altar I dedicated before her. As for me, Assur-bani-pal, the worshipper of thy mighty divinity, a life of long days, goodness of heart and stability are coming upon me. May Bit-Merodach last long under me.

(II.) Talents of the best iron, for Istar of Arbela, which Mannu-ci-Arbela in the presence of Merodach-akhe-sallim, in the month Ab, hands over, shall be lent at three per cent., unless they are given back. The 11th day of the month Sivan, during the eponymy of Bamba, in the presence of Istar-bab-cames, Kua, Surru-ikbi, Dumku-pan-sarri, and Nebo-rub-bal.

(III.) I, Sennacherib, king of multitudes, king of Assyria, have given chains of gold, heaps of ivory, a *cup* of gold, crowns and chains with them, all the riches, of which there are heaps, crystal and another precious stone, and bird's stone : one and a half manehs, two and a half *cibi* according to their weight: to Essar-haddon my son, who was afterwards named Assur-ebil-mucin-pal, according to my wish : the treasure of the temple of Amuk and . . . iriq-erba, the *harpists* of Nebo.

ADDITIONS AND CORRECTIONS.

Page 3, line 19. According to Abul-Faraj (p. 18, ed. Pococke), Shinar "is Sāmarrah," and Sāmīrūs, king of Chaldæa in the time of Serug, invented weights and measures, weaving and dyeing. The change of *m* into *ng* is paralleled by the Accadian *dimir* "god," which is also found under the form *dingir*. Otherwise a nearer explanation would be *sana-'uru* "the four cities." The Cassi, I now find, were not identical with the Sumiri or people "of the dog's language," who lived in Babylonia from immemorial times, but were an Elamite tribe, who conquered Babylonia under Khammurabi in the sixteenth (?) century B.C.

P. 4, l. 5. Later Assyrian itself shows the same interchange of *k* and *g*, as in *gadistu* in the Law-tablet by the side of *kadistu* ("sanctuary").

P. 4. Older Babylonian, especially in the vulgar dialect, presents many peculiar forms. Thus *ś* is preferred to *s*, as in *yuśannu'* "he changed"; *m* becomes *n*, as in *sun-sunu* for *sum-sunu* "their name"; the possessive pronoun *ni* "our" appears as *na*, as in *S'amśu-ilu-na; ina mukhkhi* is regularly used for the preposition *ina eli;* and we even find such corrupt forms as *baśurri* (W.A.I. iii., 43, 16) "flesh" for *biśru*, and the ungrammatical *liseli* and *lisetsbit* (iii. 43, 20, 31) instead of *luseli* and *lusatsbit* or *lusatsbat*.

P. 5, l. 7. *Birid* was not a new word, but goes back to the oldest period of the language. My mistake was caused by a hasty recollection of Norris's Dict., p. 102. In place of it, read *zilluv* (*iz-mi*) "grace," "favour." In the Persian period, we also find a final -*h* added to the third person plural of the verb, like quiescent ا in Arabic (though this is sometimes met with in the vulgar Assyrian of the contract-tablets). *Ittur* has assumed the general sense of "became," and the plural *itturunu* is an instance of the old final vowel of the third person plural, which was generally weakened to *i*.

P. 8, note 10. Change *kamets* before ה into *pathakh*.

P. 9, note 15. See a paper of mine on "The Origin of Semitic Civilization, chiefly upon Philological Evidence," in the *Transactions* of the Society of Biblical Archæology, vol. i., part 2.

P. 10, note 17. M. Neubauer informs me that in Babylonian Hebrew ר is doubled just as in Assyrian.

After "Assyrian has but one example of the substitution of *n* for the reduplication of a letter," add, "except in verbal forms." Here we not unfrequently meet with instances like *innindu* for *inniddu*, Niphal of נדה; see p. 31.

P. 13, note 23. Dr. Haug ("Old Pahlavi-Pazand Glossary," p. 53) connects the Assyrian adverbial ending with the Aramaic -*dit*, Syriac -(*ó*)*it*, which forms adverbs from substantives, adjectives, and past participles, as well as with the Hebrew ארמית. But phonology alone would exclude this explanation.

P. 14, note 26. It is not quite accurate to say that "all the older kings have Turanian names." This is not the case with Naram-Sin, or Samśu-iluna, a contemporary of Khammurabi (unless he is to be identified with the latter king), but their names admit of a sufficient explanation (p. 13). See a good paper by Mr. G. Smith on the "Early History of Babylonia," in the *Transactions* of the Society of Biblical Archæology, vol. i., part 1.

P. 15, note 29. We may add the tendency of *a* to become *i* in forms through the medium of *e*, as in *innindu* for *innandu*, and the intermixture of the Perfect-termination with the Augment of Motion, e.g. *yubta'uni*.

P. 15, note 31. Other peculiarities will be the uncertainty of gender, as in the plural *makarut* ("a measure") by the side of *makarrāt* (for *makárāt*), or *caśaptu* instead of *caśpu* ("silver").

P. 17. The same disregard of gender in the verb occurs in the Assyrian translation of a legendary account of the famous Accadian king Sargina (W.A.I. iii., 4, 7), which must be ascribed to the age of Assur-bani-pal. So upon the principle that grammatical forms get shortened, not lengthened, with the wearing of time, דִּאֵל must be later than the longer form.

P. 20. Add letters by Rawlinson, Hincks, and others in the *Athenæum*: Aug. 23, 1851 (Rawl.); Sept. 6, 1851, Sept. 20, 1851, Oct. 25, 1851, Dec. 27, 1851, Jan. 3, 1852 (Hincks); Aug. 18, 1860 (Rawl.); March 8, 1862 (Rawl.); May 31, 1862 (Rawl., first announcement of the discovery of the Assyrian Canon); July 19, 1862 (Rawl. on the Canon); July 5, 1862 (Hincks); Sept. 20, 1862 (Ménant, on Khammurabi's Inscrip.); Jan 24, 1863 (Fox Talbot); Feb. 14, 1863 (Rawl. on Taylor's Discoveries); Aug. 22, 1863 (Rawl., Early Hist., etc.); Oct. 24, 1863 (Hincks); March 18, 1867 (Rawl., Verification of Canon by eclipse); Sept. 7, 1867 (Rawl., Assyrian Calculation of Time); Oct. 18, 1868 (G. Smith, Protochaldæan Chronology); Nov. 7, 1868 (Smith); Nov. 14, 1868 (Sayce, Assyrian Poetry), Nov. 21, 1868 (Sayce), May 29, 1869 (Sayce, the Law-tablet); June 12, 1869 (Smith), June 19, 1869 (Smith), July 17, 1869 (Smith). *Journal* of Royal Asiatic Society, 1851, xiv. part 1 (Rawl. "Analysis of Babylonian Text at Behistun"); 1854, xvi. 1

(Norris, "Assyrian and Babylonian Weights and Measures"); 1855, xv. 2 (Rawl., "Notes on Hist. of Babylonia," "Orthography of some Assyrian Names"); 1860, xvii. 2 (Rawl. "Memoir on the Birs Nimrud"); 1860, xviii. 1 (Fox Talbot, "Translation of Assyrian Texts," Inscriptions of Birs Nimrud, Michaux, Bellino; (1861, xix. 2) Of Sennacherib, Nebuchadnezzar (at Senkereh), and Nabonidus; (1862, xix. 3) Of Naksh-i-Rustam; (1863, xx. 3, 4) Of Khammurabi; (1861, xix. 1) Of Broken Obelisk). *Transactions* of Society of Biblical Archæology, 1872, vol. i. part 1 : Smith, "Early Hist. of Babylonia" (important); Fox Talbot, "On an Ancient Eclipse," "On the Religious Belief of the Assyrians." Ménant on Oppert's Translations of Astrological and Portent Tablets, and Identification of the Stars, in *Journal Asiatique*, 1871, xviii. 67 (valuable and acute). Criticism of Smith's Syllabary and Assur-bani-pal by Oppert in *Journal Asiatique*, Jan. 1872, xix. 68 (already reviewed in the *Academy*, Nov. 15th, 1871). F. Lenormant, "Essai sur un Monument Mathématique Chaldéen, et sur le Système Métrique de Bab.," Paris, 1868; "Manual of the Ancient History of the East" (Engl. Edit.), vol. i., 1869; "Essai de Commentaire des Fragments de Bérose," 1872.

P. 25, note. Owing to ill-health, Mr. Smith was unable to make his Syllabary so complete as he wished. The following values may be added: 1. *kharra=samu*; 3. *essu*; 4. *citamma*; 6. *idin, belu*; 8b. *dudu*; 10. *cuda, se, gudibir=Maruduc*; 12. *gita*; 15. *nurma, cuśśu, khalacu*; 30b. *duddhu*; 30k. *śiśi, śidi*; 43. *laluruv*; 44. *turi*; 45. *gu, ni, râru, illu*; 48. *śa*; 50. *humis*; 53. *essit*; 70. *dara*; 73. *tiśkhu=ramcuti*; 76. *la, nindanu*; 88. *masadu*; 92. *malu'u*; 93. *mas*; 99. *rabdu*; 102. *ilba*; 108. *ginû, gâgunû=padanu, khaśaśu*; 112. *dhúcus, nila, mutstsa*; 118. *sana*; 135. *dü*; 136. *khibis, ginna=*

muniru; 143. *ul, nakbu;* 146. *summa;* 147. *siris;* 152. *calu,*
nasasu; 155. *urugal, mitu;* 158o. *alal=alalluv;* 159. *khut, cun=
napiaru;* 159c. *luga;* 164. *sun, lukh;* 166. *alittu, natsabu sa
etsi;* 169. *gut, khar, dapara;* 179. *pil, napakhu;* 180. *gi;*
182. *guk;* 182b. *garru, mandinu;* 187. *nadalu, etsibu, sanin,
rada, takh;* 188. *iztáti;* 191. *garru;* 192. *ugudili;* 200.
galam, galum; 201. *sem, sámu;* 203. *khur, zarakhu, calu, atsu
sa etsi u kani;* 208. *gá;* 209. *tsalam;* 212. *lugur, cū;* 215.
zak, tami; 217. *udessu;* 224. *a=dilte;* 226. *idgal;* 229.
bisseba, alala, alam=tsalamu; 232. *balag=balangu;* 237. *pakh,
rar, lib;* 238. *sana, niga=marū;* 239. *sus, nasakhu, sepus=
napakhu, Damcina;* 240. *esu;* 241. *mus;* 242. *tsir;* 246. *suplu,
mikhiltu;* 247. *igū;* 253. *náku;* 254b. *sagalum;* 255. *cizlukh
=mascanu;* 255h. *canlab;* 262. *arik, nē;* 266. *enuv, garru,
samu;* 270. *cacabu;* 272. *dim, idinnu;* 273. *sita;* 280. *ugun
=akhzētu;* 282. *pusur=samsu;* 293. *sarru, napiaru sa tammi;*
303. *khá, id, sar, cissat same;* 305. *kham;* 307. *ur;* 307c.
urus=tirtuv; 309. *lammubi;* 311. *sukh;* 318. *ga, náku;* 318f.
ara; 318h. *ir=calū naccal;* 324. *garru, sēmu;* 338d. *pusu;*
339. *girim, gil, mik;* 348. *gur;* 352. *illammi;* 354. *ligittu,
daruv=izkhu, sa issik icribi;* 355. *garru, acalu;* 355b. *khartsu;*
356. *amaru;* 359. *halacu;* 360. *rak;* 362. *ni;* 367. *sikhapcu;*
371. *khīsu;* 373. *cistu;* 377. *isi, sulsa;* 368. *sutul.* Several
characters have been omitted altogether, whose powers are
for the most part known. It would have added to the value
of the Syllabary had the meanings been attached wherever
possible.

P. 26, l. 5. Add:—The division of words sometimes takes
place without being marked by the writing, when the second
word begins with a vowel; especially if the first word is in
the *status constructus,* or is a shortened preposition, as in
adussi for *ad'ussi* " to the foundations"; *matturru* for *mat'urru*

"land of light" or "morning" (W.A.I., ii. 39, 13); *igidibbu* for *igid-ibbu* "it joins phrases" (according to Norris). Assyrian very seldom divides a word at the end of a line; now and then, however, we find a vocable not ending with the line (*e.g.* Layard 70, 3, 13).

P. 29. A good example at once of the loss of *kh* in Assyrian, and of the confusion between *m* and *v*, is *lamu* "a tablet," the Hebrew לוּחַ.

P. 29. This derivation of *katu* is due to Dr. Hincks. Many reasons, however, would rather point to an Accadian origin. Talmudic Hebrew uses קתא in the sense of "handle" (e.g. קתא הֲחַרְבָּא, like יד הֲחרב). From *katu* comes the feminine adjective *katitu*, as in *daltu la katitu* "a door without handles," by which *arcabinnu* is explained.

P. 30. *Kinnatu* "a female slave" is probably from קנה "to buy," like Talmudic בירי "slave" from ביר "to sell," according to conjecture. (Neubauer, "La Géographie du Talmud," p. 306.)

P. 31. Other similarities between Assyrian and Babylonian (Talmudic) Hebrew (as might be expected) may be pointed out. Thus like *nadinu* instead of נתן we have נדוניא "gift," quoted by Harkavy, who also notices that in the Targum (Ex. v. 7, 12, etc.) גבב="to unite," like the Assyrian *gabbu* "all" (so in the Talmud הַמְגַבֵּב "he who amasses"). The Assyrian *lamassu*, again, derived from the Accadian *lamma* or *lamaś* "colossus," seems to reappear in Rabbinic למם, and the Rabbinic וְשֶׁט "gullet" finds its analogue in the Assyrian *essdhu* (W.A.I., ii. 17, 20).

P. 34. The sharper pronunciation of *s* may have been due to Turanian influence. The earliest specimens of Babylonian Semitic write *S'amśu*.

P. 34, l. 4. Read כרסא.

P. 47, l. 19. Read *annute—annute.*

P. 50, l. 22. For S read I.

P. 50. Add:—The conjugation Niphael, which stands by the side of Shaphael, is an evidence of the artificial regularity introduced by the Assyrians into their verbal system. Niphael is mostly found in verbs whose last radical is a vowel (p. 94). But Dr. Oppert quotes also *nagarrur* and *nasallul* in the strong verb (see p. 78).

P. 51. A good instance of the aorist of the Shaphel Passive occurs in W.A.I., iii., 38, 56, where we have *yussupulu* for *yusasupulu* "(which) had been caused to be overthrown."

P. 53. The Future often takes the form *icattamu* or *icatamu* "he shall cover," from the analogy of the derived conjugations. Vulgar Babylonian actually presents us with the form *inassukhu* "he shall take away" (W.A.I., iii. 41, 11).

P. 61. l. 22. After "never the initial syllable," add: "when this expressed the force of the root."

P. 63, l. 28. For F read A.

P. 67, l. 18. *Atani* is not "wild-ass," but a river-bird, also called *cumu'u* like the *appunnu* (W.A.I., ii. 37, 55). The Accadian name seems to mean "blue rump." *Appunnu* may be compared with the Biblical אֲנָפָה, which the Targum of Jerusalem renders אבניתא.

P. 69. *Yucin, yuca'an* might be Aphel; but as the other Assyrian forms are Pael, *yucin* must be for *yuccin*, the ordinary Pael form. The late Dr. Hincks denied the existence of an Aphel in Assyrian altogether; but without good reason.

P. 80, l. 5. For Iphtaneal read Iphtanaal.

P. 94. Similarly the Hebrew עָנָה appears as עָנוּ on the Moabite Stone.

P. 98. The forms *-annini, -nini,* for the First Personal

Pronoun Suffix are given upon the authority of Dr. Oppert. I do not recollect having found them in the inscriptions.

P. 108. Add the instance of a Shaphel Passive from verbs פ׳א, which we find in *susuptu* "a royal throne," given as a synonyme of *napalsukhtu*.

P. 109. Quadriliterals admit of an inserted dental after the second radical: thus *tsimtaru* or *tsivtaru* "a spirit of the neck" (צואר).

P. 110. Since תגמול is a Piel Infinitive, it would be more nearly represented by the Arabic forms *taktâl, taktîl*, etc. We may compare the Æthiopic *ta'agaḥ* "robber," *tasâlâkî* "abuser," and the Hebrew תּוֹשָׁב or Aramaic תַּלְמִיד, from which Ewald would deduce the original personal use of the formation with ת.

P. 111. A few strange forms terminating in *â* from weak roots are found. Thus we have *mali'â* "fullness" as nominative in the syllabaries, and *imri'â* "family" (but sometimes "my family") in the contract-inscriptions. The form is generally used in the *status constructus*. It may be Aramaising, or it may be due to the influence of Accadian, where the participle was distinguished by final *â*. *Daru* "name" —a word originally borrowed from the Accadian—appears as *dâri'â* in the Accadian (W.A.I., ii., 33, 71).

P. 112. I have forgotten to speak of Compounds in Assyrian. These are rare, as in the other Semitic languages; but we meet with *bin-binu* and *lib-libbu* "grandson." These examples will show that the first part of the Compound took the form of the Construct; the second part, however, had the nominative, not the genitive, ending. See pp. 148, 165.

P. 113. Another instructive instance is the root ירק "green," "yellow" in W.A.I. ii., 26, 50, where we have *arku, rakraku, 'urriku, urik*, and *urcitu*, besides the Accadian *ara*.

P. 140. M. Neubauer has pointed out to me that a second Nisan and a second Elul are mentioned in the Talmud.

P. 140. Another measure of capacity was the *makaru*, with a double plural *makarut* (masculine) and *makarrat* (feminine). We find 100 *makarrat* of barley in a contract-tablet. Comp. Hebrew קְעָרָה or קוּר "to dig out," like כֹּר and קַב.

The Accadian name of the *lagitu* or *ligittu* was *ib*.

According to Dr. Oppert, the *ka* was a determinative prefix of measure.

According to M. Lenormant, the *kakkar* or "Equator" (but see W.A.I. iii., 51, 18) was divided into 12 *kasbi*, each containing 60 degrees (*daragi* or *dargatu*), again subdivided into 60 *sussi* or "minutes."

P. 143. I would now connect *lamu* with Hebrew לוּחַ not with לוֹהַ; see above.

P. 144. Add *akhennû* "on the other side," *akhamis* "with one another."

P. 157. Traces of a feminine in the Third Person of the Precative are, however, found in the Vulgar Babylonian: e.g. *liparrici* "may she (Papśucul) break" (W.A.I. iii., 43, 27), where the vowel of the first syllable is to be noticed (see p. 179).

P. 160. In a paper read before the Society of Biblical Archæology, April 2nd, 1872, Mr. Cull sought to connect *basu*, *kabu*, and *isu*, respectively with the Hebrew חָוָה, הָוָה, and יֵשׁ.

P. 166. The myth of the Babylonian Sargon contains a good example of the use of *ana* to express the object, where we read *Acci nis-abal ana maruti yurabba-nni Acci nis-abal ana pakid-ciri iscun-anni*, "Acci the *abal* reared me to youth; Acci the *abal* made me the woods-superintendent."

Since the foregoing was sent to the press, I have been permitted, through the great kindness of Dr. Haigh, to see the MS. notes made by the late Dr. Hincks in a copy of Dr. Oppert's Grammar (1st edit.). Dr. Hincks draws attention to the fact that *kh* in Assyrian was sometimes so strong as to approach *o* in sound, *iptakhid* being sometimes written *iptaoid*. We may compare the Hebrew שָׁחֹר by the side of the Arabic شكد, or the interchange of *kh* and *hh* with *o* in Æthiopic, as in *wacaya* and *wakhaya* "to shine," *zĕcyr* and *zĕkhyr* "memorial." Dr. Hincks gives the following list of Assyrian Ordinal Numbers: *makhru* "first," *sannu* (fem. *sanutu*) "second" (*nn* for *nw* or *ny*), *salsu* (fem. *salistu* "third," *rib'u* (fem. *rib'atu*) "fourth," *khansu* (fem. *khamistu*) "fifth," *sib'u* (fem. *sib'utu*) "seventh," and by analogy *sidu*, *siditu* "sixth," *simanu*, *simattu* "eighth," *esru*, *esritu* "tenth." He makes *sunnu*, *rub'u*, etc., collectives, "a pair," etc.; and this is certainly one of the uses of *sunnu*, pl. *sunne*. He adds another conjugation, "of which the 1st Aorist is '*upekil*," e.g. *usepic* from שָׁפַךְ, *unecis* from נכם. Considering, however, the interchange of *e* with *i* on the one hand, and *a* on the other, this seems a needless refinement (see p. 79). The following list of concave verbs in which *t* in Iphteal precedes the root is also given: דוך "to kill," בוא "to go," איב "to be an enemy," דין "to judge," כון "to be sure," מות "to die," תור "to be," and טוב "to be good."

THE END.

STEPHEN AUSTIN AND SONS, PRINTERS, HERTFORD.

LINGUISTIC PUBLICATIONS

OF

TRÜBNER & CO.,

8 AND 60, PATERNOSTER ROW, LONDON, E.C.

Ahlwardt.—THE DIVÁNS OF THE SIX ANCIENT ARABIC POETS, Ennábiga, 'Antara, Tarafa, Zuhair, 'Algama, and Imruolqais; chiefly according to the MSS. of Paris, Gotha, and Leyden, and the collection of their Fragments: with a complete list of the various readings of the Text. Edited by W. AHLWARDT, Professor of Oriental Languages at the University of Geifswald. 8vo. pp. xxx. 340, sewed. 1870. 12s.

Alabaster.—THE WHEEL OF THE LAW: Buddhism illustrated from Siamese Sources by the Modern Buddhist, a Life of Buddha, and an account of the Phra Bat. By HENRY ALABASTER, Esq., Interpreter of Her Majesty's Consulate-General in Siam; Member of the Royal Asiatic Society. Demy 8vo. pp. lviii. and 324. 1871. 14s.

Alcock.—A PRACTICAL GRAMMAR of the JAPANESE LANGUAGE. By Sir RUTHERFORD ALCOCK, Resident British Minister at Jeddo. 4to. pp. 61, sewed. 18s.

Alcock.—FAMILIAR DIALOGUES in JAPANESE, with English and French Translations, for the use of Students. By Sir RUTHERFORD ALCOCK. 8vo. pp. viii. and 40, sewed. Paris and London, 1863. 5s.

Alger.—THE POETRY OF THE ORIENT. By WILLIAM ROUNSEVILLE ALGER, 8vo. cloth, pp. xii. and 337. 9s.

Alif Lailat wa Lailat.—THE ARABIAN NIGHTS. 4 vols. 4to. pp. 495, 493, 442, 434. Cairo, A.H. 1279 (1862). £2 2s.

This celebrated Edition of the Arabian Nights is now, for the first time, offered at a price which makes it accessible to Scholars of limited means.

Andrews.—A DICTIONARY OF THE HAWAIIAN LANGUAGE, to which is appended an English-Hawaiian Vocabulary, and a Chronological Table of Remarkable Events. By LORRIN ANDREWS. 8vo. pp. 560, cloth. £1 11s. 6d.

Arabic, Persian, and Turkish Books (A Catalogue of). Printed in the East. Constantly for sale by Trübner and Co., 8 and 60, Paternoster Row, London. CONTENTS.—Arabic, Persian, and Turkish Books printed in Egypt.—Arabic Books printed in Oudh.—Persian Literature printed in Oudh.—Editions of the Koran printed in Oudh.—Arabic Books printed at Bombay.—Persian Books printed at Bombay.—Arabic Literature printed at Tunis.—Arabic Literature printed in Syria. 16mo. pp. 68. Price 1s.

Asher.—ON THE STUDY OF MODERN LANGUAGES IN GENERAL, and of the English Language in particular. An Essay. By DAVID ASHER, Ph.D. 12mo. pp. viii. and 80, cloth. 2s.

Asiatic Society.—JOURNAL OF THE ROYAL ASIATIC SOCIETY OF GREAT BRITAIN AND IRELAND, from the Commencement to 1863. First Series, complete in 20 Vols. 8vo., with many Plates. Price £10; or, in Single Numbers, as follows:—Nos. 1 to 14, 6s. each; No. 15, 2 Parts, 4s. each; No. 16, 2 Parts, 4s. each; No. 17, 2 Parts, 4s. each; No. 18, 6s. These 18 Numbers form Vols. I. to IX.—Vol. X., Part 1, op.; Part 2, 5s.; Part 3, 5s.—Vol. XI., Part 1, 6s.; Part 2 not published.—Vol. XII., 2 Parts, 6s. each.—Vol. XIII., 2 Parts, 6s. each.—Vol. XIV., Part 1, 5s.; Part 2 not published.—Vol. XV., Part 1, 6s.; Part 2, with Maps, 10s.—Vol. XVI., 2 Parts, 6s. each.—Vol. XVII., 2 Parts, 6s. each.—Vol. XVIII., 2 Parts, 6s. each.—Vol. XIX., Parts 1 to 4, 16s.—Vol. XX., 3 Parts, 4s. each.

Asiatic Society.—JOURNAL OF THE ROYAL ASIATIC SOCIETY OF GREAT BRITAIN AND IRELAND. *New Series.* Vol. I. In Two Parts. pp. iv. and 490. Price 16s.

CONTENTS.—I. Vajra-chhedikā, the "Kin Kong King," or Diamond Sūtra. Translated from the Chinese by the Rev. S. Beal, Chaplain, R.N.—II. The Páramitá-hridaya Sútra, or, in Chinese, "Mo ho-pô-ye-po-lo-mih-to-sin-king," *i.e.* "The Great Páramitá Heart Sútra." Translated from the Chinese by the Rev. S. Beal, Chaplain, R.N.—III. On the Preservation of National Literature in the East. By Colonel F. J. Goldsmid.—IV. On the Agricultural, Commercial, Financial, and Military Statistics of Ceylon. By E. R. Power, Esq.—V. Contributions to a Knowledge of the Vedic Theogony and Mythology. By J. Muir, D.C.L., LL.D.—VI. A Tabular List of Original Works and Translations, published by the late Dutch Government of Ceylon at their Printing Press at Colombo. Compiled by Mr. Mat. P. J. Ondaatje, of Colombo.—VII. Assyrian and Hebrew Chronology compared, with a view of showing the extent to which the Hebrew Chronology of Ussher must be modified, in conformity with the Assyrian Canon. By J. W. Bosanquet, Esq.—VIII. On the existing Dictionaries of the Malay Language. By Dr. H. N. van der Tuuk.—IX. Bilingual Readings: Cuneiform and Phœnician. Notes on some Tablets in the British Museum, containing Bilingual Legends (Assyrian and Phœnician). By Major-General Sir H. Rawlinson, K.C.B., Director R.A.S.—X. Translations of Three Copper-plate Inscriptions of the Fourth Century A.D., and Notices of the Châlukya and Gurjjara Dynasties. By Professor J. Dowson, Staff College, Sandhurst.—XI. Yama and the Doctrine of a Future Life, according to the Rig-Yajur-, and Atharva-Vedas. By J. Muir, Esq., D.C.L., LL.D.—XII. On the Jyotisha Observation of the Place of the Colures, and the Date derivable from it. By William D. Whitney, Esq., Professor of Sanskrit in Yale College, New Haven, U.S.—Note on the preceding Article. By Sir Edward Colebrooke, Bart., M.P., President R.A.S.—XIII. Progress of the Vedic Religion towards Abstract Conceptions of the Deity. By J. Muir, Esq., D.C.L., LL.D.—XIV. Brief Notes on the Age and Authenticity of the Work of Aryabhata, Varáhamihira, Brahmagupta, Bhuttotpala, and Bhâskarâchârya. By Dr. Bháu Dájí, Honorary Member R.A.S.—XV. Outlines of a Grammar of the Malagasy Language. By H. N. Van der Tuuk.—XVI. On the Identity of Xandrames and Krananda. By Edward Thomas, Esq.

Vol. II. In Two Parts. pp. 522. Price, 16s.

CONTENTS.—I. Contributions to a Knowledge of Vedic Theogony and Mythology. No. 2. By J. Muir, Esq.—II. Miscellaneous Hymns from the Rig- and Atharva-Vedas. By J. Muir, Esq.—III. Five hundred questions on the Social Condition of the Natives of Bengal. By the Rev. J. Long.—IV. Short account of the Malay Manuscripts belonging to the Royal Asiatic Society. By Dr. H. N. van der Tuuk.—V. Translation of the Amitábha Sútra from the Chinese. By the Rev. S. Beal, Chaplain Royal Navy.—VI. The initial coinage of Bengal. By Edward Thomas, Esq.—VII. Specimens of an Assyrian Dictionary. By Edwin Norris, Esq.—VIII. On the Relations of the Priests to the other classes of Indian Society in the Vedic age. By J. Muir, Esq.—IX. On the Interpretation of the Veda. By the same.—X. An attempt to Translate from the Chinese a work known as the Confessional Services of the great compassionate Kwan Yin, possessing 1000 hands and 1000 eyes. By the Rev. S. Beal, Chaplain Royal Navy.—XI. The Hymns of the Gaupáyanas and the Legend of King Asamáti. By Professor Max Müller, M.A., Honorary Member Royal Asiatic Society.—XII. Specimen Chapters of an Assyrian Grammar. By the Rev. E. Hincks, D.D., Honorary Member Royal Asiatic Society.

Vol. III. In Two Parts. pp. 516. With Photograph. 22s.

CONTENTS.—I. Contributions towards a Glossary of the Assyrian Language. By H. F. Talbot.—II. Remarks on the Indo-Chinese Alphabets. By Dr. A. Bastian.—III. The poetry of Mohamed Rabadan, Arragonese. By the Hon. H. E. J. Stanley.—IV. Catalogue of the Oriental Manuscripts in the Library of King's College, Cambridge. By Edward Henry Palmer, B.A., Scholar of St. John's College, Cambridge; Member of the Royal Asiatic Society; Membre de la Société Asiatique de Paris.—V. Description of the Amravati Tope in Guntur. By J. Fergusson, Esq., F.R.S.—VI. Remarks on Prof. Brockhaus' edition of the Kathâsarit-sâgara, Lambaka IX. XVIII. By Dr. H. Kern, Professor of Sanskrit in the University of Leyden.—VII. The source of Colebrooke's Essay "On the Duties of a Faithful Hindu Widow." By Fitzedward Hall, Esq., M.A., D.C.L. Oxon. Supplement: Further detail of proofs that Colebrooke's Essay, "On the Duties of a Faithful Hindu Widow," was not indebted to the Vivâdabhangârnava. By Fitzedward Hall, Esq.—VIII. The Sixth Hymn of the First Book of the Rig Veda. By Professor Max Müller, M.A., Hon. M.R.A.S.—IX. Sassanian Inscriptions. By E. Thomas, Esq.—X. Account of an Embassy from Morocco to Spain in 1690 and 1691. By the Hon. H. E. J. Stanley.—XI. The Poetry of Mohamed Rabadun, of Arragon. By the Hon. H. E. J. Stanley.—XII. Materials for the History of India for the Six Hundred Years of Mohammadan rule, previous to the Foundation of the British Indian Empire. By Major W. Nassau Lees, LL.D., Ph.D.—XIII. A Few Words concerning the Hill people inhabiting the Forests of the Cochin State. By Captain G. E. Fryer, Madras Staff Corps, M.R.A.S.—XIV. Notes on the Bhojpuri Dialect of Hindi, spoken in Western Behar. By John Beames, Esq., B.C.S., Magistrate of Chumparun.

Vol. IV. In Two Parts. pp. 521. 16s.

CONTENTS.—I. Contribution towards a Glossary of the Assyrian Language. By H. F. Talbot. Part II.—II. On Indian Chronology. By J. Fergusson, Esq., F.R.S.—III. The Poetry of Mohamed Rabadan of Arragon. By the Hon. H. E. J. Stanley.—IV. On the Magar Language of Nepal. By John Beames, Esq., B.C.S.—V. Contributions to the Knowledge of Parsee Literature. By Edward Sachau, Ph.D.—VI. Illustrations of the Lamaist System in Tibet, drawn from Chinese Sources. By Wm. Frederick Mayers, Esq., of H.B.M. Consular Service, China.—VII. Khuddaka Pátha, a Páli Text, with a Translation and Notes. By R. C. Childers, late of the Ceylon Civil Service.—VIII. An Endeavour to elucidate Rashiduddin's Geographical Notices of India. By Col. H. Yule, C.B.—IX. Sassanian Inscriptions explained by the Pahlavi of the

Pârsis. By E. W. West, Esq.—X. Some Account of the Senbyú Pagoda at Mengún, near the Burmese Capital, in a Memorandum by Capt. E. H. Sladan, Political Agent at Mandalé; with Remarks on the Subject by Col. Henry Yule, C.B.—XI. The Brhat-Sanhitá; or, Complete System of Natural Astrology of Varâha-Mihira. Translated from Sanskrit into English by Dr. H. Kern.—XII. The Mohammedan Law of Evidence, and its influence on the Administration of Justice in India. By N. B. E. Baillie, Esq.—XIII. The Mohammedan Law of Evidence in connection with the Administration of Justice to Foreigners. By N. B. E. Baillie, Esq.—XIV. A Translation of a Bactrian Páli Inscription. By Prof. J. Dowson.—XV. Indo-Parthian Coins. By E. Thomas, Esq.

Vol. V. Part I. pp. 197.

CONTENTS.—I. Two Játakas. The original Páli Text, with an English Translation. By V. Fausböll.—II. On an Ancient Buddhist Inscription at Keu-yung kwan, in North China. By A. Wylie.—III. The Brhat Sanhitá; or, Complete System of Natural Astrology of Varâha-Mihira Translated from Sanskrit into English by Dr. H. Kern.—IV. The Pongol Festival in Southern India. By Charles E. Gover.—V. The Poetry of Mohamed Rabadan, of Arragon. By the Right Hon. Lord Stanley of Alderley.—VI. Essay on the Creed and Customs of the Jangams. By Charles P. Brown.—VII. On Malabar, Coromandel, Quilon, etc. By C. P. Brown.—VIII. On the Treatment of the Nexus in the Neo-Aryan Languages of India. By John Beames, B.C.S.—IX. Some Remarks on the Great Tope at Sánchi. By the Rev. S. Beal.—X. Ancient Inscriptions from Mathura. Translated by Professor J. Dowson.—Note to the Mathura Inscriptions. By Major-General A. Cunningham.

Asiatic Society.—TRANSACTIONS OF THE ROYAL ASIATIC SOCIETY OF GREAT BRITAIN AND IRELAND. Complete in 3 vols. 4to., 80 Plates of Facsimiles, etc., cloth. London, 1827 to 1835. Published at £9 5s.; reduced to £3 3s.

The above contains contributions by Professor Wilson, G. C. Haughton, Davis, Morrison, Colebrooke, Humboldt, Dorn, Grotefend, and other eminent Oriental scholars.

Auctores Sanscriti. Edited for the Sanskrit Text Society, under the supervision of THEODOR GOLDSTÜCKER. Vol. I., containing the Jaimíníya-Nyúya-Málá-Vistara. Parts I. to V., pp. 1 to 400, large 4to. sewed. 10s. each part.

Axon.—THE LITERATURE OF THE LANCASHIRE DIALECT. A Bibliographical Essay. By WILLIAM E. A. AXON, F.R.S.L. Fcap. 8vo. sewed. 1870. 1s.

Bachmaier.—PASIGRAPHICAL DICTIONARY AND GRAMMAR. By ANTON BACHMAIER, President of the Central Pasigraphical Society at Munich. 18mo. cloth, pp. viii.; 26; 160. 1870. 3s. 6d.

Bachmaier.—PASIGRAPHISCHES WÖRTERBUCH ZUM GEBRAUCHE FÜR DIE DEUTSCHE SPRACHE. Verfasst von ANTON BACHMAIER, Vorsitzendem des Central-Vereins für Pasigraphie in München. 18mo. cloth, pp. viii.; 32; 128; 120. 1870. 2s. 6d.

Bachmaier.—DICTIONNAIRE PASIGRAPHIQUE, PRÉCEDÉ DE LA GRAMMAIRE. Redigé par ANTOINE BACHMAIER, Président de la Société Centrale de Pasigraphie à Munich. 18mo. cloth, pp. vi. 26; 168; 150. 1870. 2s. 6d.

Ballad Society's Publications.—Subscriptions—Small paper, one guinea, and large paper, three guineas, per annum.

1868.

1. BALLADS FROM MANUSCRIPTS. Vol. I. Ballads on the condition of England in Henry VIII.'s and Edward VI.'s Reigns (including the state of the Clergy, Monks, and Friars), on Wolsey and Anne Boleyn. Part I. Edited by F. J. FURNIVALL, M.A. 8vo.
2. BALLADS FROM MANUSCRIPTS. Vol. I. Part 2. [*In the Press.*
3. BALLADS FROM MANUSCRIPTS. Vol. II. Part 1. The Poore Mans Pittance. By Richard Williams. Edited by F. J. FURNIVALL, M.A. 8vo.

1869.

4. THE ROXBURGHE BALLADS. Part 1. With short Notes by W. CHAPPELL, Esq., F.S.A., author of "Popular Music of the Olden Time," etc., etc., and with copies of the Original Woodcuts, drawn by Mr. RUDOLPH BLIND and Mr. W. H. HOOPER, and engraved by Mr. J. H. RIMBAULT and Mr. HOOPER. 8vo.

Ballad Society's Publications—*continued.*
1870.

5. THE ROXBURGHE BALLADS. Vol. I. Part II. With short Notes by W. CHAPPELL, Esq., F.S.A., and with copies of the Original Woodcuts, drawn by Mr. RUDOLPH BLIND and Mr. W. H. HOOPER, and engraved by Mr. J. H. RIMBAULT and Mr. HOOPER.

Ballantyne.—ELEMENTS OF HINDÍ AND BRAJ BHÁKÁ GRAMMAR. By the late JAMES R. BALLANTYNE, LL.D. Second edition, revised and corrected Crown 8vo., pp. 44, cloth. 5s.

Ballantyne.—FIRST LESSONS IN SANSKRIT GRAMMAR; together with an Introduction to the Hitopadésa. Second edition. By JAMES R. BALLANTYNE, LL.D., Librarian of the India Office. 8vo. pp. viii. and 110, cloth. 1869. 5s.

Bartlett.—DICTIONARY OF AMERICANISMS: a Glossary of Words and Phrases colloquially used in the United States. By JOHN R. BARTLETT. Second Edition, considerably enlarged and improved. 1 vol. 8vo., pp. xxxii. and 524, cloth. 16s.

Beal.—TRAVELS OF FAH HIAN AND SUNG-YUN, Buddhist Pilgrims from China to India (400 A.D. and 518 A.D.) Translated from the Chinese, by S. BEAL (B.A. Trinity College, Cambridge), a Chaplain in Her Majesty's Fleet, a Member of the Royal Asiatic Society, and Author of a Translation of the Pratimōksha and the Amithába Sûtra from the Chinese. Crown 8vo. pp. lxxiii. and 210, cloth, ornamental, with a coloured map, 10s. 6d.

Beal.—A CATENA OF BUDDHIST SCRIPTURES FROM THE CHINESE. By S. BEAL, B.A., Trinity College, Cambridge; a Chaplain in Her Majesty's Fleet, etc. 8vo. cloth, pp. xiv. and 436. 1871. 15s.

Beames.—OUTLINES OF INDIAN PHILOLOGY. With a Map, showing the Distribution of the Indian Languages. By JOHN BEAMES. Second enlarged and revised edition. Crown 8vo. cloth, pp. viii. and 96. 5s.

Beames.—NOTES ON THE BHOJPURÍ DIALECT OF HINDÍ, spoken in Western Behar. By JOHN BEAMES, Esq., B.C.S., Magistrate of Chumparun. 8vo. pp. 26, sewed. 1868. 1s. 6d.

Bell.—ENGLISH VISIBLE SPEECH FOR THE MILLION, for communicating the Exact Pronunciation of the Language to Native or Foreign Learners, and for Teaching Children and illiterate Adults to Read in few Days. By ALEXANDER MELVILLE BELL, F.E.I.S., F.R.S.S.A., Lecturer on Elocution in University College, London. 4to. sewed, pp. 16. 1s.

Bell.—VISIBLE SPEECH; the Science of Universal Alphabetics, or Self-Interpreting Physiological Letters, for the Writing of all Languages in one Alphabet. Illustrated by Tables, Diagrams, and Examples. By ALEXANDER MELVILLE BELL, F.E.I.S., F.R.S.A., Professor of Vocal Physiology, etc. 4to., pp. 156, cloth. 15s.

Bellew.—A DICTIONARY OF THE PUKKHTO, OR PUKSHTO LANGUAGE, on a New and Improved System. With a reversed Part, or English and Pukkhto. By H. W. BELLEW, Assistant Surgeon, Bengal Army. Super Royal 8vo., pp. xii. and 356, cloth. 42s.

Bellew.—A GRAMMAR OF THE PUKKHTO OR PUKSHTO LANGUAGE, on a New and Improved System. Combining Brevity with Utility, and Illustrated by Exercises and Dialogues. By H. W. BELLEW, Assistant Surgeon, Bengal Army. Super-royal 8vo., pp. xii. and 156, cloth. 21s.

Bellows.—ENGLISH OUTLINE VOCABULARY, for the use of Students of the Chinese, Japanese, and other Languages. Arranged by JOHN BELLOWS. With Notes on the writing of Chinese with Roman Letters. By Professor SUMMERS, King's College, London. Crown 8vo., pp. 6 and 368, cloth. 6s.

Bellows.—OUTLINE DICTIONARY, FOR THE USE OF MISSIONARIES, Explorers, and Students of Language. By MAX MÜLLER, M.A., Taylorian Professor in the University of Oxford. With an Introduction on the proper use of the ordinary English Alphabet in transcribing Foreign Languages. The Vocabulary compiled by JOHN BELLOWS. Crown 8vo. Limp morocco, pp. xxxi. and 368. 7s. 6d

Benfey.—A PRACTICAL GRAMMAR OF THE SANSKRIT LANGUAGE, for the use of Early Students. By THEODOR BENFEY, Professor of Sanskrit in the University of Göttingen. Second, revised and enlarged, edition. Royal 8vo. pp. viii. and 296, cloth. 10s. 6d.

Beurmann.—VOCABULARY OF THE TIGRÉ LANGUAGE. Written down by MORITZ VON BEURMANN. Published with a Grammatical Sketch. By Dr. A. MERX, of the University of Jena. pp. viii. and 78, cloth. 3s. 6d.

Bholanauth Chunder.—THE TRAVELS OF A HINDOO TO VARIOUS PARTS OF BENGAL and Upper India. By BHOLANAUTH CHUNDER, Member of the Asiatic Society of Bengal. With an Introduction by J. Talboys Wheeler, Esq., Author of "The History of India." Dedicated, by permission, to His Excellency Sir John Laird Mair Lawrence, G.C.B., G.C.S.I., Viceroy and Governor-General of India, etc. In 2 volumes, crown 8vo., cloth, pp. xxv. and 440, viii. and 410. 21s.

Bigandet.—THE LIFE OR LEGEND OF GAUDAMA, the Buddha of the Burmese, with Annotations. The ways to Neibban, and Notice on the Phongyies, or Burmese Monks. By the Right Reverend P. BIGANDET, Bishop of Ramatha, Vicar Apostolic of Ava and Pegu. 8vo. sewed, pp. xi., 538, and v. 18s.

Bleek.—A COMPARATIVE GRAMMAR OF SOUTH AFRICAN LANGUAGES. By W. H. I. BLEEK, Ph.D. Volume I. I. Phonology. II. The Concord. Section 1. The Noun. 8vo. pp. xxxvi. and 322, cloth. 16s.

Bleek.—REYNARD IN SOUTH AFRICA; or, Hottentot Fables. Translated from the Original Manuscript in Sir George Grey's Library. By Dr. W. H. I. BLEEK, Librarian to the Grey Library, Cape Town, Cape of Good Hope. In one volume, small 8vo., pp. xxxi. and 94, cloth. 3s. 6d.

Bombay Sanskrit Series. Edited under the superintendence of G. BÜHLER, Ph. D., Professor of Oriental Languages, Elphinstone College, and F. KIELHORN, Ph. D., Superintendent of Sanskrit Studies, Deccan College.

Already published.

1. PANCHATANTRA IV. AND V. Edited, with Notes, by G. BÜHLER, Ph. D. Pp. 84, 16. 4s. 6d.
2. NÁGOJÍBHATTA'S PARIBHÁSHENDUŚEKHARA. Edited and explained by F. KIELHORN, Ph. D. Part I., the Sanskrit Text and various readings. pp. 116. 8s. 6d.
3. PANCHATANTRA II. AND III. Edited, with Notes, by G. BÜHLER, Ph. D. Pp. 86, 14, 2. 5s. 6d.
4. PANCHATANTRA I. Edited, with Notes, by F. KIELHORN, Ph.D. Pp. 114, 53. 6s. 6d.
5. KÁLIDÁSA's RAGHUVAMŚA. With the Commentary of Mallinátha. Edited, with Notes, by SHANKAR P. PANDIT, M.A. Part I. Cantos I.-VI. 9s.
6. KÁLIDÁSA's MÁLAVIKÁGNIMITRA. Edited, with Notes, by SHANKAR P. PANDIT, M.A. 8s.

Bottrell.—TRADITIONS AND HEARTHSIDE STORIES OF WEST CORNWALL. By WILLIAM BOTTRELL (an old Celt). Demy 12mo. pp. vi. 292, cloth. 1870. 6s.

Boyce.—A GRAMMAR OF THE KAFFIR LANGUAGE.— By WILLIAM B. BOYCE, Wesleyan Missionary. Third Edition, augmented and improved, with Exercises, by WILLIAM J. DAVIS, Wesleyan Missionary. 12mo. pp. xii. and 164, cloth. 8s.

Bowditch.—SUFFOLK SURNAMES. By N. I. BOWDITCH. Third Edition, 8vo. pp. xxvi. and 758, cloth. 7s. 6d.

Brice.—A ROMANIZED HINDUSTANI AND ENGLISH DICTIONARY. Designed for the use of Schools and for Vernacular Students of the Language. Compiled by NATHANIEL BRICE. New Edition, Revised and Enlarged. Post

Brinton.—THE MYTHS OF THE NEW WORLD. A Treatise on the Symbolism and Mythology of the Red Races of America. By DANIEL G. BRINTON, A.M., M.D. Crown 8vo. cloth, pp viii. and 308. 10s. 6d.

Brown.—THE DERVISHES; or, ORIENTAL SPIRITUALISM. By JOHN P. BROWN, Secretary and Dragoman of the Legation of the United States of America at Constantinople. With twenty-four Illustrations. 8vo. cloth, pp. viii. and 415. 14s.

Brown.—CARNATIC CHRONOLOGY. The Hindu and Mahomedan Methods of Reckoning Time explained: with Essays on the Systems; Symbols used for Numerals, a new Titular Method of Memory, Historical Records, and other subjects. By CHARLES PHILIP BROWN, Member of the Royal Asiatic Society; late of the Madras Civil Service; Telugu Translator to Government; Senior Member of the College Board, etc.; Author of the Telugu Dictionaries and Grammar, etc. 4to. sewed, pp. xii. and 90. 10s. 6d.

Brown.—SANSKRIT PROSODY AND NUMERICAL SYMBOLS EXPLAINED. By CHARLES PHILIP BROWN, Author of the Telugu Dictionary, Grammar, etc., Professor of Telugu in the University of London. Demy 8vo. pp. 64, cloth. 3s. 6d.

Buddhaghosha.—BUDDHAGHOSHA'S PARABLES: translated from Burmese by Captain H. T. ROGERS, R.E. With an Introduction containing Buddha's Dhammapadam, or, Path of Virtue; translated from Pali by F. MAX MÜLLER. 8vo. pp. 378, cloth. 12s. 6d.

Burgess.—SURYA-SIDDHANTA (Translation of the): A Text-book of Hindu Astronomy, with Notes and an Appendix, containing additional Notes and Tables, Calculations of Eclipses, a Stellar Map, and Indexes. By Rev. EBENEZER BURGESS, formerly Missionary of the American Board of Commissioners of Foreign Missions in India; assisted by the Committee of Publication of the American Oriental Society. 8vo. pp. iv. and 354, boards. 15s.

Burnell.—CATALOGUE OF A COLLECTION OF SANSKRIT MANUSCRIPTS. By A. C. BURNELL, M.R.A.S., Madras Civil Service. PART I. *Vedic Manuscripts.* Fcap. 8vo. pp. 64, sewed. 1870. 2s.

Byington.—GRAMMAR OF THE CHOCTAW LANGUAGE. By the Rev. CYRUS BYINGTON. Edited from the Original MSS. in the Library of the American Philosophical Society, by D. G. BRINTON, A.M., M.D., Member of the American Philosophical Society, the Pennsylvania Historical Society, Corresponding Member of the American Ethnological Society, etc. 8vo. sewed, pp. 56. 12s.

Calcutta Review.—THE CALCUTTA REVIEW. Published Quarterly. Price 8s. 6d.

Callaway.—IZINGANEKWANE, NENSUMANSUMANE, NEZINDABA, ZABANTU (Nursery Tales, Traditions, and Histories of the Zulus). In their own words, with a Translation into English, and Notes. By the Rev. HENRY CALLAWAY, M.D. Volume I., 8vo. pp. xiv. and 378, cloth. Natal, 1866 and 1867. 16s.

Callaway.— THE RELIGIOUS SYSTEM OF THE AMAZULU.
Part I.—Unkulunkulu; or, the Tradition of Creation as existing among the Amazulu and other Tribes of South Africa, in their own words, with a translation into English, and Notes. By the Rev. Canon CALLAWAY, M.D. 8vo. pp. 128, sewed. 1868. 4s.

Canones Lexicographici; or, Rules to be observed in Editing the New English Dictionary of the Philological Society, prepared by a Committee of the Society. 8vo., pp. 12, sewed. 6d.

Carpenter.—THE LAST DAYS IN ENGLAND OF THE RAJAH RAMMOHUN ROY. By MARY CARPENTER, of Bristol. With Five Illustrations. 8vo. pp. 272, cloth. 7s. 6d.

Carr.—ఆంధ్రలోకోక్తిచంద్రిక. A COLLECTION OF TELUGU PROVERBS, Translated, Illustrated, and Explained; together with some Sanscrit Proverbs printed in the Devnâgarî and Telugu Characters. By Captain M. W. CARR, Madras Staff Corps. One Vol. and Supplemnt, royal 8vo. pp. 488 and 148. 31s. 6d

Catlin.—O-KEE-PA. A Religious Ceremony of the Mandans. By GEORGE CATLIN. With 13 Coloured Illustrations. 4to. pp. 60, bound in cloth, gilt edges. 14s.

Chalmers.—THE ORIGIN OF THE CHINESE; an Attempt to Trace the connection of the Chinese with Western Nations in their Religion, Superstitions, Arts, Language, and Traditions. By JOHN CHALMERS, A.M. Foolscap 8vo. cloth, pp. 78. 2s. 6d.

Chalmers.—THE SPECULATIONS ON METAPHYSICS, POLITY, AND MORALITY OF "THE OLD PHILOSOPHER" LAU TSZE. Translated from the Chinese, with an Introduction by John Chalmers, M.A. Fcap. 8vo. cloth, xx. and 62. 4s. 6d.

Chalmers.—AN ENGLISH AND CANTONESE POCKET-DICTIONARY, for the use of those who wish to learn the spoken language of Canton Province. By JOHN CHALMERS, M.A. Third edition. Crown 8vo., pp. iv. and 146. Hong Kong, 1871. 15s.

Charnock.—LUDUS PATRONYMICUS; or, the Etymology of Curious Surnames. By RICHARD STEPHEN CHARNOCK, Ph.D., F.S.A., F.R.G.S. Crown 8vo., pp. 182, cloth. 7s. 6d.

Charnock.—VERBA NOMINALIA; or Words derived from Proper Names. By RICHARD STEPHEN CHARNOCK, Ph. Dr. F.S.A., etc. 8vo. pp. 326, cloth. 14s.

Charnock.—THE PEOPLES OF TRANSYLVANIA. Founded on a Paper read before THE ANTHROPOLOGICAL SOCIETY OF LONDON, on the 4th of May, 1869. By RICHARD STEPHEN CHARNOCK, Ph.D., F.S.A., F.R.G.S. Demy 8vo. pp. 36, sewed. 1870. 2s. 6d.

Chaucer Society's Publications. Subscription, two guineas per annum.
1868. *First Series.*

CANTERBURY TALES. Part I.
I. The Prologue and Knight's Tale, in 6 parallel Texts (from the 6 MSS. named below), together with Tables, showing the Groups of the Tales, and their varying order in 38 MSS. of the Tales, and in the old printed editions, and also Specimens from several MSS. of the "Moveable Prologues" of the Canterbury Tales,—The Shipman's Prologue, and Franklin's Prologue,—when moved from their right places, and of the substitutes for them.
II. The Prologue and Knight's Tale from the Ellesmere MS.
III. „ „ „ „ „ „ „ Hengwrt „ 154.
IV. „ „ „ „ „ „ „ Cambridge „ Gg. 4. 27.
V. „ „ „ „ „ „ „ Corpus „ Oxford.
VI. „ „ „ „ „ „ „ Petworth „
VII. „ „ „ „ „ „ „ Lansdowne „ 851.
Nos. II. to VII. are separate Texts of the 6-Text edition of the Canterbury

Chaucer Society's Publications—*continued.*

1868. *Second Series.*

ON EARLY ENGLISH PRONUNCIATION, with especial reference to Shakspere and Chaucer, containing an investigation of the Correspondence of Writing with Speech in England, from the Anglo-Saxon period to the present day, preceded by a systematic notation of all spoken sounds, by means of the ordinary printing types. Including a re-arrangement of Prof. F. J. Child's Memoirs on the Language of Chaucer and Gower, and Reprints of the Rare Tracts by Salesbury on English, 1547, and Welsh, 1567, and by Barcley on French, 1521. By ALEXANDER J. ELLIS, F.R.S., etc., etc. Part I. On the Pronunciation of the xivth, xvth, xviith, and xviiith centuries.

ESSAYS ON CHAUCER; His Words and Works. Part I. 1. Ebert's Review of Sandras's *E'tude sur Chaucer, considéré comme Imitateur des Trouvères*, translated by J. W. Van Rees Hoets, M.A., Trinity Hall, Cambridge, and revised by the Author.—II. A Thirteenth Century Latin Treatise on the *Chilindre*: "For by my *chilindre* it is prime of day" (*Shipmannes Tale*). Edited, with a Translation, by Mr. EDMUND BROCK, and illustrated by a Woodcut of the Instrument from the Ashmole MS. 1522.

A TEMPORARY PREFACE to the Six-Text Edition of Chaucer's Canterbury Tales. Part I. Attempting to show the true order of the Tales, and the Days and Stages of the Pilgrimage, etc., etc. By F. J. FURNIVALL, Esq., M.A., Trinity Hall, Cambridge.

1869. *First Series.*

VIII. The Miller's, Reeve's, Cook's, and Gamelyn's Tales: Ellesmere MS.
IX.   „   „   „   „   „   „   „   Hengwrt „
X.   „   „   „   „   „   „   „   Cambridge „
XI.   „   „   „   „   „   „   „   Corpus „
XII. „   „   „   „   „   „   „   Petworth „
XIII. „   „   „   „   „   „   „   Lansdowne „

These are separate issues of the 6-Text Chaucer's Canterbury Tales, Part II.

1869. *Second Series.*

ENGLISH PRONUNCIATION, with especial reference to Shakspere and Chaucer. By ALEXANDER J. ELLIS, F.R.S. Part II.

1870. *First Series.*

XIV. The Miller's, Reeve's, and Cook's Tales, with an Appendix of the Spurious Tale of Gamelyn, in Six parallel Texts.

Childers.—KNUDDAKA PATHA. A Páli Text, with a Translation and Notes. By R. C. CHILDERS, late of the Ceylon Civil Service. 8vo. pp. 32, stitched. 1s. 6d.

Childers.—A PÁLI-ENGLISH DICTIONARY, with Sanskrit Equivalents, and with numerous Quotations, Extracts, and References. Compiled by R. C. CHILDERS, late of the Ceylon Civil Service. [*In preparation.*

Chronique DE ABOU-DJAFAR-MOHAMMED-BEN-DJARIR-BEN-YEZID TABARI. Traduite par Monsieur HERMANN ZOTENBERG. Vol. I. 8vo. pp. 608. Vol. II. 8vo. pp. ii. and 252, sewed. 7s. 6d. each. (*To be completed in Four Volumes.*)

Clarke.—TEN GREAT RELIGIONS: an Essay in Comparative Theology. By JAMES FREEMAN CLARKE. 8vo. cloth, pp. x. and 528. 1871. 14s.

Colenso.—FIRST STEPS IN ZULU-KAFIR: An Abridgement of the Elementary Grammar of the Zulu-Kafir Language. By the Right Rev. JOHN W. COLENSO, Bishop of Natal. 8vo. pp. 86, cloth. Ekukanyeni, 1859. 4s. 6d.

Colenso.—ZULU-ENGLISH DICTIONARY. By the Right Rev. JOHN W. COLENSO, Bishop of Natal. 8vo. pp. viii. and 552, sewed. Pietermaritzburg, 1861. 15s.

Colenso.—FIRST ZULU-KAFIR READING BOOK, two parts in one. By the Right Rev. JOHN W. COLENSO, Bishop of Natal. 16mo. pp. 44, sewed. Natal. 1s.

Colenso.—SECOND ZULU-KAFIR READING BOOK. By the same. 16mo. pp. 108, sewed. Natal. 3s.

Colenso.—FOURTH ZULU-KAFIR READING BOOK. By the same. 8vo. pp. 160, cloth. Natal, 1859. 7s.

Colenso.—Three Native Accounts of the Visits of the Bishop of Natal in September and October, 1859, to Upmande, King of the Zulus; with Explanatory Notes and a Literal Translation, and a Glossary of all the Zulu Words employed in the same: designed for the use of Students of the Zulu Language. By the Right Rev. JOHN W. COLENSO, Bishop of Natal. 16mo. pp. 160, stiff cover. Natal, Maritzburg, 1860. 4s. 6d.

Coleridge.—A GLOSSARIAL INDEX to the Printed English Literature of the Thirteenth Century. By HERBERT COLERIDGE, Esq. 8vo. pp. 104, cloth. 2s. 6d.

Colleccao de Vocabulos e Frases usados na Provincia de S. Pedro, do Rio Grande do Sul, no Brasil. 12mo. pp. 32, sewed. 1s.

Contopoulos.—A LEXICON OF MODERN GREEK-ENGLISH AND ENGLISH MODERN GREEK. By N. CONTOPOULOS.
Part I. Modern Greek-English. 8vo. cloth, pp. 460. 12s.
Part II. English-Modern Greek. 8vo. cloth, pp. 582. 15s.

Cunningham.—THE ANCIENT GEOGRAPHY OF INDIA. I. The Buddhist Period, including the Campaigns of Alexander, and the Travels of Hwen-Thsang. By ALEXANDER CUNNINGHAM, Major-General, Royal Engineers (Bengal Retired). With thirteen Maps. 8vo. pp. xx. 590, cloth. 1870. 28s.

Cunningham.—AN ESSAY ON THE ARIAN ORDER OF ARCHITECTURE, as exhibited in the Temples of Kashmere. By Captain (now Major-General) ALEXANDER CUNNINGHAM. 8vo. pp. 86, cloth. With seventeen large folding Plates. 18s.

Cunningham.—THE BHILSA TOPES; or, Buddhist Monuments of Central India: comprising a brief Historical Sketch of the Rise, Progress, and Decline of Buddhism; with an Account of the Opening and Examination of the various Groups of Topes around Bhilsa. By Brev.-Major Alexander Cunningham, Bengal Engineers. Illustrated with thirty-three Plates. 8vo. pp. xxxvi. 370, cloth. 1854. 21s.

Delepierre.—REVUE ANALYTIQUE DES OUVRAGES ÉCRITS EN CENTONS, depuis les Temps Anciens, jusqu'au xixième Siècle. Par un Bibliophile Belge. Small 4to. pp. 508, stiff covers. 1868. 30s.

Delepierre.—ESSAI HISTORIQUE ET BIBLIOGRAPHIQUE SUR LES RÉBUS. Par Octave Delepierre. 8vo. pp. 24, sewed. With 15 pages of Woodcuts. 1870. 3s. 6d.

Dennys.—CHINA AND JAPAN. A complete Guide to the Open Ports of those countries, together with Pekin, Yeddo, Hong Kong, and Macao; forming a Guide Book and Vade Mecum for Travellers, Merchants, and Residents in general; with 56 Maps and Plans. By WM. FREDERICK MAYERS, F.R.G.S. H.M.'s Consular Service; N. B. DENNYS, late H.M.'s Consular Service; and CHARLES KING, Lieut. Royal Marine Artillery. Edited by N. B. DENNYS. In one volume. 8vo. pp. 600, cloth. £2 2s.

Digest of Hindu Law, from the Replies of the Shastris in the several Courts of the Bombay Presidency. With an Introduction, Notes, and Appendix. Edited by Raymond West and Johann Georg Bühler. Vol. I. 8vo. cloth. £3 3s. Vol. II. 8vo. pp. v. 118, cloth. 12s.

Döhne.—A ZULU-KAFIR DICTIONARY, etymologically explained, with copious Illustrations and examples, preceded by an introduction on the Zulu-Kafir Language. By the Rev. J. L. DÖHNE. Royal 8vo. pp. xlii. and 418, sewed. Cape Town, 1857. 21s.

Döhne.—THE FOUR GOSPELS IN ZULU. By the Rev. J. L. DÖHNE, Missionary to the American Board, C.F.M. 8vo. pp. 208, cloth. Pietermaritzburg, 1866. 5s.

Doolittle.—AN ENGLISH AND CHINESE DICTIONARY. By the Rev. JUSTUS DOOLITTLE. China. [*In the Press.*

Early English Text Society's Publications. Subscription, one guinea per annum.

1. EARLY ENGLISH ALLITERATIVE POEMS. In the West-Midland Dialect of the Fourteenth Century. Edited by R. MORRIS, Esq., from an unique Cottonian MS. 16s.
2. ARTHUR (about 1440 A.D.). Edited by F. J. FURNIVALL, Esq., from the Marquis of Bath's unique MS. 4s.
3. ANE COMPENDIOUS AND BREUE TRACTATE CONCERNYNG YE OFFICE AND DEWTIE OF KYNGIS, etc. By WILLIAM LAUDER. (1556 A.D.) Edited by F. HALL, Esq., D.C.L. 4s.
4. SIR GAWAYNE AND THE GREEN KNIGHT (about 1320-30 A.D.). Edited by R. MORRIS, Esq., from an unique Cottonian MS. 10s.
5. OF THE ORTHOGRAPHIE AND CONGRUITIE OF THE BRITAN TONGUE; a treates, noe shorter than necessarie, for the Schooles, be ALEXANDER HUME. Edited for the first time from the unique MS. in the British Museum (about 1617 A.D.), by HENRY B. WHEATLEY, Esq. 4s.
6. LANCELOT OF THE LAIK. Edited from the unique MS. in the Cambridge University Library (ab. 1500), by the Rev. WALTER W. SKEAT, M.A. 8s.
7. THE STORY OF GENESIS AND EXODUS, an Early English Song, of about 1250 A.D. Edited for the first time from the unique MS. in the Library of Corpus Christi College, Cambridge, by R. MORRIS, Esq. 8s.
8. MORTE ARTHURE; the Alliterative Version. Edited from ROBERT THORNTON's unique MS. (about 1440 A.D.) at Lincoln, by the Rev. GEORGE PERRY, M.A., Prebendary of Lincoln. 7s.
9. ANIMADVERSIONS UPPON THE ANNOTACIONS AND CORRECTIONS OF SOME IMPERFECTIONS OF IMPRESSIONES OF CHAUCER'S WORKES, reprinted in 1598; by FRANCIS THYNNE. Edited from the unique MS. in the Bridgewater Library. By G. H. KINGSLEY, Esq., M.D. 4s.
10. MERLIN, OR THE EARLY HISTORY OF KING ARTHUR. Edited for the first time from the unique MS. in the Cambridge University Library (about 1450 A.D.), by HENRY B. WHEATLEY, Esq. Part I. 2s. 6d.
11. THE MONARCHE, and other Poems of Sir David Lyndesay. Edited from the first edition by JOHNE SKOTT, in 1552, by FITZEDWARD HALL, Esq., D.C.L. Part I. 3s.
12. THE WRIGHT'S CHASTE WIFE, a Merry Tale, by Adam of Cobsam (about 1462 A.D.), from the unique Lambeth MS. 306. Edited for the first time by F. J. FURNIVALL, Esq., M.A. 1s.
13. SEINTE MARHERETE, þE MEIDEN ANT MARTYR. Three Texts of ab. 1200, 1310, 1330 A.D. First edited in 1862, by the Rev. OSWALD COCKAYNE, M.A., and now re-issued. 2s.
14. KYNG HORN, with fragments of Floriz and Blauncheflur, and the Assumption of the Blessed Virgin. Edited from the MSS. in the Library of the University of Cambridge and the British Museum, by the Rev. J. RAWSON LUMBY. 3s. 6d.
15. POLITICAL, RELIGIOUS, AND LOVE POEMS, from the Lambeth MS. No. 306, and other sources. Edited by F. J. FURNIVALL, Esq., M.A. 7s. 6d.
16. A TRETICE IN ENGLISH breuely drawe out of þ book of Quintis essencijs in Latyn, þ Hermys þ prophete and king of Egipt after þ flood of Noe, fader of Philosophris, hadde by reuelacions of an auugil of God to him sente. Edited from the Sloane MS. 73, by F. J. FURNIVALL, Esq., M.A. 1s.
17. PARALLEL EXTRACTS from 29 Manuscripts of PIERS PLOWMAN, with Comments, and a Proposal for the Society's Three-text edition of this Poem. By the Rev. W. SKEAT, M.A. 1s.
18. HALI MEIDENHEAD, about 1200 A.D. Edited for the first time from the MS. (with a translation) by the Rev. OSWALD COCKAYNE, M.A. 1s.

Early English Text Society's Publications—*continued.*

19. THE MONARCHE, and other Poems of Sir David Lyndesay. Part II., the Complaynt of the King's Papingo, and other minor Poems. Edited from the First Edition by F. HALL, Esq., D.C.L. 3s. 6d.
20. SOME TREATISES BY RICHARD ROLLE DE HAMPOLE. Edited from Robert of Thornton's MS. (ab. 1440 A.D.), by Rev. GEORGE G. PERRY, M.A. 1s.
21. MERLIN, OR THE EARLY HISTORY OF KING ARTHUR. Part II. Edited by HENRY B. WHEATLEY, Esq. 4s.
22. THE ROMANS OF PARTENAY, OR LUSIGNEN. Edited for the first time from the unique MS. in the Library of Trinity College, Cambridge, by the Rev. W. W. SKEAT, M.A. 6s.
23. DAN MICHEL'S AYENBITE OF INWYT, or Remorse of Conscience, in the Kentish dialect, 1340 A.D. Edited from the unique MS. in the British Museum, by RICHARD MORRIS, Esq. 10s. 6d.
24. HYMNS OF THE VIRGIN AND CHRIST; THE PARLIAMENT OF DEVILS, and Other Religious Poems. Edited from the Lambeth MS. 853, by F. J. FURNIVALL, M.A. 3s.
25. THE STACIONS OF ROME, and the Pilgrim's Sea-Voyage and Sea-Sickness, with Clene Maydenhod. Edited from the Vernon and Porkington MSS., etc., by F. J. FURNIVALL, Esq., M.A. 1s.
26. RELIGIOUS PIECES IN PROSE AND VERSE. Containing Dan Jon Gaytrigg's Sermon; The Abbaye of S. Spirit; Sayne Jon, and other pieces in the Northern Dialect. Edited from Robert of Thorntone's MS. (ab. 1460 A.D.), by the Rev. G. PERRY, M.A. 2s.
27. MANIPULUS VOCABULORUM: a Rhyming Dictionary of the English Language, by PETER LEVINS (1570). Edited, with an Alphabetical Index, by HENRY B. WHEATLEY. 12s.
28. THE VISION OF WILLIAM CONCERNING PIERS PLOWMAN, together with Vita de Dowel, Dobet et Dobest. 1362 A.D., by WILLIAM LANGLAND. The earliest or Vernon Text; Text A. Edited from the Vernon MS., with full Collations, by Rev. W. W. SKEAT, M.A. 7s.
29. OLD ENGLISH HOMILIES AND HOMILETIC TREATISES. (Sawles Warde and the Wohunge of Ure Lauerd: Ureisuns of Ure Louerd and of Ure Lefdi, etc.) of the Twelfth and Thirteenth Centuries. Edited from MSS. in the British Museum, Lambeth, and Bodleian Libraries; with Introduction, Translation, and Notes. By RICHARD MORRIS. *First Series.* Part I. 7s.
30. PIERS, THE PLOUGHMAN'S CREDE (about 1394). Edited from the MSS. by the Rev. W. W. SKEAT, M.A. 2s.
31. INSTRUCTIONS FOR PARISH PRIESTS. By JOHN MYRC. Edited from Cotton MS. Claudius A. II., by EDWARD PEACOCK, Esq., F.S.A., etc., etc. 4s.
32. THE BABEES BOOK, Aristotle's A B C, Urbanitatis, Stans Puer ad Mensam, The Lytille Childrenes Lytil Boke. THE BOKES OF NURTURE of Hugh Rhodes and John Russell, Wynkyn de Worde's Boke of Kervynge, The Booke of Demeanor, The Boke of Curtasye, Seager's Schoole of Vertue, etc., etc. With some French and Latin Poems on like subjects, and some Forewords on Education in Early England. Edited by F. J. FURNIVALL, M.A., Trin. Hall, Cambridge. 15s.
33. THE BOOK OF THE KNIGHT DE LA TOUR LANDRY, 1372. A Father's Book for his Daughters, Edited from the Harleian MS. 1764, by THOMAS WRIGHT, Esq., M.A., and Mr. WILLIAM ROSSITER. 8s.
34. OLD ENGLISH HOMILIES AND HOMILETIC TREATISES. (Sawles Warde, and the Wohunge of Ure Lauerd: Ureisuns of Ure Louerd and of Ure Lefdi, etc.) of the Twelfth and Thirteenth Centuries. Edited from MSS. in the British Museum, Lambeth, and Bodleian Libraries; with Introduction, Translation, and Notes, by RICHARD MORRIS. *First Series.* Part 2. 8s.

Early English English Text Society's Publications—*continued.*

35. SIR DAVID LYNDESAY'S WORKS. PART 3. The Historie of ane Nobil and Wailzeand Sqvyer, WILLIAM MELDRUM, umqvhyle Laird of Cleische and Bynnis, compylit be Sir DAVID LYNDESAY of the Mont *alias* Lyoun King of Armes. With the Testament of the said Williame Meldrum, Squyer, compylit alswa be Sir Dauid Lyndesay, etc. Edited by F. HALL, D.C.L. 2s.

36. MERLIN, OR THE EARLY HISTORY OF KING ARTHUR. A Prose Romance (about 1450–1460 A.D.), edited from the unique MS. in the University Library, Cambridge, by HENRY B. WHEATLEY. With an Essay on Arthurian Localities, by J. S. STUART GLENNIE, Esq. Part III. 1869. 12s.

37. SIR DAVID LYNDESAY'S WORKS. Part IV. Ane Satyre of the thrie estaits, in commendation of vertew and vitvperation of vyce. Maid be Sir DAVID LINDESAY, of the Mont, *alias* Lyon King of Armes. At Edinbvrgh. Printed be Robert Charteris, 1602. Cvm privilegio regis. Edited by F. HALL, Esq., D.C.L. 4s.

38. THE VISION OF WILLIAM CONCERNING PIERS THE PLOWMAN, together with Vita de Dowel, Dobet, et Dobest, Secundum Wit et Resoun, by WILLIAM LANGLAND (1377 A.D.). The "Crowley" Text; or Text B. Edited from MS. Laud Misc. 581, collated with MS. Rawl. Poet. 38, MS. B. 15. 17. in the Library of Trinity College, Cambridge, MS. Dd. 1. 17. in the Cambridge University Library, the MS. in Oriel College, Oxford, MS. Bodley 814, etc. By the Rev. WALTER W. SKEAT, M.A., late Fellow of Christ's College, Cambridge. 10s. 6d.

39. THE "GEST HYSTORIALE" OF THE DESTRUCTION OF TROY. An Alliterative Romance, translated from Guido De Colonna's "Hystoria Troiana." Now first edited from the unique MS. in the Hunterian Museum, University of Glasgow, by the Rev. GEO. A. PANTON and DAVID DONALDSON. Part I. 10s. 6d.

40. ENGLISH GILDS. The Original Ordinances of more than One Hundred Early English Gilds : Together with the olde usages of the cite of Wynchestre; The Ordinances of Worcester; The Office of the Mayor of Bristol; and the Customary of the Manor of Tettenhall-Regis. From Original MSS. of the Fourteenth and Fifteenth Centuries. Edited with Notes by the late TOULMIN SMITH, Esq., F.R.S. of Northern Antiquaries (Copenhagen). With an Introduction and Glossary, etc., by his daughter, LUCY TOULMIN SMITH. And a Preliminary Essay, in Five Parts, ON THE HISTORY AND DEVELOPMENT OF GILDS, by LUJO BRENTANO, Doctor Juris Utriusque et Philosophiæ. 21s.

41. THE MINOR POEMS OF WILLIAM LAUDER, Playwright, Poet, and Minister of the Word of God (mainly on the State of Scotland in and about 1568 A.D., that year of Famine and Plague). Edited from the Unique Originals belonging to S. CHRISTIE-MILLER, Esq., of Britwell, by F. J. FURNIVALL, M.A., Trin. Hall, Camb. 3s.

42. BERNARDUS DE CURA REI FAMULIARIS, with some Early Scotch Prophecies, etc. From a MS., KK 1. 5, in the Cambridge University Library. Edited by J. RAWSON LUMBY, M.A., late Fellow of Magdalen College, Cambridge. 2s.

Early English Text Society's Publications—*continued.*

45. KING ALFRED'S WEST-SAXON VERSION OF GREGORY'S PASTORAL CARE. With an English translation, the Latin Text, Notes, and an Introduction Edited by HENRY SWEET, Esq., of Balliol College, Oxford. Part I. 10s.

Extra Series. Subscriptions—Small paper, one guinea; large paper, two guineas, per annum.

1. THE ROMANCE OF WILLIAM OF PALERNE (otherwise known as the Romance of William and the Werwolf). Translated from the French at the command of Sir Humphrey de Bohun, about A.D. 1350, to which is added a fragment of the Alliterative Romance of Alisaunder, translated from the Latin by the same author, about A.D. 1340; the former re-edited from the unique MS. in the Library of King's College, Cambridge, the latter now first edited from the unique MS. in the Bodleian Library, Oxford. By the Rev. WALTER W. SKEAT, M.A. 8vo. sewed, pp. xliv. and 328. £1 6s.

2. ON EARLY ENGLISH PRONUNCIATION, with especial reference to Shakspere and Chaucer; containing an investigation of the Correspondence of Writing with Speech in England, from the Anglo-Saxon period to the present day, preceded by a systematic Notation of all Spoken Sounds by means of the ordinary Printing Types; including a re-arrangement of Prof. F. J. Child's Memoirs on the Language of Chaucer and Gower, and reprints of the rare Tracts by Salesbury on English, 1547, and Welsh, 1567, and by Barcley on French, 1521. By ALEXANDER J. ELLIS, F.R.S. Part I. On the Pronunciation of the XIVth, XVIth, XVIIth, and XVIIIth centuries. 8vo. sewed, pp. viii. and 416. 10s.

3. CAXTON'S BOOK OF CURTESYE, printed at Westminster about 1477-8, A.D., and now reprinted, with two MS. copies of the same treatise, from the Oriel MS. 79, and the Balliol MS. 354. Edited by FREDERICK J. FURNIVALL, M.A. 8vo. sewed, pp. xii. and 58. 5s.

4. THE LAY OF HAVELOK THE DANE; composed in the reign of Edward I., about A.D. 1280. Formerly edited by Sir F. MADDEN for the Roxburghe Club, and now re-edited from the unique MS. Laud Misc. 108, in the Bodleian Library, Oxford, by the Rev. WALTER W. SKEAT, M.A. 8vo. sewed, pp. lv. and 160. 10s.

5. CHAUCER'S TRANSLATION OF BOETHIUS'S "DE CONSOLATIONE PHILOSOPHIE." Edited from the Additional MS. 10,340 in the British Museum. Collated with the Cambridge Univ. Libr. MS. Ii. 3. 21. By RICHARD MORRIS. 8vo. 12s.

6. THE ROMANCE OF THE CHEVELERE ASSIGNE. Re-edited from the unique manuscript in the British Museum, with a Preface, Notes, and Glossarial Index, by HENRY H. GIBBS, Esq., M.A. 8vo. sewed, pp. xviii. and 38. 3s.

7. ON EARLY ENGLISH PRONUNCIATION, with especial reference to Shakspere and Chaucer. By ALEXANDER J. ELLIS, F.R.S., etc., etc. Part II. On the Pronunciation of the XIIIth and previous centuries, of Anglo-Saxon, Icelandic, Old Norse and Gothic, with Chronological Tables of the Value of Letters and Expression of Sounds in English Writing. 10s.

8. QUEENE ELIZABETHES ACHADEMY, by Sir HUMPHREY GILBERT. A Booke of Precedence, The Ordering of a Funerall, etc. Varying Versions of the Good Wife, The Wise Man, etc., Maxims, Lydgate's Order of Fools, A Poem on Heraldry, Occleve on Lords' Men, etc., Edited by F. J. FURNIVALL, M.A., Trin. Hall, Camb. With Essays on Early Italian and German Books of Courtesy, by W. M. ROSSETTI, Esq., and E. OSWALD, Esq. 8vo. 13s.

Early English Text Society's Publications—*continued.*

9. THE FRATERNITYE OF VACABONDES, by JOHN AWDELEY (licensed in 1560-1, imprinted then, and in 1565), from the edition of 1575 in the Bodleian Library. A Caueat or Warening for Commen Cursetors vulgarely called Vagabones, by THOMAS HARMAN, ESQUIRE. From the 3rd edition of 1567, belonging to Henry Huth, Esq., collated with the 2nd edition of 1567, in the Bodleian Library, Oxford, and with the reprint of the 4th edition of 1573. A Sermon in Praise of Thieves and Thievery, by PARSON HABEN OR HYBERDYNE, from the Lansdowne MS. 98, and Cotton Vesp. A. 25. Those parts of the Groundworke of Conny-catching (ed. 1592), that differ from *Harman's Caueat*. Edited by EDWARD VILES & F. J. FURNIVALL. 8vo. 7s. 6d.

10. THE FYRST BOKE OF THE INTRODUCTION OF KNOWLEDGE, made by Andrew Borde, of Physycke Doctor. A COMPENDYOUS REGYMENT OF A DYETARY OF HELTH made in Mountpyllier, compiled by Andrewe Boorde, of Physycke Doctor. BARNES IN THE DEFENCE OF THE BEARDE: a treatyse made, answerynge the treatyse of Doctor Borde upon Berdes. Edited, with a life of Andrew Boorde, and large extracts from his Brevyary, by F. J. FURNIVALL, M.A., Trinity Hall, Camb. 8vo. 18s.

11. THE BRUCE; or, the Book of the most excellent and noble Prince, Robert de Broyss, King of Scots: compiled by Master John Barbour, Archdeacon of Aberdeen. A.D. 1375. Edited from MS. G 23 in the Library of St. John's College, Cambridge, written A.D. 1487; collated with the MS. in the Advocates' Library at Edinburgh, written A.D. 1489, and with Hart's Edition, printed A.D. 1616; with a Preface, Notes, and Glossarial Index, by the Rev. WALTER W. SKEAT, M.A. Part I. 8vo. 12s.

12. ENGLAND IN THE REIGN OF KING HENRY THE EIGHTH. A Dialogue between Cardinal Pole and Thomas Lupset, Lecturer in Rhetoric at Oxford. By THOMAS STARKEY, Chaplain to the King. Edited, with Preface, Notes, and Glossary, by J. M. COWPER. And with an Introduction containing the Life and Letters of Thomas Starkey, by the Rev. J. S. BREWER, M.A. Part II. 12s.

(Part I., Starkey's Life and Letters, is in preparation.

13. A SUPPLICACYON FOR THE BEGGARS. Written about the year 1529, by SIMON FISH. Now re-edited by FREDERICK J. FURNIVALL. With a Supplycacion to our moste Soueraigne Lorde Kynge Henry the Eyght (1544 A.D.), A Supplication of the Poore Commons (1546 A.D.), The Decaye of England by the great multitude of Shepe (1550-3 A.D.). Edited by J. MEADOWS COWPER. 6s.

Edda Saemundar Hinns Froda—The Edda of Saemund the Learned. From the Old Norse or Icelandic. Part I. with a Mythological Index. 12mo. pp. 152, cloth, 3s. 6d. Part II. with Index of Persons and Places. By BENJAMIN THORPE. 12mo. pp. viii. and 172, cloth. 1866. 4s.; or in 1 Vol. complete, 7s. 6d.

Edkins.—CHINA'S PLACE IN PHILOLOGY. An attempt to show that the Languages of Europe and Asia have a common origin. By the Rev. JOSEPH EDKINS. Crown 8vo, pp. xxiii.—403, cloth.

Edkins.—A VOCABULARY OF THE SHANGHAI DIALECT. By J. EDKINS. 8vo. half-calf, pp. vi. and 151. Shanghai, 1869. 21s.

Edkins.—A GRAMMAR OF COLLOQUIAL CHINESE, as exhibited in the Shanghai Dialect. By J. EDKINS, B.A. Second edition, corrected. 8vo. half-calf, pp. viii. and 225. Shanghai, 1868. 21s.

Edkins.—A GRAMMAR OF THE CHINESE COLLOQUIAL LANGUAGE, commonly called the Mandarin Dialect. By JOSEPH EDKINS. Second edition. 8vo. half-calf, pp. viii. and 279. Shanghai, 1864. £1 10s.

Eger and Grime; an Early English Romance. Edited from Bishop Percy's Folio Manuscript, about 1650 A.D. By JOHN W. HALES, M.A., Fellow and late Assistant Tutor of Christ's College, Cambridge, and FREDERICK J. FURNIVALL, M.A., of Trinity Hall, Cambridge. 1 vol. 4to. (only 100 copies printed), bound in the Roxburghe style. pp. 64. Price 10s. 6d.

Eitel.—HANDBOOK FOR THE STUDENT OF CHINESE BUDDHISM. By the Rev. E. J. EITEL, of the London Missionary Society. Crown 8vo. pp. viii., 224, cloth, 18s.

Eitel.—THREE LECTURES ON BUDDHISM. By the Rev. E. J. EITEL.
(*In the Press.*)

Elliot.—THE HISTORY OF INDIA, as told by its own Historians. The Muhammadan Period. Edited from the Posthumous Papers of the late Sir H. M. ELLIOT, K.C.B., East India Company's Bengal Civil Service, by Prof. JOHN DOWSON, M.R.A.S., Staff College, Sandhurst. Vols. I. and II. With a Portrait of Sir H. M. Elliot. 8vo. pp xxxii. and 542, x. and 580, cloth. 18s. each. Vol. III. 8vo. pp. xii. and 627, cloth. 24s.

Elliot.—MEMOIRS ON THE HISTORY, FOLK-LORE, AND DISTRIBUTION OF THE RACES OF THE NORTH WESTERN PROVINCES OF INDIA; being an amplified Edition of the original Supplementary Glossary of Indian Terms. By the late Sir HENRY M. ELLIOT, K.C.B., of the Hon. East India Company's Bengal Civil Service. Edited, revised, and re-arranged, by JOHN BEAMES, M.R.A.S., Bengal Civil Service; Member of the German Oriental Society, of the Asiatic Societies of Paris and Bengal, and of the Philological Society of London. In 2 vols. demy 8vo., pp. xx., 370, and 396, cloth. With two Lithographic Plates, one full-page coloured Map, and three large coloured folding Maps. 36s.

Ellis.—THE ASIATIC AFFINITIES OF THE OLD ITALIANS. By ROBERT ELLIS, B.D., Fellow of St. John's College, Cambridge, and author of "Ancient Routes between Italy and Gaul." Crown 8vo. pp. iv. 156, cloth. 1870. 5s.

English and Welsh Languages.—THE INFLUENCE OF THE ENGLISH AND Welsh Languages upon each other, exhibited in the Vocabularies of the two Tongues. Intended to suggest the importance to Philologers, Antiquaries, Ethnographers, and others, of giving due attention to the Celtic Branch of the Indo-Germanic Family of Languages. Square, pp. 30, sewed. 1869. 1s.

Etherington.—THE STUDENT'S GRAMMAR OF THE HINDÍ LANGUAGE. By the Rev. W. ETHERINGTON, Missionary, Benares. Crown 8vo. pp. xii. 220. xlviii. cloth. 1870. 10s. 6d.

Ethnological Society of London (The Journal of the). Edited by Professor HUXLEY, F.R.S., President of the Society; GEORGE BUSK, Esq., F.R.S.; Sir JOHN LUBBOCK, Bart., F.R.S.; Colonel A. LANE FOX, Hon. Sec.; THOMAS WRIGHT, Esq., Hon. Sec.; HYDE CLARKE, Esq.; Sub-Editor; and Assistant Secretary, J. H. LAMPREY, Esq. Published Quarterly.

Vol. I., No. 1. April, 1869. 8vo. pp. 88, sewed. 3s.

CONTENTS.—Flint Instruments from Oxfordshire and the Isle of Thanet. (Illustrated.) By Colonel A. Lane Fox.—The Westerly Drifting of Nomads. By H. H. Howorth.—On the Lion Shilling. By Hyde Clarke.—Letter on a Marble Armlet. By H. W. Edwards.—On a Bronze Spear from Lough Gur, Limerick. (Illustrated.) By Col. A. Lane Fox.—On Chinese Charms. By W. H. Black.—Proto-ethnic Condition of Asia Minor. By Hyde Clarke.—On Stone Implements from the Cape. (Illustrated.) By Sir J. Lubbock.—Cromlechs and Megalithic Structures. By H. M. Westropp.—Remarks on Mr. Westropp's Paper. By Colonel A. Lane Fox.—Stone Implements from San José. By A. Steffens.—On Child-bearing in Australia and New Zealand. By J. Hooker, M.D.—On a Pseudo-cromlech on Mount Alexander, Australia. By Acheson.—The Cave Cannibals of South Africa. By Layland.—Reviews: Wallace's Malay Archipelago (with illustrations); Fryer's Hill Tribes of India (with an illustration); Reliquiæ Aquitanicæ, etc.—Method of Photographic Measurement of the Human Frame (with an illustration). By J. H. Lamprey.—Notes and Queries.

Vol. I., No. 2. July, 1869. 8vo. pp. 117, sewed. 3s.

CONTENTS.—Ordinary Meeting, March 9, 1869 (held at the Museum of Practical Geology), Professor Huxley, F.R.S., President, in the Chair. Opening Address of the President.—On the Characteristics of the population of Central and South India (Illustrated). By Sir Walter Elliot.—On the Races of India as traced in existing Tribes and Castes (With a Map). By G. Campbell, Esq.—Remarks by Mr. James Fergusson.—Remarks by Mr. Walter Dendy.—Ordinary Meeting, January 23rd, 1869. Professor Huxley, F.R.S., President, in the Chair. On the Lepchas. By Dr. A. Campbell, late Superintendent of Darjeeling.—On Prehistoric Archæology of India (Illustrated). By Colonel Meadows Taylor, C.S.I., M.R.A.S., M.R.I.A., etc.—Appendix I. Extract from description of the Pandoo Coolies in Malabar. By J. Babington, Esq. (Read before the Literary Society of Bombay, December 20th, 1820. Published in Volume III. of the Society's Transactions).—Appendix II. Extract from a letter from Captain, now Colonel, A. Doria, dated Camp Katangrich, April 12th, 1852.—On some of the Mountain Tribes of the North Western frontier of India. By Major Fosbery, V.C.—On Permanence of type in the Human Race. By Sir William Denison.—Notes and Reviews.—Ethnological Notes and Queries.—Notices of Ethnology.

Vol. I., No. 3. October, 1869. pp. 137, sewed. 3s.
CONTENTS.— On the Excavation of a large raised Stone Circle or Barrow, near the Village of Wurreegaon, one mile from the military station of Kamptee, Central Provinces of India (Illustrated). By Major George Godfrey Pearse, Royal Artillery.—Remarks by Dr. Hooker on Dr. Campbell's paper.—North-American Ethnology: Address of the President.—On the Native Races of New Mexico (Illustrated). By Dr. A. W. Bell.—On the Arapahoes, Kiowas, and Comanches. By Morton C. Fisher.—The North-American Indians: a Sketch of some of the hostile Tribes; together with a brief account of General Sheridan's Campaign of 1868 against the Sioux, Cheyenne, Arapaboe, Kiowa, and Comanche Indians. By William Blackmore.—Notes and Reviews: The Ethnological Essays of William Ewart Gladstone. Juventus Mundi, the Gods and Men of the Homeric Age. By the Right Hon. William Ewart Gladstone. (The Review by Hyde Clarke, Esq.)—Notes and Queries.—Classification Committee.

Vol. I., No. 4. January, 1870. pp. 98, sewed. 3s.
CONTENTS.—On New Zealand and Polynesian Ethnology: On the Social Life of the ancient Inhabitants of New Zealand, and on the national character it was likely to form. By Sir George Grey, K.C.B.—Notes on the Maories of New Zealand and some Melanesians of the south-west Pacific. By the Bishop of Wellington.—Observations on the Inhabitants and Antiquities of Easter Island. By J. L. Palmer.—On the westerly drifting of Nomades from the fifth to the nineteenth century. Part II. The Scljuks, Ghaznevides, etc. By H. H. Howorth, Esq.—Settle Cave Exploration.—Index.—Contents.—Report of the Council.—List of Fellows.

Vol. II., No. 1. April, 1870. 8vo. sewed, pp. 96. 3s.
CONTENTS:—On the Proposed Exploration of Stonehenge by a Committee of the British Association. By Col. A. Lane Fox.—On the Chinese Race, their Language, Government, Social Institutions, and Religion. By C. T. Gardner. Appendix I.: On Chinese Mythological and Legendary History II.: On Chinese Time.—Discussion.—On the Races and Languages of Dardistan. By Dr. G. W. Leitner.—Discussion.—Extract from a Communication by Munphool, Pundit to the Political Department, India Office, on the Relations between Gilgit, Chitral, and Kashmir.—On Quartzite Implements from the Cape of Good Hope. By Sir G. Grey.—Discussion.— Note on a supposed Stone Implement from County Wicklow, Ireland. By F. Atcheson.—Note on the Stature of American Indians of the Chipewyan Tribe. By Major-General Lefroy—Report on the Present State and Condition of Pre-historic Remains in the Channel Islands. By Lieut. S. P. Oliver.—Appendix: The Opening and Restoration of the Cromlech of Le Couperon.—Discussion—Description and Remarks upon an Ancient Celtaria from China, which has been supposed to be that of Confucius. By George Busk.—Discussion.—On the Westerly Drifting of Nomades, from the 5th to the 19th Century. Part III. The Comans and Petchenegs. By H. H. Howorth.—Review.—Notes and Queries.—Illustrated.

Vol. II., No. 2. July, 1870. 8vo. sewed, pp. 95. 3s.
CONTENTS:—On the Kitai and Kara-Kitai. By Dr. G. Oppert.—Discussion.—Note on the Use of the New Zealand Mere. By Colonel A. Lane Fox.—On Certain Pre-historic Remains discovered in New Zealand, and on the Nature of the Deposits in which they occurred. By Dr. Julius Haast.—Discussion.—On the Origin of the Tasmanians, geologically considered. By James Bonwick.—Discussion.—On a Frontier Line of Ethnology and Geology. By H. H. Howorth.—Notes on the Nicobar Islanders. By G. M. Atkinson.—On the Discovery of Flint and Chert under a Submerged Forest in West Somerset. By W. Boyd Dawkins.—Discussion.—Remarks by Dr. A. Campbell, introductory to the Rev. R. J. Mapleton's Report.—Report on Pre-historic Remains in the Neighbourhood of the Crinan Canal, Argyllshire. By the Rev. R. J. Mapleton.—Discussion.—Supplementary Remarks to a Note on an Ancient Chinese Calva. By George Busk.—On Discoveries in Recent Deposits in Yorkshire. By C. Monkman.—Discussion.—On the Natives of Naga, in Luzon, Philippine Islands.—By Dr. Jagor.—On the Koords. By Major F. Millinger.—On the Westerly Drifting of Nomades, from the 5th to the 19th Century. Part IV. The Circassians and White Kazars. By H. H. Howorth.—Notes and Queries.—Illustrated.

Vol. II., No. 3. October, 1870. 8vo. sewed, pp. 176. 3s.
CONTENTS:—On the Aymara Indians of Bolivia and Peru. By David Forbes. Appendix: A. Table of Detailed Measurements of Aymara Indians. B. Substances used as Medicines by the Aymara Indians, and their Names for Diseases. C. Vocabulary of Aymara Words—Discussion.—On the Opening of Two Cairns near Bangor, North Wales. By Colonel A. Lane Fox.—Discussion.—On the Earliest Phases of Civilization. By Hodder M. Westropp.—On Current British Mythology and Oral Traditions. By J. F. Campbell.—Note on a Cist with Engraved Stones on the Poltalloch Estate, Argyllshire. By the Rev. R. J. Mapleton.—Discussion—On the Tribal System and Land Tenure in Ireland under the Brehon Laws. By Hodder M. Westropp.

Gesenius' Hebrew Grammar. Translated from the 17th Edition. By Dr. T. J. CONANT. With grammatical Exercises and a Chrestomathy by the Translator. 8vo. pp. xvi. and 364, cloth. 20s.

Gesenius' Hebrew and English Lexicon of the Old Testament, including the Biblical Chaldee, from the Latin. By EDWARD ROBINSON. Fifth Edition. 8vo. pp. xii. and 1160, cloth. 36s.

God.—BOOK OF GOD. By ☉. 8vo. cloth. Vol. I.: The Apocalypse. pp. 647. 12s. 6d.—Vol II. An Introduction to the Apocalypse, pp. 752. 14s.— Vol. III. A Commentary on the Apocalypse, pp. 854. 16s.

God.—THE NAME OF GOD IN 405 LANGUAGES. Ἀγνώστῳ Θεῷ. 32mo. pp 64, sewed. 2d.

Goldstücker.—A DICTIONARY, SANSKRIT AND ENGLISH, extended and improved from the Second Edition of the Dictionary of Professor H. H. WILSON, with his sanction and concurrence. Together with a Supplement, Grammatical Appendices, and an Index, serving as a Sanskrit-English Vocabulary. By THEODOR GOLDSTÜCKER. Parts I. to VI. 4to. pp. 400. 1856-1863. 6s. each.

Goldstücker.—A COMPENDIOUS SANSKRIT-ENGLISH DICTIONARY, for the Use of those who intend to read the easier Works of Classical Sanskrit Literature. By THEODOR GOLDSTÜCKER. Small 4to. pp. 900, cloth. [*In preparation.*

Goldstücker.—PANINI: His Place in Sanskrit Literature. An Investigation of some Literary and Chronological Questions which may be settled by a study of his Work. A separate impression of the Preface to the Facsimile of MS. No. 17 in the Library of Her Majesty's Home Government for India, which contains a portion of the MANAVA-KALPA-SUTRA, with the Commentary of KUMARILA-SWAMIN. By THEODOR GOLDSTÜCKER. Imperial 8vo. pp. 268, cloth. 12s.

Grammatography.—A MANUAL OF REFERENCE to the Alphabets of Ancient and Modern Languages. Based on the German Compilation of F. BALLHORN. Royal 8vo. pp. 80, cloth. 7s. 6d.

The "Grammatography" is offered to the public as a compendious introduction to the reading of the most important ancient and modern languages. Simple in its design, it will be consulted with advantage by the philological student, the amateur linguist, the bookseller, the corrector of the press, and the diligent compositor.

ALPHABETICAL INDEX.

Afghan (or Pushto). Amharic. Anglo-Saxon. Arabic. Arabic Ligatures. Aramaic. Archaic Characters. Armenian. Assyrian Cuneiform. Bengali. Bohemian (Czechian). Bugis. Burmese. Canarese (or Carnátaca). Chinese. Coptic. Croato-Glagolitic. Cufic. Cyrillic (or Old Slavonic). Czechian (or Bohemian). Danish. Demotic. Estrangelo. Ethiopic. Etruscan. Georgian. German. Glagolitic. Gothic. Greek. Greek Ligatures. Greek (Archaic). Gujerati (or Guzzeratte). Hieratic. Hieroglyphics. Hebrew. Hebrew (Archaic). Hebrew (Rabbinical). Hebrew (current hand). Hebrew (Judæo-German). Hungarian. Illyrian. Irish. Italian (Old). Japanese. Javanese. Lettish. Mantshu. Median Cuneiform. Modern Greek (Romaic). Mongolian. Numidian. Old Slavonic (or Cyrillic). Palmyrenian. Persian. Persian Cuneiform. Phœnician. Polish. Pushto (or Afghan). Romaic (Modern Greek). Russian. Runes. Samaritan. Sanscrit. Servian. Slavonic (Old). Sorbian (or Wendish). Swedish. Syriac. Tamil. Telugu. Tibetan. Turkish. Wallachian. Wendish (or Sorbian). Zend.

Grey.—HANDBOOK OF AFRICAN, AUSTRALIAN, AND POLYNESIAN PHILOLOGY, as represented in the Library of His Excellency Sir George Grey, K.C.B., Her Majesty's High Commissioner of the Cape Colony. Classed, Annotated, and Edited by Sir GEORGE GREY and Dr. H. I. BLEEK.

Vol. I. Part 1.—South Africa. 8vo. pp. 186. 7s. 6d.
Vol. I. Part 2.—Africa (North of the Tropic of Capricorn). 8vo. pp. 70. 2s.
Vol. I. Part 3.—Madagascar. 8vo. pp. 24. 1s.
Vol. II. Part 1.—Australia. 8vo. pp. iv. and 44. 1s. 6d.
Vol. II. Part 2.—Papuan Languages of the Loyalty Islands and New Hebrides, comprising those of the Islands of Nengone, Lifu, Aneitum, Tana, and others. 8vo. p. 12. 6d.
Vol. II. Part 3.—Fiji Islands and Rotuma (with Supplement to Part II., Papuan Languages, and Part I., Australia). 8vo. pp. 34. 1s.

Vol. II. Part 4.—New Zealand, the Chatham Islands, and Auckland Islands. 8vo. pp. 76. 3s. 6d.
Vol. II. Part 4 (*continuation*).—Polynesia and Borneo. 8vo. pp. 77-154. 3s. 6d.
Vol. III. Part I.—Manuscripts and Incunables. 8vo. pp. viii. and 24. 2s.
Vol. IV. Part 1.—Early Printed Books. England. 8vo. pp. vi. and 266.

Grey.—MAORI MEMENTOS: being a Series of Addresses presented by the Native People to His Excellency Sir George Grey, K.C.B., F.R.S. With Introductory Remarks and Explanatory Notes; to which is added a small Collection of Laments, etc. By CH. OLIVER B. DAVIS. 8vo. pp. iv. and 228, cloth. 12s.

Green.—SHAKESPEARE AND THE EMBLEM-WRITERS: an Exposition of their Similarities of Thought and Expression. Preceded by a View of the Emblem-Book Literature down to A.D. 1616. By HENRY GREEN, M.A. In one volume, pp. xvi. 572, profusely illustrated with Woodcuts and Photolith. Plates, elegantly bound in cloth gilt, large medium 8vo. £1 11s. 6d; large imperial 8vo. £2 12s. 6d. 1870.

Griffith.—SCENES FROM THE RAMAYANA, MEGHADUTA, ETC. Translated by RALPH T. H. GRIFFITH, M.A., Principal of the Benares College. Second Edition. Crown 8vo. pp. xviii., 244, cloth. 6s.
CONTENTS.—Preface—Ayodhya—Ravan Doomed—The Birth of Rama—The Heir apparent—Manthara's Guile—Dasaratha's Oath—The Step-mother—Mother and Son—The Triumph of Love—Farewell!—The Hermit's Son—The Trial of Truth—The Forest—The Rape of Sita—Rama's Despair—The Messenger Cloud—Khumbakarna—The Suppliant Dove—True Glory—Feed the Poor—The Wise Scholar.

Griffith.—THE RÁMÁYAN OF VÁLMIKI. Translated into English verse. By RALPH T. H. GRIFFITH, M.A., Principal of the Benares College. Vol. I., containing Books I. and II. 8vo pp. xxxii. 440, cloth. 1870. 18s.

—— Vol. II., containing Book II., with additional Notes and Index of Names. 8vo. cloth, pp. 504. 18s.

Grout.—THE ISIZULU: a Grammar of the Zulu Language; accompanied with an Historical Introduction, also with an Appendix. By Rev. LEWIS GROUT. 8vo. pp. lii. and 432, cloth. 21s.

Haug.—ESSAYS ON THE SACRED LANGUAGE, WRITINGS, AND RELIGION OF THE PARSEES. By MARTIN HAUG, Dr. Phil. Superintendent of Sanskrit Studies in the Poona College. 8vo. pp. 278, cloth. [*Out of print*.

Haug.—A LECTURE ON AN ORIGINAL SPEECH OF ZOROASTER (Yasna 45), with remarks on his age. By MARTIN HAUG, Ph.D. 8vo. pp. 28, sewed. Bombay, 1865. 2s.

Haug.—OUTLINE OF A GRAMMAR OF THE ZEND LANGUAGE. By MARTIN HAUG, Dr. Phil. 8vo. pp. 82, sewed. 14s.

Haug.—THE AITAREYA BRAHMANAM OF THE RIG VEDA: containing the Earliest Speculations of the Brahmans on the meaning of the Sacrificial Prayers, and on the Origin, Performance, and Sense of the Rites of the Vedic Religion. Edited, Translated, and Explained by MARTIN HAUG, Ph.D., Superintendent of Sanskrit Studies in the Poona College, etc., etc. In 2 Vols. Crown 8vo. Vol. I. Contents, Sanskrit Text, with Preface, Introductory Essay, and a Map of the Sacrificial Compound at the Soma Sacrifice, pp. 312. Vol. II. Translation with Notes, pp. 544. £3 3s.

Haug.—AN OLD ZAND-PAHLAVI GLOSSARY. Edited in the Original Characters, with a Transliteration in Roman Letters, an English Translation, and an Alphabetical Index. By DESTUR HOSHENGJI JAMASPJI, High-priest of the Parsis in Malwa, India. Revised with Notes and Introduction by MARTIN HAUG, Ph.D., late Superintendent of Sanscrit Studies in the Poona College, Foreign Member of the Royal Bavarian Academy. Published by order of the Government of Bombay. 8vo. sewed, pp. lvi. and 132. 15s.

Haug.—AN OLD PAHLAVI-PAZAND GLOSSARY. Edited, with an Alphabetical Index, by DESTUR HOSHANGJI JAMASPJI ASA, High Priest of the Parsis in Malwa, India. Revised and Enlarged, with an Introductory Essay on the Pahlavi Language, by MARTIN HAUG, Ph.D. Published by order of the Government of Bombay. 8vo. pp. xvi. 152, 268, sewed. 1870. 28s.

Haug.—ESSAY ON THE PAHLAVI LANGUAGE. By MARTIN HAUG, Ph. D., Professor of Sanscrit and Comparative Philology at the University of Munich, Member of the Royal Bavarian Academy of Sciences, etc. (From the PAHLAVI-PAZAND GLOSSARY, edited by DESTUR HOSHANGJI and M. HAUG.) 8vo. pp. 152, sewed. 1870. 3s. 6d.

Haug.—THE RELIGION OF THE ZOROASTRIANS, as contained in their Sacred Writings. With a History of the Zend and Pehlevi Literature, and a Grammar of the Zend and Pehlevi Languages. By MARTIN HAUG, Ph.D., late Superintendent of Sanscrit Studies in the Poona College. 2 vols. 8vo. [*In preparation.*

Heaviside.—AMERICAN ANTIQUITIES; or, the New World the Old, and the Old World the New. By JOHN T. C. HEAVISIDE. 8vo. pp. 46, sewed. 1s. 6d.

Hepburn.—A JAPANESE AND ENGLISH DICTIONARY. With an English and Japanese Index. By J. C. HEPBURN, A.M., M.D. Imperial 8vo. cloth, pp. xii., 560 and 132. 5l. 5s.

Hernisz.—A GUIDE TO CONVERSATION IN THE ENGLISH AND CHINESE LANGUAGES, for the use of Americans and Chinese in California and elsewhere. By STANISLAS HERNISZ. Square 8vo. pp. 274, sewed. 10s. 6d.

The Chinese characters contained in this work are from the collections of Chinese groups, engraved on steel, and cast into moveable types, by Mr. Marcellin Legrand, engraver of the Imperial Printing Office at Paris. They are used by most of the missions to China.

Hincks.—SPECIMEN CHAPTERS OF AN ASSYRIAN GRAMMAR. By the late Rev. E. HINCKS, D.D., Hon. M.R.A.S. 8vo., pp. 44, sewed. 1s.

History of the Sect of Maharajahs; or, VALLABHACHARYAS IN WESTERN INDIA. With a Steel Plate. 8vo. pp. 384, cloth. 12s.

Hoffmann.—SHOPPING DIALOGUES, in Japanese, Dutch, and English. By Professor J. HOFFMANN. Oblong 8vo. pp. xiii. and 44, sewed. 3s.

Hoffmann.—A JAPANESE GRAMMAR. By J. J. HOFFMANN, Ph. Doc., Member of the Royal Academy of Sciences, etc., etc. Published by command of His Majesty's Minister for Colonial Affairs. Imp. 8vo. pp. viii. 352, sewed. 12s. 6d.

Historia y fundacion de la Ciudad de Tlaxcala, y sus cuatro caveceras. Sacada por Francisco de Loaiza de lengua Castellana á esta Mexicana. Año de 1718. Con una Traduccion Castellana, publicado por S. Leon Reinisch. In one volume folio, with 25 Photographic Plates. [*In preparation.*

Howse.—A GRAMMAR OF THE CREE LANGUAGE. With which is combined an analysis of the Chippeway Dialect. By JOSEPH HOWSE, Esq., F.R.G.S. 8vo. pp. xx. and 324, cloth. 7s. 6d.

Hunter.—A COMPARATIVE DICTIONARY OF THE LANGUAGES OF INDIA AND HIGH ASIA, with a Dissertation, based on The Hodgson Lists, Official Records, and Manuscripts. By W. W. HUNTER, B.A., M.R.A.S., Honorary Fellow, Ethnological Society, of Her Majesty's Bengal Civil Service. Folio, pp. vi. and 224, cloth. £3 2s.

Ikhwánu-s Safá.—IKHWÁNU-S SAFÁ; or, BROTHERS OF PURITY. Describing the Contention between Men and Beasts as to the Superiority of the Human Race. Translated from the Hindustáni by Professor J. DOWSON, Staff College, Sandhurst. Crown 8vo. pp. viii. and 156, cloth. 7s.

Inman.—ANCIENT FAITHS EMBODIED IN ANCIENT TIMES; or, an attempt to trace the Religious Belief, Sacred Rites, and Holy Emblems of certain Nations, by an interpretation of the names given to children by Priestly authority, or assumed by prophets, kings and hierarchs. By THOMAS INMAN, M.D., Liverpool. 2 vols. 8vo. pp. 1. and 1028, cloth, illustrated with numerous plates and woodcuts. £3.

Inman.—ANCIENT PAGAN AND MODERN CHRISTIAN SYMBOLISM EXPOSED AND EXPLAINED. By THOMAS INMAN, M.D. (London), Physician to the Royal Infirmary, Liverpool. 8vo. pp. xvi. 68, stiff covers, with numerous Illustrations. 1870. 5s.

Jaeschke.—A Short Practical Grammar of the Tibetan Language, with special Reference to the Spoken Dialects. By H. A. Jaeschke, Moravian Missionary. 8vo. sewed, pp. ii. and 56. 2s. 6d.

Jaeschke.—Romanized Tibetan and English Dictionary, each word being re-produced in the Tibetan as well as in the Roman character. By H. A. Jaeschke, Moravian Missionary. 8vo. pp. ii. and 158, sewed. 5s.

Julien.—Syntaxe Nouvelle de la Langue Chinoise.
Vol. I.—Fondée sur la position des mots, suivie de deux traités sur les particules et les principaux termes de grammaire, d'une table des idiotismes, de fables, de légendes et d'apologues traduits mot à mot. 8vo. sewed. 1869. 20s.

Vol. II.—Fondée sur la position des mots confirmée par l'analyse d'un texte ancien, suivie d'un petit Dictionnaire du Roman des Deux Cousines, et de Dialogues dramatiques traduits mot à mot, par M. Stanislas Julien, de l'Institut. 8vo. pp. 436, sewed. 1870. 20s.

Justi.—Handbuch der Zendsprache, von Ferdinand Justi. Altbactrisches Woerterbuch. Grammatik Chrestomathie. Four parts, 4to. sewed, pp. xxii. and 424. Leipzig, 1864. 24s.

Kafir Essays, and other Pieces; with an English Translation. Edited by the Right Rev. the Bishop of Grahamstown. 32mo. pp. 84, sewed. 2s 6d.

Kalidasa.—Raghuvansa. By Kalidasa. No. 1. (Cantos 1-3.) With Notes and Grammatical Explanations, by Rev. K. M. Banerjea, Second Professor of Bishop's College, Calcutta; Member of the Board of Examiners, Fort-William; Honorary Member of the Royal Asiatic Society, London. 8vo. sewed, pp. 70. 4s. 6d.

Kern.—The Brhat-Sanhitá; or, Complete System of Natural Astrology of Varâha-Mihira. Translated from Sanskrit into English by Dr. H. Kern, Professor of Sanskrit at the University of Leyden. 8vo. pp. 50, stitched. Part I. 2s. [Will be completed in Nine Parts.

Khirad-Afroz (The Illuminator of the Understanding). By Maulaví Hafízu'd-dín. A new edition of the Hindústání Text, carefully revised, with Notes, Critical and Explanatory. By Edward B. Eastwick, M.P., F.R.S., F.S.A., M.R.A.S., Professor of Hindústání at the late East India Company's College at Haileybury. 8vo. cloth, pp. xiv. and 321. 18s.

Kidd.—Catalogue of the Chinese Library of the Royal Asiatic Society. By the Rev. S. Kidd. 8vo. pp. 58, sewed. 1s.

Kielhorn.—A Grammar of the Sanskrit Language. By F. Kielhorn, Ph.D., Superintendent of Sanskrit Studies in Deccan College. Registered under Act xxv. of 1867. Demy 8vo. pp. xvi. 260. cloth. 1870. 10s. 6d.

Kistner.—Buddha and his Doctrines. A Biographical Essay. By Otto Kistner. Imperial 8vo., pp. iv. and 32, sewed. 2s. 6d.

Koran (The). Arabic text, lithographed in Oudh, A.H. 1284 (1867). 16mo. pp. 942, bound in red goatskin, Oriental style, silver tooling. 7s. 6d.
The printing, as well as the outer appearance of the book, is extremely tasteful, and the characters, although small, read very easily. As a cheap edition for reference this is preferable to any other, and its price puts it within the reach of every Oriental scholar. It is now first imported from India.

Laghu Kaumudí. A Sanskrit Grammar. By Varadarája. With an English Version, Commentary, and References. By James R. Ballantyne, LL.D., Principal of the Sanskrit College, Benares. 8vo. pp. xxxvi. and 424, cloth. £1 11s. 6d.

Lee.—A Translation of the Bálávatáro: a Native Grammar of the Pali Language. With the Romanized Text, the Nagari Text, and Copious Explanatory Notes. By Lionel F. Lee. In one vol. 8vo. (In preparation).

Legge.—The Chinese Classics. With a Translation, Critical and Exegetical Notes, Prolegomena, and Copious Indexes. By James Legge, D.D., of the London Missionary Society. In seven vols. Vol. I. containing Confucian Analects, the Great Learning, and the Doctrine of the Mean. 8vo. pp. 526, cloth. £2 2s.—Vol. II., containing the Works of Mencius. 8vo. pp. 634, cloth. £2 2s.—Vol. III. Part I. containing the First Part of the Shoo-King, or the Books of T. Aug, the Books of Yu, the Books of Hea. the Books of Shang, and the Prolegomena. Royal 8vo. pp. viii. and 280, cloth. £2 2s.—Vol. III. Part II. containing the Fifth Part of the Shoo-King, or the Books of Chow, and the Indexes. Royal 8vo. pp. 281—736, cloth. £2 2s.

Legge.—The Life and Teachings of Confucius, with Explanatory Notes. By James Legge, D.D. Reproduced for General Readers from the Author's work, "The Chinese Classics," with the original Text. Second edition. Crown 8vo. cloth, pp. vi. and 338. 10s. 6d.

Leigh.—The Religion of the World. By H. Stone Leigh. 12mo. pp. xii. 66, cloth. 1869. 2s. 6d.

Leitner.—The Races and Languages of Dardistan. By G. W. Leitner, M.A., Ph.D., Honorary Fellow of King's College London, etc.; late on Special Duty in Kashmir. 4 vols. 4to. [In the Press.

Leland.—Hans Breitmann's Party. With other Ballads. By Charles G. Leland. Eighth Edition. Square, pp. xvi. and 74, sewed. 1s.

Leland.—Hans Breitmann's Christmas. With other Ballads. By Charles G. Leland. Second edition. Square, pp. 80, sewed. 1s.

Leland.—Hans Breitmann as a Politician. By Charles G. Leland. Second edition. Square, pp. 72, sewed. 1s.

Leland.—Hans Breitmann in Church. With other Ballads. By Charles G. Leland. With an Introduction and Glossary. Square, pp. 80, sewed. 1870. 1s.

Leland.—Breitmann Ballads. *Four Series complete.* Contents:—Hans Breitmann's Party. Hans Breitmann's Christmas. Hans Breitmann as a Politician. Hans Breitmann in Church. With other Ballads. By Charles G. Leland. With Introductions and Glossaries. Square, pp. 300, cloth. 1870. 4s. 6d.

Leland.—Hans Breitmann as an Uhlan. Six New Ballads, with a Glossary. Square, sewed, pp. 72. 1s.

Leland.—The Breitmann Ballads. Complete in 1 vol., including Nineteen Ballads illustrating his Travels in Europe (never before printed), with Comments by Fritz Schwackenhammer. By Charles G. Leland. Crown 8vo. handsomely bound in cloth, pp. xxviii. and 292. 6s.

Lesley.—Man's Origin and Destiny, Sketched from the Platform of the Sciences, in a Course of Lectures delivered before the Lowell Institute, in Boston, in the Winter of 1865-6. By J. P. Lesley, Member of the National Academy of the United States, Secretary of the American Philosophical Society. Numerous Woodcuts. Crown 8vo. pp. 392, cloth. 10s. 6d.

Liherien hag Avielen; or, the Catholic Epistles and Gospels for the Day up to Ascension. Translated for the first time into the Brehonec of Brittany. Also in three other parallel columns a New Version of the same into Breizounec (commonly called Breton and Armorican); a Version into Welsh, mostly new, and closely resembling the Breton; and a Version Gaelic or Manx or Cernaweg; with Illustrative Articles by Christoll Terrien and Charles Waring Saxton, D.D. Ch. Ch., Oxford. The Penitential Psalms are also added. Oblong 4to. pp. 156, sewed. 5s.

Lobscheid.—English and Chinese Dictionary, with the Punti and Mandarin Pronunciation. By the Rev. W. Lobscheid, Knight of Francis Joseph, C.M.I.R.G.S.A., N.Z.B.S.V., etc. Folio, pp. viii. and 2016. In Four Parts. £8 8s.

Lobscheid.—CHINESE AND ENGLISH DICTIONARY, Arranged according to the Radicals. By the Rev. W. LOBSCHEID, Knight of Francis Joseph, C.M.I.R.G.S.A., N.Z.B.S.V., &c. 1 vol. imp. 8vo. double columns, pp. 600, bound. £2 8s.

Ludewig (Hermann E.)—The LITERATURE OF AMERICAN ABORIGINAL LANGUAGES. With Additions and Corrections by Professor WM. W. TURNER. Edited by NICOLAS TRÜBNER. 8vo. fly and general Title, 2 leaves; Dr. Ludewig's Preface, pp. v.—viii.; Editor's Preface, pp. iv.—xii.; Biographical Memoir of Dr. Ludewig, pp. xiii.—xiv.; and Introductory Biographical Notices, pp. xiv.—xxiv., followed by List of Contents. Then follow Dr. Ludewig's Bibliotheca Glottica, alphabetically arranged, with Additions by the Editor, pp. 1—209; Professor Turner's Additions, with those of the Editor to the same, also alphabetically arranged, pp. 210—246; Index, pp. 247—256; and List of Errata, pp. 257, 258. Handsomely bound in cloth. 10s. 6d.

Macgowan.—A MANUAL OF THE AMOY COLLOQUIAL. By Rev. J. MACGOWAN, of the London Missionary Society. 8vo. sewed, pp. xvii. and 200. Amoy, 1871. £1 1s.

Maclay and Baldwin.—AN ALPHABETIC DICTIONARY OF THE CHINESE LANGUAGE IN THE FOOCHOW DIALECT. By Rev. R. S. MACLAY, D.D., of the Methodist Episcopal Mission, and Rev. C. C. BALDWIN, A.M., of the American Board of Mission. 8vo. half-bound, pp. 1132. Foochow, 1871. £4 4s.

Maha-Vira-Charita; or, the Adventures of the Great Hero Rama. An Indian Drama in Seven Acts. Translated into English Prose from the Sanskrit of Bhavabhūti. By JOHN PICKFORD, M.A. Crown 8vo. cloth.

Manava-Kalpa-Sutra; being a portion of this ancient Work on Vaidik Rites, together with the Commentary of KUMARILA-SWAMIN. A Facsimile of the MS. No. 17, in the Library of Her Majesty's Home Government for India. With a Preface by THEODOR GOLDSTÜCKER. Oblong folio, pp. 268 of letterpress and 121 leaves of facsimiles. Cloth. £4 4s.

Manipulus Vocabulorum; A Rhyming Dictionary of the English Language. By Peter Levins (1570) Edited, with an Alphabetical Index, by HENRY B. WHEATLEY. 8vo. pp. xvi. and 370, cloth. 14s.

Manning.—AN INQUIRY INTO THE CHARACTER AND ORIGIN OF THE POSSESSIVE AUGMENT in English and in Cognate Dialects. By the late JAMES MANNING, Q.A.S., Recorder of Oxford. 8vo. pp. iv. and 90. 2s.

Markham.—QUICHUA GRAMMAR and DICTIONARY. Contributions towards a Grammar and Dictionary of Quichua, the Language of the Yncas of Peru; collected by CLEMENTS R. MARKHAM, F.S.A., Corr. Mem. of the University of Chile. Author of "Cuzco and Lima," and "Travels in Peru and India." In one vol. crown 8vo., pp. 223, cloth. £1. 1s.

Markham.—OLLANTA: A DRAMA IN THE QUICHUA LANGUAGE. Text, Translation, and Introduction, By CLEMENTS R. MARKHAM, F.R.G.S. Crown 8vo., pp. 128, cloth. 7s. 6d.

Marsden.—NUMISMATA ORIENTALIA ILLUSTRATA. The Plates of the Oriental Coins, Ancient and Modern, of the Collection of the late William Marsden, F.R.S., etc., etc., engraved from drawings made under his direction 4to. pp. iv. (explanatory advertisement). cloth, gilt top. £1 11s. 6d.

Mason.—BURMAH: its People and Natural Productions; or Notes on the Nations, Fauna, Flora, and Minerals of Tenasserim, Pegu, and Burmah By Rev. F. MASON, D.D., M.R.A.S., Corresponding Member of the American Oriental Society, of the Boston Society of Natural History, and of the Lyceum of Natural History, New York. 8vo. pp. xviii. and 914, cloth. Rangoon 1860. 30s.

Mason.—THE PALI TEXT OF KACHCHAYANO'S GRAMMAR, WITH ENGLISH ANNOTATIONS. By FRANCIS MASON, D.D. I. The Text Aphorisms, 1 to 673 II. The English Annotations, including the various Readings of six independent Burmese Manuscripts, the Singalese Text on Verbs, and the Cambodian Text on Syntax. To which is added a Concordance of the Aphorisms. In Two Parts. 8vo. sewed, pp. 208, 75, and 28. Toongoo, 1871. £1 12s.

Mathurāprasāda Misra.—A TRILINGUAL DICTIONARY, being a comprehensive Lexicon in English, Urdú, and Hindí, exhibiting the Syllabication, Pronunciation, and Etymology of English Words, with their Explanation in English, and in Urdú and Hindí in the Roman Character. By MATHURÁPRASÁDA MISRA, Second Master, Queen's College, Benares. 8vo. pp. xv. and 1330, cloth. Benares, 1865. £2 2s.

Mayers.—ILLUSTRATIONS OF THE LAMAIST SYSTEM IN TIBET, drawn from Chinese Sources. By WILLIAM FREDERICK MAYERS, Esq., of Her Britannic Majesty's Consular Service, China. 8vo. pp. 24, sewed. 1869. 1s. 6d.

Medhurst.—CHINESE DIALOGUES, QUESTIONS, and FAMILIAR SENTENCES, literally translated into English, with a view to promote commercial intercourse and assist beginners in the Language. By the late W. H. MEDHURST, D.D. A new and enlarged Edition. 8vo. pp. 226. 18s.

Megha-Duta (The). (Cloud-Messenger.) By Kālidāsa. Translated from the Sanskrit into English verse, with Notes and Illustrations. By the late H. H. WILSON, M.A., F.R.S., Boden Professor of Sanskrit in the University of Oxford, etc., etc. The Vocabulary by FRANCIS JOHNSON, sometime Professor of Oriental Languages at the College of the Honourable the East India Company, Haileybury. New Edition. 4to. cloth, pp. xi. and 180. 10s. 6d.

Memoirs read before the ANTHROPOLOGICAL SOCIETY OF LONDON, 1863 1864. 8vo., pp. 542, cloth. 21s.

Memoirs read before the ANTHROPOLOGICAL SOCIETY OF LONDON, 1865-6. Vol. II. 8vo., pp. x. 464, cloth. 21s.

Merx.—GRAMMATICA SYRIACA, quam post opus Hoffmanni refecit ADALBERTUS MERX, Phil. Dr. Theol. Lic. in Univ. Litt. Jenensi Priv. Docens.
Particula I. Royal 8vo. pp. 136, sewed. 7s.
Particula II. Royal 8vo. pp. 137-388, sewed. 10s. 6d.

Moffat.—THE STANDARD ALPHABET PROBLEM; or the Preliminary Subject of a General Phonic System, considered on the basis of some important facts in the Sechwana Language of South Africa, and in reference to the views of Professors Lepsius, Max Müller, and others. A contribution to Phonetic Philology. By ROBERT MOFFAT, junr., Surveyor, Fellow of the Royal Geographical Society. 8vo. pp. xxviii. and 174, cloth. 7s. 6d.

Molesworth.—A DICTIONARY, MÁRATHI and ENGLISH. Compiled by J. T. MOLESWORTH, assisted by GEORGE and THOMAS CANDY. Second Edition, revised and enlarged. By J. T. MOLESWORTH. Royal 4to. pp. xxx and 922, boards. Bombay, 1857. £3 3s.

Morfill.—THE SLAVES: their Ethnology, early History, and popular Traditions, with some account of Slavonic Literature. Being the substance of a course of Lectures delivered at Oxford. By W. R. MORFILL, M.A.
[*In preparation.*]

Morley.—A DESCRIPTIVE CATALOGUE of the HISTORICAL MANUSCRIPTS in the ARABIC and PERSIAN LANGUAGES preserved in the Library of the Royal Asiatic Society of Great Britain and Ireland. By WILLIAM H. MORLEY, M.R.A.S. 8vo. pp. viii. and 160, sewed. London, 1854. 2s. 6d.

Morrison.—A DICTIONARY OF THE CHINESE LANGUAGE. By the Rev. R. MORRISON, D.D. Two vols. Vol. I. pp. x. and 762; Vol. II. pp. 828, cloth. Shanghae, 1865. £6 6s.

Muhammed.—THE LIFE OF MUHAMMED. Based on Muhammed Ibn Ishak By Abd El Malik Ibn Hisham. Edited by Dr. FERDINAND WÜSTENFELD. One volume containing the Arabic Text. 8vo. pp. 1026, sewed. Price 21s. Another volume, containing Introduction, Notes, and Index in German. 8vo. pp. lxxii. and 266, sewed. 7s. 6d. Each part sold separately. The text based on the Manuscripts of the Berlin, Leipsic, Gotha and Leyden Libraries, has been carefully revised by the learned editor, and printed with the utmost exactness.

Muir.—ORIGINAL SANSKRIT TEXTS, on the Origin and History of the People of India, their Religion and Institutions. Collected, Translated, and Illustrated by JOHN MUIR, Esq., D.C.L., LL.D., Ph.D.

Vol. I. Mythical and Legendary Accounts of the Origin of Caste, with an Inquiry into its existence in the Vedic Age. Second Edition, re-written and greatly enlarged. 8vo. pp. xx. 532, cloth. 1868. 21s.

Vol. II. *A New Edition is in preparation.*

Vol. III. The Vedas: Opinions of their Authors, and of later Indian Writers, on their Origin, Inspiration, and Authority. Second Edition, revised and enlarged. 8vo. pp. xxxii. 312, cloth. 1868. 16s.

Vol. IV. Comparison of the Vedic with the later representation of the principal Indian Deities. 8vo pp. xii. 440, cloth. 1863. 15s.

Vol. V. Contributions to a Knowledge of the Cosmogony, Mythology, Religious Ideas, Life and Manners of the Indians in the Vedic Age. 8vo. pp. xvi. 492, cloth, 1870. 21s.

Müller (Max).—THE SACRED HYMNS OF THE BRAHMINS, as preserved to us in the oldest collection of religious poetry, the Rig-Veda-Sanhita, translated and explained. By F. MAX MÜLLER, M.A., Fellow of All Souls' College; Professor of Comparative Philology at Oxford; Foreign Member of the Institute of France, etc., etc. In 8 vols. Volume I. 8vo. pp. clii. and 264. 12s. 6d.

Müller (Max).—A NEW EDITION OF THE HYMNS OF THE RIG-VEDA IN THE SANHITÁ TEXT, without the Commentary of the Sáyana. Based upon the Editio princeps of Max Müller. Large 8vo. of about 800 pages. [*In preparation.*

"The above New Edition of the Sanhitá Text of the Rig-Veda, without the Commentary of Sáyana, will contain foot-notes of the names of the Authors, Deities, and Metres. It will be comprised in about fifty large 8vo. sheets, and will be carefully corrected and revised by Prof. F. Max Müller. The price to subscribers before publication will be 24s. per copy. After publication the price will be 36s. per copy.

Müller (Max).—LECTURE ON BUDDHIST NIHILISM. By F. MAX MÜLLER, M.A., Professor of Comparative Philology in the University of Oxford; Member of the French Institute, etc. Delivered before the General Meeting of the Association of German Philologists, at Kiel, 28th September, 1869. (Translated from the German.) Sewed. 1869. 1s.

Naphegyi.—THE ALBUM OF LANGUAGE, illustrated by the Lord's Prayer in one hundred languages, with historical descriptions of the principal languages, interlinear translation and pronunciation of each prayer, a dissertation on the languages of the world, and tables exhibiting all known languages, dead and living. By G. NAPHEGYI, M.D., A.M., Member of the "Sociedad Geográfica y Estadistica" of Mexico, and "Mejoras Materiales" of Texoco, of the Numismatic and Antiquarian Society of Philadelphia, etc. In one splendid folio volume of 322 pages, illuminated frontispiece and title-page, elegantly bound in cloth, gilt top. £2 10s.

CONTENTS.—Preface (pp. 2).—Introduction.—Observations on the Origin of Language (pp. 12).—Authors of Collections of the Lord's Prayer (pp. 8).—Families of Language (pp. 13).—Alphabets (pp. 25). The Lord's Prayer in the following languages (each accompanied by a transliteration into Roman characters, a translation into English, and a Monograph of the language), printed in the original characters.

A. ARYAN FAMILY.—1. Sanskrit. 2. Bengalee. 3. Moltanee. 4. Hindoostanee. 5. Gipsy. 6. Greek. 7. Modern Greek. 8. Latin. 9. Italian. 10. French. 11. Spanish. 12. Portuguese. 13. Celtic. 14. Welsh. 15. Cornish. 16. Irish. 17. Gothic. 18. Anglo-Saxon. 19. Old Saxon and Dano-Saxon. 20. English (4 varieties). 21. German (4 varieties). 22. Dutch. 23. Runic. 24. Wallachian. 25. Icelandic. 26. Danish. 27. Norwegian. 28. Swedish. 29 Lithuanian. 30. Old Prussian. 31. Servian. 32. Sclavonic. 33. Polavian. 34. Bohemian. 35. Polish. 36. Russian. 37. Bulgaric. 38. Armenian. 39. Armenian-Turkish. 40. Albanian. 41. Persian.

B. SEMITIC FAMILY.—1. Hebrew. 2. Chaldee. 3. Samaritan. 4. Syriac. 5. Syro-Chaldaic. 6. Carshun. 7. Arabic. 8. Æthiopic. 9. Amharic.

C. TURANIAN FAMILY.—1. Turkish. 2. Hungarian. 3. Finnish. 4. Estonian. 5. Lapponian. 6. Laplandic (Dialect of Umå-Lappmark). 7. Basque. 8. Javanese. 9. Hawaiian. 10. Maori (New Zealandic). 11. Malay. 12. Ceylonese. 13. Moorish. 14. Coptic. 15. Berber. 16. Hottentot. 17. Susuic. 18. Burmese. 19. Siamese. 20. Mongolian. 21. Chinese. 22. Kalmuk. 23. Cashmere.

D. AMERICAN FAMILY.—1. Cherokee. 2. Delawar. 3. Micmac. 4. Totonac. 5. Othomi. 6. Cora. 7. Kolusic. 8. Greenland. 9. Mexican. 10. Misteklo. 11. Mayu. 12. Brazilian. 13. Chiquitic. 14. Amaric.

Nayler.—COMMONSENSE OBSERVATIONS ON THE EXISTENCE OF RULES (not yet reduced to System in any work extant) regarding THE ENGLISH LANGUAGE; on the pernicious effects of yielding blind obedience to so-called authorities, whether DICTIONARY-COMPILERS, GRAMMAR-MAKERS, or SPELLING-BOOK MANUFACTURERS, instead of examining and judging for ourselves on all questions that are open to investigation; followed by a Treatise, entitled PRONUNCIATION MADE EASY; also an ESSAY ON THE PRONUNCIATION OF PROPER NAMES. By B. S. NAYLER, accredited Elocutionist to the most celebrated Literary Societies in London. 8vo. pp. iv. 148, boards. 1869. 5s.

Newman.—A DICTIONARY OF MODERN ARABIC —1. Anglo-Arabic Dictionary. 2. Anglo-Arabic Vocabulary. 3. Arabo-English Dictionary. By F. W. NEWMAN, Emeritus Professor of University College, London. In 2 vols. crown 8vo., pp. xvi. and 376—464, cloth. £1 1s.

Newman.—A HANDBOOK OF MODERN ARABIC, consisting of a Practical Grammar, with numerous Examples, Dialogues, and Newspaper Extracts, in a European Type. By F. W. NEWMAN, Emeritus Professor of University College, London; formerly Fellow of Balliol College, Oxford. Post 8vo. pp. xx. and 192, cloth. London, 1866. 6s.

Newman.—THE TEXT OF THE IGUVINE INSCRIPTIONS, with interlinear Latin Translation and Notes. By FRANCIS W. NEWMAN, late Professor of Latin at University College, London. 8vo. pp. xvi. and 54, sewed. 2s.

Newman.—ORTHOËPY: or, a simple mode of Accenting English, for the advantage of Foreigners and of all Learners. By FRANCIS W. NEWMAN, Emeritus Professor of University College, London. 8vo. pp. 28, sewed. 1869. 1s.

Notley.—A COMPARATIVE GRAMMAR OF THE FRENCH, ITALIAN, SPANISH, AND PORTUGUESE LANGUAGES. By EDWIN A. NOTLEY. Crown oblong 8vo. cloth, pp. xv. and 396. 7s. 6d.

Oriental Text Society.—(*The Publications of the Oriental Text Society*.)

1. THEOPHANIA; or, Divine Manifestations of our Lord and Saviour. By EUSEBIUS, Bishop of Cæsarea. Syriac. Edited by Prof. S. LEE. 8vo. 1842. 15s.
2. ATHANASIUS's FESTAL LETTERS, discovered in an ancient Syriac Version. Edited by the Rev. W. CURETON. 8vo. 1848. 15s.
3. SHAHRASTANI: Book of Religious and Philosophical Sects, in Arabic. Two Parts. 8vo. 1842. 30s.
4. UMDAT AKIDAT AHL AL SUNNAT WA AL TAMAAT; Pillar of the Creed of the Sunnites. Edited in Arabic by the Rev. W. CURETON. 8vo. 1843. 5s.
5. HISTORY OF THE ALMOHADES. Edited in Arabic by Dr. R. P. A. DOZY. 8vo. 1347. 10s. 6d.
6. SAMA VEDA. Edited in Sanskrit by Rev. G. STEVENSON. 8vo. 1843. 12s.
7. DASA KUMARA CHARITA. Edited in Sanskrit by Professor H. H. WILSON. 8vo. 1846. £1 4s.
8. MAHA VIRA CHARITA, or a History of Rama. A Sanskrit Play. Edited by F. H. TRITHEN. 8vo. 1848. 15s.
9. MAZHZAN UL ASRAR: The Treasury of Secrets. By NIZAMI. Edited in Persian by N. BLAND. 4to. 1844. 10s. 6d.
10. SALAMAN-U-UBSAL; A Romance of Jami (Dshami). Edited in Persian by F. FALCONER. 4to. 1843. 10s.
11. MIRKHOND's HISTORY OF THE ATABEKS. Edited in Persian by W. H. MORLEY. 8vo. 1850. 12s.
12. TUHFAT-UL-AHRAR; the Gift of the Noble. A Poem. By Jami

Osburn.—THE MONUMENTAL HISTORY of EGYPT, as recorded on the Ruins of her Temples, Palaces, and Tombs. By WILLIAM OSBURN. Illustrated with Maps, Plates, etc. 2 vols. 8vo. pp. xii. and 461 ; vii. and 643, cloth. £2 2s.
Vol. I.—From the Colonization of the Valley to the Visit of the Patriarch Abram.
Vol. II.—From the Visit of Abram to the Exodus.

Palmer.—EGYPTIAN CHRONICLES, with a harmony of Sacred and Egyptian Chronology, and an Appendix on Babylonian and Assyrian Antiquities. By WILLIAM PALMER, M.A., and late Fellow of Magdalen College, Oxford. 2 vols., 8vo. cloth, pp. lxxiv. and 428, and viii. and 636. 1861. 12s.

Pand-Námah.—THE PAND-NÁMAH ; or, Books of Counsels. By ADARBÁD MÁRÁSPAND. Translated from Pehlevi into Gujerathi, by Harbad Sheriarjee Dadabhoy. And from Gujerathi into English by the Rev. Shapurji Edalji. Fcap. 8vo. sewed. 1870. 6d.

Pandit.—A PANDIT'S REMARKS ON PROFESSOR MAX MÜLLER'S TRANSLATION of the "Rig-Veda." Sanskrit and English. Fcap. 8vo. sewed. 1870. 6d.

Paspati.—ÉTUDES SUR LES TCHINGHIANÉS (GYPSIES) OU BOHÉMIENS DE L'EMPIRE OTTOMAN. Par ALEXANDRE G. PASPATI, M.D. Large 8vo. sewed, pp. xii. and 652. Constantinople, 1871. 28s.

Patell.—COWASJEE PATELL'S CHRONOLOGY, containing corresponding Dates of the different Eras used by Christians, Jews, Greeks, Hindús, Mohamedans, Parsees, Chinese, Japanese, etc. By COWASJEE SORABJEE PATELL. 4to. pp. viii. and 184, cloth. 50s.

Pauthier.—LE LIVRE DE MARCO POLO, Citoyen de Vénise, Conseiller Privé et Commissaire Impérial de Khoubilal-Khaán. Rédigé en français sous sa dictée en 1298 par Rusticien de Pise ; Publié pour la première fois d'après trois manuscrits inédits de la Bibliothèque Impériale de Paris, présentant la rédaction primitive du Livre, revue par Marco Polo lui-même et donneé par lui, en 1307, à Thiébault de Cépoy, accompagnée des Variantes, de l'Explication des mots hors d'usage, et de commentaires géographiques et historiques, tirés des écrivains orientaux, principalement Chinois, avec une Carte générale de l'Asie par M. G. PAUTHIER. Two vols. roy. 8vo. pp. clvi. 832. With Map and View of Marco Polo's House at Venice. £1 8s.

Pazand.—THE BOOK OF THE MAINYO-I-KHARD. The Pazand and Sanskrit Texts (in Roman characters) as arranged by Neriosengh Dhaval, in the fifteenth century. With an English translation, a Glossary of the Pazand texts, containing the Sanskrit, Rosian, and Pahlavi equivalents, a sketch of Pazand Grammar, and an Introduction. By E. W. WEST. 8vo. sewed, pp. 484. 1871. 16s.

Percy.—BISHOP PERCY'S FOLIO MANUSCRIPTS—BALLADS AND ROMANCES. Edited by John W. Hales, M.A., Fellow and late Assistant Tutor of Christ's College, Cambridge ; and Frederick J. Furnivall, M.A., of Trinity Hall, Cambridge ; assisted by Professor Child, of Harvard University, Cambridge, U.S.A., W. Chappell, Esq., etc. In 3 volumes. Vol. I., pp. 610 ; Vol. 2, pp. 681. ; Vol. 3, pp. 640. Demy 8vo. half-bound, £4 4s. Extra demy 8vo. half-bound, on Whatman's ribbed paper, £6 6s. Extra royal 8vo., paper covers, on Whatman's best ribbed paper, £10 10s. Large 4to., paper covers, on Whatman's best ribbed paper, £12.

Perny.—DICTIONNAIRE FRANÇAIS-LATIN-CHINOIS DE LA LANGUE MANDARINE PARLÉE. Par PAUL PERNY. M.A., de la Congrégation des Missions Etrangères. 4to. pp. viii. 459, sewed. £2 2s.

Perny.—GRAMMAIRE PRATIQUE DE LA LANGUE MANDARINE PARLÉE. Par PAUL PERNY, M.A., de la Congrégation des Missions Etrangères.
[*In the Press.*

Perny.—PROVERBES CHINOIS, RECUEILLIS ET MIS EN ORDRE. Par PAUL PERNY, M.A., de la Congrégation des Missions Etrangères. 12mo. pp. iv. 135. 3s.

Perrin.—ENGLISH-ZULU DICTIONARY. New Edition, revised by J. A. BRICKHILL, Interpreter to the Supreme Court of Natal. 12mo. pp. 226, cloth, Pietermaritzburg, 1865. 5s.

Philological Society.—PROPOSALS for the Publication of a NEW ENGLISH DICTIONARY. 8vo. pp. 32, sewed. 6d.

Pierce the Ploughman's Crede (about 1394 Anno Domini). Transcribed and Edited from the MS. of Trinity College, Cambridge, R. 3, 15. Collated with the MS. Bibl. Reg. 18. B. xvii. in the British Museum, and with the old Printed Text of 1553, to which is appended "God spede the Plough" (about 1500 Anno Domini), from the Lansdowne MS. 762. By the Rev. WALTER W. SKEAT, M.A., late Fellow of Christ's College, Cambridge. pp. xx. and 75, cloth. 1867. 2s. 6d.

Prakrita-Prakasa; or, The Prakrit Grammar of Vararuchi, with the Commentary (Manorama) of Bhamaha. The first complete edition of the Original Text with Various Readings from a Collation of Six Manuscripts in the Bodleian Library at Oxford, and the Libraries of the Royal Asiatic Society and the East India House; with copious Notes, an English Translation, and Index of Prakrit words, to which is prefixed an easy Introduction to Prakrit Grammar. By EDWARD BYLES COWELL, of Magdalen Hall, Oxford, Professor of Sanskrit at Cambridge. Second issue, with new Preface, and corrections. 8vo. pp. xxxii. and 204. 14s.

Priaulx.—QUÆSTIONES MOSAICÆ; or, the first part of the Book of Genesis compared with the remains of ancient religions. By OSMOND DE BEAUVOIR PRIAULX. 8vo. pp. viii. and 548, cloth. 12s.

Raja-Niti.—A COLLECTION OF HINDU APOLOGUES, in the Braj Bháshá Language. Revised edition. With a Preface, Notes, and Supplementary Glossary. By FITZEDWARD HALL, Esq. 8vo. cloth, pp. 204. 21s.

Ram Raz.—Essay on the ARCHITECTURE of the HINDUS. By RAM RAZ, Native Judge and Magistrate of Bangalore, Corresponding Member of the R.A.S. of Great Britain and Ireland. With 48 plates. 4to. pp. xiv. and 64, sewed. London, 1834. Original selling price, £1 11s. 6d., reduced (for a short time) to 12s.

Rask.—A GRAMMAR OF THE ANGLO-SAXON TONGUE. From the Danish of Erasmus Rask, Professor of Literary History in, and Librarian to, the University of Copenhagen, etc. By BENJAMIN THORPE, Member of the Munich Royal Academy of Sciences, and of the Society of Netherlandish Literature, Leyden. Second edition, corrected and improved. 18mo. pp. 200, cloth. 5s. 6d.

Rawlinson.—A COMMENTARY ON THE CUNEIFORM INSCRIPTIONS OF BABYLONIA AND ASSYRIA, including Readings of the Inscription on the Nimrud Obelisk, and Brief Notice of the Ancient Kings of Nineveh and Babylon, Read before the Royal Asiatic Society, by Major H. C. RAWLINSON. 8vo., pp. 84, sewed. London, 1850. 2s. 6d.

Rawlinson.—OUTLINES OF ASSYRIAN HISTORY, from the Inscriptions of Nineveh. By Lieut. Col. RAWLINSON, C.B., followed by some Remarks by A. H. LAYARD, Esq., D.C.L. 8vo., pp. xliv., sewed. London, 1852. 1s.

Renan.—AN ESSAY ON THE AGE AND ANTIQUITY OF THE BOOK OF NABATHÆAN AGRICULTURE. To which is added an Inaugural Lecture on the Position of the Shemitic Nations in the History of Civilization. By M. ERNEST RENAN, Membre de l'Institut. Crown 8vo., pp. xvi. and 148, cloth. 3s. 6d.

Revue Celtique.—THE REVUE CELTIQUE, a Quarterly Magazine for Celtic Philology, Literature, and History. Edited with the assistance of the Chief Celtic Scholars of the British Islands and of the Continent, and Conducted by H. GAIDOZ. 8vo. Subscription, £1 per annum.

Ridley.—KAMILAROI, DIPPIL, AND TURRUBUL. Languages Spoken by Australian Aborigines. By Rev. WM. RIDLEY, M.A., of the University of Sydney; Minister of the Presbyterian Church of New South Wales. Printed by authority. Small 4to. cloth. pp. vi. and 90. 30s.

Thomas.—EARLY SASSANIAN INSCRIPTIONS, SEALS AND COINS, illustrating the Early History of the Sassanian Dynasty, containing Proclamations of Ardeshir Babek, Sapor I., and his Successors. With a Critical Examination and Explanation of the Celebrated Inscription in the Hájíábad Cave, demonstrating that Supor, the Conqueror of Valerian, was a Professing Christian. By EDWARD THOMAS, Esq. 8vo. cloth, pp. 148, Illustrated. 7s. 6d.

Thomas.—THE CHRONICLES OF THE PATHÁN KINGS OF DEHLI. Illustrated by Coins, Inscriptions, and other Antiquarian Remains. By EDWARD THOMAS, F.R.A.S., late of the East India Company's Bengal Civil Service. With numerous Copperplates and Woodcuts. Demy 8vo. cloth, pp. xxiv. and 467. 1871. 28s.

Thomas.—ESSAYS ON INDIAN ANTIQUITIES: following up the Discoveries of James Prinsep, with specimens of his Engravings, and selections from his Useful Tables, and embodying the most recent investigations into the History, Palæography, and Numismatics of Ancient India. By EDWARD THOMAS, late of the East India Company's Bengal Civil Service. In 2 vols. 8vo., profusely illustrated. [*In preparation.*

Thomas.—THE THEORY AND PRACTICE OF CREOLE GRAMMAR. By J. J. THOMAS. Port of Spain (Trinidad), 1869. One vol. 8vo. boards, pp. viii. and 135. 12s.

Thonissen.—ÉTUDES SUR L'HISTOIRE DU DROIT CRIMINEL DES PEUPLES Anciens (Inde Brahmanique, E'gypte, Judée), par J. J. THONISSEN, Professeur à l'Université Catholique de Louvain, Membre de l'Academie Royale de Belgique. 2 vols. 8vo. pp. xvi. 248, 320, sewed. 1869. 12s.

Thorpe.—DIPLOMATARIUM ANGLICUM ÆVI SAXONICI. A Collection of English Charters, from the reign of King Æthelberht of Kent, A.D., DCV., to that of William the Conqueror. Containing: I. Miscellaneous Charters. II. Wills. III. Guilds. IV. Manumissions and Acquittances. With a Translation of the Anglo-Saxon. By the late BENJAMIN THORPE, Member of the Royal Academy of Sciences at Munich, and of the Society of Netherlandish Literature at Leyden. 8vo. pp. xlii. and 682, cloth. 1865. £1 1s.

Tindall.—A GRAMMAR AND VOCABULARY OF THE NAMAQUA-HOTTENTOT LANGUAGE. By HENRY TINDALL, Wesleyan Missionary. 8vo., pp. 124, sewed. 6s.

Van der Tuuk.—OUTLINES OF A GRAMMAR OF THE MALAGASY LANGUAGE. By H. N. VAN DER TUUK. 8vo., pp. 28, sewed. 1s.

Van der Tuuk.—SHORT ACCOUNT OF THE MALAY MANUSCRIPTS BELONGING TO THE ROYAL ASIATIC SOCIETY. By H. N. VAN DER TUUK. 8vo., pp. 52. 2s. 6d.

Vishnu-Purana (The); a System of Hindu Mythology and Tradition. Translated from the original Sanskrit, and Illustrated by Notes derived chiefly from other Puráṇas. By the late H. H. WILSON, M.A., F.R.S., Boden Professor of Sanskrit in the University of Oxford, etc., etc. Edited by FITZEDWARD HALL. In 6 vols. 8vo. Vol. I. pp. cxl. and 200; Vol. II. pp. 343; Vol. III. pp. 348; Vol. IV. pp. 346 cloth; Vol. V. pp. 392, cloth. Price 10s. 6d. each. [*Vol. VI. in preparation.*

Wade.—YÜ-YEN TZÚ-ERH CHI. A progressive course designed to assist the Student of Colloquial Chinese, as spoken in the Capital and the Metropolitan Department. In eight parts, with Key, Syllabary, and Writing Exercises. By THOMAS FRANCIS WADE, C.B., Secretary to Her Britannic Majesty's Legation, Peking. 3 vols. 4to. Progressive Course, pp. xx. 296 and 16; Syllabary, pp. 126 and 36; Writing Exercises, pp. 48; Key, pp. 174 and 140, sewed. £4.

Wade.—WÊN-CHIEN TZÚ-ERH CHI. A series of papers selected as specimens of documentary Chinese, designed to assist Students of the language,

Wake.—CHAPTERS ON MAN. With the Outlines of a Science of comparative Psychology. By C. STANILAND WAKE, Fellow of the Anthropological Society of London. Crown 8vo. pp. viii. and 344, cloth. 7s. 6d.

Watson.—INDEX TO THE NATIVE AND SCIENTIFIC NAMES OF INDIAN AND OTHER EASTERN ECONOMIC PLANTS AND PRODUCTS, originally prepared under the authority of the Secretary of State for India in Council. By JOHN FORBES WATSON, M.A., M.D., F.L.S., F.R.A.S., etc., Reporter on the Products of India. Imperial 8vo., cloth, pp. 650. £1 11s. 6d.

Watts.—ESSAYS ON LANGUAGE AND LITERATURE. By THOMAS WATTS, late of the British Museum. Reprinted, with Alterations and Additions, from the Transactions of the Philological Society, and elsewhere. In 1 vol. 8vo.
[*In preparation.*

Webster.—AN INTRODUCTORY ESSAY TO THE SCIENCE OF COMPARATIVE THEOLOGY; with a Tabular Synopsis of Scientific Religion. By EDWARD WEBSTER, of Ealing, Middlesex. Read in an abbreviated form as a Lecture to a public audience at Ealing, on the 3rd of January, 1870, and to an evening congregation at South Place Chapel, Finsbury Square, London, on the 27th of February, 1870. 8vo. pp. 28, sewed. 1870. 1s.

Wedgwood.—A DICTIONARY OF THE ENGLISH LANGUAGE. By HENSLEIGH WEDGWOOD, M.A. late Fellow of Christ's College, Cambridge. Vol. I. (A to D) 8vo., pp. xxiv. 508, cloth, 14s.; Vol. II. (E to P) 8vo. pp. 578, cloth, 14s.; Vol. III., Part I. (Q to Sy), 8vo. pp. 366, 10s. 6d.; Vol. III. Part II. (T to W) 8vo. pp. 200, 5s. 6d. completing the Work. Price of the complete work, £2 4s.

" Dictionaries are a class of books not usually esteemed light reading; but no intelligent man were to be pitied who should find himself sunt np on a rainy day in a lonely house in the dreariest part of Salisbury Plain, with no other means of recreation than that which Mr. Wedgwood's Dictionary of Etymology could afford him. He would read it through from cover to cover at a sitting, and only regret that he had not the second volume to begin upon forthwith. It is a very able book, of great research, full of delightful surprises, a repertory of the fairy tales of linguistic science."—*Spectator.*

Wedgwood.—ON THE ORIGIN OF LANGUAGE. By HENSLEIGH WEDGWOOD, late Fellow of Christ's College, Cambridge. Fcap. 8vo. pp. 172, cloth. 3s. 6d.

Wékey.—A GRAMMAR OF THE HUNGARIAN LANGUAGE, with appropriate Exercises, a Copious Vocabulary, and Specimens of Hungarian Poetry. By SIGISMUND WÉKEY, late Aide-de-Camp to Kossuth. 12mo., pp. xii. and 150, sewed. 4s. 6d.

Wheeler.—THE HISTORY OF INDIA FROM THE EARLIEST AGES. By J. TALBOYS WHEELER, Assistant Secretary to the Government of India in the Foreign Department, Secretary to the Indian Record Commission, author of "The Geography of Herodotus," etc. etc. Vol. I., The Vedic Period and the Maha Bharata. 8vo. cloth, pp. lxxv. and 576. 18s.

Vol. II., The Ramayana and the Brahmanic Period. 8vo. cloth, pp. lxxxviii. and 680, with 2 Maps. 21s.

Whitney.—ATHARVA VEDA PRÁTIÇÁKHYA; or, Çáunakíyá Caturádhyáyiká (The). Text, Translation, and Notes. By WILLIAM D. WHITNEY, Professor of Sanskrit in Yale College. 8vo. pp. 286, boards. 12s.

Whitney.—LANGUAGE AND THE STUDY OF LANGUAGE: Twelve Lectures on the Principles of Linguistic Science. By WILLIAM DWIGHT WHITNEY, Professor of Sanskrit, etc., in Yale College. Second Edition, augmented by an Analysis. Crown 8vo. cloth, pp. xii. and 504. 10s. 6d.

Whitney.—TÁITTIRÍYA-PRÁTIÇÁKHYA, with its Commentary, the Tribháshyaratna: Text, Translation, and Notes. By W. D. WHITNEY, Prof. of Sanskrit in Yale College, New Haven. 8vo. pp. 469. 1871. 25s.

Wilkins.—THE BHAGAVAT-GEETA; or, Dialogues of Kreeshna and Arjoon. Translated by CHAS. WILKINS. A faithful reprint of the now very scarce Original London Edition of 1785, made at the Bradsheet Press, New York. In one vol. 8vo. Beautifully printed with old face type on laid paper. 261 copies were produced of this edition, of which only a few now remain. 12s.

Williams.—FIRST LESSONS IN THE MAORI LANGUAGE, with a Short Vocabulary. By W. L. WILLIAMS, B.A. Square 8vo., pp. 80, cloth, London, 1862. 10s.

Williams.—LEXICON CORNU-BRITANNICUM. A Dictionary of the Ancient Celtic Language of Cornwall, in which the words are elucidated by copious examples from the Cornish works now remaining, with translations in English. The synonyms are also given in the cognate dialects of Welsh, Armoric, Irish, Gaelic, and Manx, showing at one view the connexion between them. By the Rev. ROBERT WILLIAMS, M.A., Christ Church, Oxford, Parish Curate of Llangadwaladr and Rhydycroesan, Denbighshire. Sewed. 3 parts, pp. 400. £2 5s.

Williams.—A DICTIONARY, ENGLISH AND SANSCRIT. By MONIER WILLIAMS, M.A. Published under the Patronage of the Honourable East India Company. 4to. pp. xii. 862, cloth. London, 1855. £3 3s.

Wilson.—Works of the late HORACE HAYMAN WILSON, M.A., F.R.S., Member of the Royal Asiatic Societies of Calcutta and Paris, and of the Oriental Society of Germany, etc., and Boden Professor of Sanskrit in the University of Oxford. Vols I. and II. Also, under this title, ESSAYS AND LECTURES chiefly on the Religion of the Hindus, by the late H. H. WILSON, M.A., F.R.S. etc. Collected and edited by Dr. REINHOLD ROST. 2 vols. cloth, pp. xiii. and 399, vi. and 416. 21s.

Wilson.—Works of the late HORACE HAYMAN WILSON, M.A., F.R.S., Member of the Royal Asiatic Societies of Calcutta and Paris, and of the Oriental Society of Germany, etc., and Boden Professor of Sanskrit in the University of Oxford. Vols. III, IV. and V. Also, under the title of Essays Analytical, Critical, and Philological, on subjects connected with Sanskrit Literature. Collected and Edited by Dr. REINHOLD ROST. 3 vols. 8vo. pp. 408, 406, and 390, cloth. Price 36s

Wilson.—Works of the Late HORACE HAYMAN WILSON. Vols. VI. VII. VIII, IX. and X. Also, under the title of the Vishṇu Purâṇâ, a system, of Hindu mythology and tradition. Translated from the original Sanskrit, and Illustrated by Notes derived chiefly from other Purâṇâs. By the late H. H. WILSON, Boden Professor of Sanskrit in the University of Oxford, etc., etc. Edited by FITZEDWARD HALL, M.A., D.C.L., Oxon. Vols. I. to V. 8vo., pp. cxl. and 200; 344; 344; 346, cloth. 2l. 12s. 6d. [*Vol. VI. in the press.*

Wilson.—SELECT SPECIMENS OF THE THEATRE OF THE HINDUS. Translated from the Original Sanskrit. By HORACE HAYMAN WILSON, M.A., F.R.S. Third corrected edition. 2 vols. 8vo. [*Nearly ready.*

CONTENTS.

Vol. I.—Preface—Treatise on the Dramatic System of the Hindus—Dramas translated from the Original Sanskrit—The Mrichchakati, or the Toy Cart—Vikrama and Urvasi, or the Hero and the Nymph—Uttara Ramá Cheritra, or continuation of the History of Ramá.

Vol. II.—Dramas translated from the Original Sanskrit—Malátí and Mádhava, or the Stolen Marriage—Mudrá Rakshasa, or the Signet of the Minister—Retnávali, or the Necklace—Appendix, containing short accounts of different Dramas.

Wilson.—THE PRESENT STATE OF THE CULTIVATION OF ORIENTAL LITERATURE. A Lecture delivered at the Meeting of the Royal Asiatic Society. By the Director, Professor H. H. WILSON. 8vo., pp. 26, sewed. London, 1852. 6d.

Wise.—COMMENTARY ON THE HINDU SYSTEM OF MEDICINE. By T. A. WISE, M.D., Bengal Medical Service. 8vo., pp. xx. and 432, cloth. 7s. 6d.

Wylie.—NOTES ON CHINESE LITERATURE; with introductory Remarks on the Progressive Advancement of the Art; and a list of translations from the Chinese, into various European Languages. By A. WYLIE, Agent of the British and Foreign Bible Society in China. 4to. pp. 296, cloth. Price, 1l. 10s.

Yates.—A BENGÁLÍ GRAMMAR. By the late Rev. W. YATES, D.D. Reprinted, with improvements, from his Introduction to the Bengáli Language, Edited by I. WENGER. Fcap. 8vo., pp. iv. and 150, bds. Calcutta, 1864. 3s. 6d.

www.ingramcontent.com/pod-product-compliance
Lightning Source LLC
Chambersburg PA
CBHW021821230426
43669CB00008B/822